I WOULD LIE TO YOU IF I COULD

PITT POETRY SERIES

Ed Ochester, Editor

I WOULD LIE TO YOU IF I COULD

INTERVIEWS
WITH
TEN
AMERICAN
POETS

CHARD deNIORD

UNIVERSITY OF PITTSBURGH PRESS

Published by the University of Pittsburgh Press, Pittsburgh, Pa., 15260

Manufactured in the United States of America
Printed on acid-free paper
10 9 8 7 6 5 4 3 2 1

Cataloging-in-Publication data is available from the Library of Congress

ISBN 13: 978-0-8229-6534-3

Cover art: Liz Hawkes deNiord
Cover design: Alex Wolfe

For Liz

The most sublime act is to set another before you.

— WILLIAM BLAKE

CONTENTS

INTRODUCTION

T hese interviews took place over the past five years, with the exception of Galway Kinnell's interview, which took place in 2009 and appeared in an abridged form in the *American Poetry Review* in 2010. Unlike my first book of interviews, *Sad Friends, Drowned Lovers, Stapled Songs: Conversations and Reflections on Twentieth-Century American Poets*, in which I focused on interviewing renowned senior poets—Jack Gilbert, Lucille Clifton, Ruth Stone, Galway Kinnell, Robert Bly, Maxine Kumin, and Donald Hall—I have chosen to concentrate in this collection on a vital cross section of American poets that represents various age groups, ethnic identities, and social backgrounds. These mostly midcareer and senior poets— Natasha Trethewey, Jane Hirshfield, Martín Espada, Stephen Kuusisto, Stephen Sandy, Ed Ochester, Carolyn Forché, Peter Everwine, Galway Kinnell, and Annie Wright, James Wright's widow—testify to what Walt Whitman called the "broad and narrow zones" of America's poetic landscape.

In their progress over the past fifty years, arbiters and publishers of American poetry have worked with a long overdue commitment at replacing the palace on Mount Parnassus, formerly reserved for mostly white male poets, with a big tent, sending invitations to women and ethnically diverse poets who had previously been excluded for reasons that appear in retrospect only misogynistic, racist, and antithetical to the inherently demotic spirit of poetry itself.

While these interviews make only a small start at representing the diverse crowd of American poets, they nonetheless provide a small but revealing window into contemporary American poetry. Since the genesis of the internet, poetry has, like Google News and social media, streamed rampantly across the invisible wires of the World Wide Web. One might in fact be tempted to say that the unedited glut of poetry that appears on myriad websites has rendered poetry a drowned literary river. Any serious reader of poetry feels overwhelmed by the unmanageable abundance of poetry that has swamped the new poetry market. I hope these interviews help, at least, in providing critical signposts for the diverse range and arc of American poetry during the last fifty years. During each of the interviews, I felt the poets' responses to my questions added up to formidable ironic parts that were greater than the whole, while at the same time remaining a part of the whole.

The poets I chose to interview for this book encompass a wide range of aesthetic, social, and ethnic voices. They of course speak for themselves but do so in ways that reverberate deeply in genuine and generous ways. Each testifies to the demotic nature of poetry itself as a charged language that appeals to the human spirit with a self-enriching diversity. As individuals with their own transpersonal stories, they have emerged onto the national stage with news that informs universally, witnessing memorably to their respective insights into what it means and feels like to be alive today as a poet and citizen in America. They talk about their poems and development as poets self-effacingly out of deference to their struggles of truth-telling, what Natasha Trethewey describes as the "the narrative" and "the meta-narrative—the way [one] both remembers and forgets, the erasures, and how intricately intertwined memory and forgetting always are."

As with the other interviews I've conducted over the past ten years, I was initially interested in what "hurt" my subjects "into poetry"—that phrase that W. H. Auden used in his elegy for W. B. Yeats. What mad America like Yeats's "mad Ireland" had spurred them to write poetry in their various towns and purlieus? Each provided his or her own memorable answers, addressing his or her respective hurts directly with bittersweet responses, confessions, disquisitions, and definitions that surprise as much as they enlighten.

Chard deNiord,
Putney, Vermon

I WOULD LIE TO YOU IF I COULD

Natasha Trethewey. Photo © Nancy Crampton

1 / *Natasha Trethewey*

Natasha Trethewey was born in Gulfport, Mississippi, to poet, professor, and Canadian emigrant Eric Trethewey and social worker Gwendolyn Ann Turnbough. The daughter of a mixed-race marriage, Trethewey experienced her parents' divorce when she was six. She subsequently spent time in Atlanta, Georgia, with her mother and in New Orleans, Louisiana, with her father. Trethewey studied English at the University of Georgia, earned an MA in English and creative writing from Hollins University, and received an MFA in poetry from the University of Massachusetts, Amherst.

Trethewey's first collection, *Domestic Work* (2000), won the Cave Canem Prize for a first book by an African American poet. *Domestic Work* explores the lives and jobs of working-class people, particularly black men and women in the South. Based in part on her grandmother's life, the poems are particularly attuned to the vivid imagery of her characters' lives and the region itself. The book effortlessly blends free verse and traditional forms, including ballads and sonnets.

Trethewey is adept at combining the personal and the historical in her work. Her second book, *Bellocq's Ophelia* (2002), is about a fictional prostitute in New Orleans in the early 1900s. For the book, Trethewey researched the lives of the women in the red-light district, many of whom were multiracial. She commented that the project combined "the details of my own mixed-race experience in the Deep South" with facts about the real women's lives.

Her third book of poems, *Native Guard* (2006), won the 2007 Pulitzer Prize in poetry. The book contains elegies to her mother, who died while Trethewey was in college, and a sonnet sequence in the voice of a black soldier fighting in the Civil War. Her recent work includes a book of creative nonfiction, *Beyond Katrina: A Meditation on the Mississippi Gulf Coast* (2010), and the poetry collection *Thrall* (2012). The latter book examines historical representations of mixed-race families, focusing on fathers and children, through a series of poems that treat portrait art of the eighteenth century.

Trethewey's many honors and awards include fellowships from the Guggenheim Foundation, the Rockefeller Foundation, the National Endowment for the Arts, and the Radcliffe Institute, where she was a Bunting fellow. She has held appointments at Duke University, as the Lehman Brady Joint Chair Professor of Documentary and American Studies; the University of North Carolina–Chapel Hill; and Yale University, where she was the James Weldon Johnson Fellow in African American Studies at the Beinecke Library.

The recipient of a Mississippi Governor's Award for Excellence in the Arts, Trethewey was named the 2008 Georgia Woman of the Year. She has been inducted into both the Fellowship of Southern Writers and the Georgia Writers Hall of Fame. In 2012 she was named poet laureate of the state of Mississippi and the nineteenth poet laureate of the United States.

This interview took place on stage at the Palm Beach Poetry Festival on January 23, 2014.

———————

Chard deNiord (CD): I'd like to begin with that turning point in your life when you decided to become a poet. I know you attended the University of Georgia as an undergraduate, then worked for a while as a social worker before earning your master's degree in English at Hollins University and your MFA at the University of Massachusetts and additional graduate work there in American studies. But there must have been a particularly eventful moment when you decided you were going to take writing seriously and pursue it as a career.

Natasha Trethewey (NT): You know, one of the things I've realized is that the more you tell a story about something, the more the story changes. And so, for that reason, I keep trying to tell the truest version of that moment to my recollection. As an undergraduate, I never took any creative writing classes. That was when you still registered by the alphabet, and by the time I registered for those desirable classes, with a T I never got to get into any of them. But when I left, I tried to write a poem for the first time in undergraduate school after my mother died, and it was just an attempt out of sheer necessity to make sense of that loss. It was a terrible poem, and I asked a professor of mine if I could bring it to her office to show it to her. But I lost the courage to do so, and I never did. It was a good thing because it was a horrible poem. It had this image of me ... well, what I wrote was that I felt like I was "sinking into an ocean of despair," and the word *sinking* went down the page like that, and there was that little pool of cliché at the bottom that the word just went right into. So I never showed that poem, and I'd been an English major, and when I graduated my father talked me into applying to Hollins, but as a fiction writer. So I went to Hollins thinking that, because I loved short fiction so much, I wanted to write stories. In my first semester I had Marianne Gingher, who's a wonderful novelist, as a professor. I remember a friend of mine, who was a poet, daring me to write a poem. I remembered how bad this poem from freshman year had been, so I knew I couldn't do it. But I decided to take the dare just to prove how bad it would be. I wrote the poem, and actually it wasn't that bad, and I gave it to Marianne Gingher—I put it in her mailbox. The next time I saw her, she came running down the hall to say, "Oh, Tasha, you're a poet!" I think it had more to do with the fact that I wasn't a very good fiction writer, and she was hoping that I would find a new avenue for whatever talents I might have. From then on I started writing poems. So then, you know, one turns to poems not to write them sometimes but to read them and to be comforted by them. So there's a different story about turning to poetry for that reason, which is also about grief for me, but a very different moment of deciding, again, to write them.

CD: This reminds me of Auden's famous line about Yeats in his elegy for him, "In Memory of W. B. Yeats."

NT: That "mad Ireland hurt him into poetry."

CD: Yes.

NT: It's a line that I say often too because I certainly feel "hurt into poetry." Not just by the tremendous grief that I felt over losing my mother, but also by having been born in Mississippi in a certain period in our history and all the things that go with that.

CD: It's fascinating that almost thirty years after you decided to pursue a career in writing, you wrote a poem called "Calling," which is about your call to become a poet at the early age of three. Of course you hadn't started to write poetry then, but you define a particular moment as a significant event in your life when you, in the presence of your parents in Monterrey, Mexico, with your mother "kneeling at the altar of the Black Virgin," received your call to become a poet. I wonder if you could read that?

NT: Oh, I'd love to.

Calling
Mexico 1969

Why not make a fiction
       of the mind's fictions? I want to say
    it begins like this: the trip
       a pilgrimage, my mother
kneeling at the altar of the Black Virgin,
       enthralled—light streaming in
          a window, the sun
       at her back, holy water
    in a bowl she must have touched.

What's left is palimpsest—one memory
    bleeding into another, overwriting it.
        How else to explain
            what remains? The sound
  of water in a basin I know is white,
      the sun behind her, light streaming in,
        her face—
  as if she were already dead—blurred
    as it will become.

I want to imagine her before
    the altar, rising to meet us, my father
        lifting me
    toward her outstretched arms.
What else to make
    of the mind's slick confabulations?
        What comes back
is the sun's dazzle on a pool's surface,
    light filtered through water

closing over my head, my mother—her body
    between me and the high sun, a corona of light
      around her face. Why not call it
a vision? What I know is this:
I was drowning and saw a dark Madonna;
      someone pulled me through
  the water's bright ceiling
    and I rose, initiate,
    from one life into another.

CD: A remarkably mystical poem.

NT: Thank you. I think that's part of the story of realizing that no matter how many times I try to explain the "moment" that I decided to become a poet, none of it's exactly right—there are so many moments along the way that perhaps that moment, farthest back in the memory, is the one that initiated that genuine calling. I think of it also, in the poem, as a calling toward something else—toward not just the need to write poetry but to have a particular vision about what it is I want to write, to be drawn to, as I am deeply drawn to a sense of social justice. I think that for me the poem is also about that particular calling as well.

CD: In your book *Beyond Katrina* you talk about not being a religious person. Yet at the same time, perhaps you possess a more insightful view ironically into what that calling meant to you as a nonreligious poet. I'm referring to the way you conflate your mother with the "dark Madonna" in your early memory of her in Monterrey.

NT: Yes, I think that I was always drawn to language, so the language of ceremony is always interesting to me. Those words that I heard on Sundays, or during the week when the ladies' group would come to my grandmother's house for Bible study, and they also had a secular meaning outside of what I was learning. But the imagery was something that stuck with me, and I remember being fascinated about learning that my mother, after her death, a woman who had grown up in the Baptist Church, who lived her whole life across the street from the Baptist church that her aunt founded, became a Catholic convert. I never knew this about my mother, but I did know that she made certain gestures which I, of course, understood to be Catholic, and that she performed certain other rituals. But I never knew why, and when I began to think about why—I was thinking about that around the time I wrote this poem, too—I started thinking about that particular historical moment, and of course there are a lot of black Catholics in the Gulf Coast region from New Orleans to Mobile, so plenty of people she knew would have been Catholic. But I also thought that my mother might have chosen to convert because the people in the Catholic faith . . . the church was, at that point, a little out front of integration in the South, and the church seemed more liberal to her, perhaps, than the Baptist church she had grown up in. That would be one reason. The other reason is that I imagined that on that trip to Mexico, to be confronted with the Black Virgin—with an image of black womanhood that she would have never seen growing up in that society—might be very attractive to her.

CD: And a little exotic.

NT: That would have been before her conversion.

CD: In more secular terms, you've talked about your inclination to bear witness to injustice and discrimination pretty early on. There's a poem in your first book, *Domestic Work*, in which you write about advice that a woman named Sugar gave you. Is that her name?

NT: That's right. She was my great-aunt, Sugar.

CD: You write of her in your poem "Gathering":

> Under ripe figs, green,
> hard as jewels, these we save,
> hold in deep white bowls.
> She put them to the light
> on the windowsill, tells me
> *to wait, learn, patience.*
>
> I touched them each day,
> watched them turn gold, grow sweet,
> and give sweetness back.
>
> I begin to see
> our lives are like this—we take
> what we need of light.
>
> We glisten, preserve
> hand-picked days in memory,
> our minds' dark pantry.

I'm fascinated by this advice to wait and learn in light of what you have called "measured syntax" and patience in your work, which you have claimed is "necessary for being able to lift that heavy arm of history up."

NT: You know, I think of Sugar, my great-aunt, as one of my muses in the way that the poem suggests, because of the kind of advice she'd give. She was also someone who was very precise about things, and I love precision—I think because of her. She was also someone who would convey messages to you not just with words, but also with gesture, which, of course, in the mind becomes image. I can remember a time she came to my grandmother's back door—they lived side by side. We didn't know it yet, but she was suffering from Alzheimer's, but we just called her senile, not knowing anything else. So she started to lose a lot of things, so her communication became very different. I remember how she always used to make fig preserves because she had this huge fig tree. She came to the back door one day and knocked on it—the kitchen door—and I opened it, and all she did was stand there and hold out her palm, which had these three underripe figs in it. Then she said nothing, and I knew to take them and wait.

CD: And they ripened.

NT: Yes.

CD: I would like to turn to some of the paintings you write about in your new book, *Thrall*—Renaissance paintings for the most part, but also eighteenth-, nineteenth-, and twentieth-century paintings, drawings, and photographs that focus on mixed-race or *casta* images by such painters and artists as Juan Rodríguez Juárez, Miguel Cabrera, Juan de Pareja, Diego Velázquez, George Fuller, and Robert Frank. You follow a strategy in many of these ekphrastic poems of describing the painting, then developing your description into an extended metaphor. Which of these paintings would you like to discuss first?

NT: Do you mind if I start with the poem titled "Knowledge"? This one will allow me to talk a little bit about process and the advice we get from other writers that can be so useful. It would probably be easier to read this one than anything from the section called "Taxonomy," because "Taxonomy" is really where this began for me. "Knowledge" is crucial.

CD: There's a lot in this poem about your own personal history as well.

NT: Indeed. Okay, this is "Knowledge":

Knowledge
After a chalk drawing by J. H. Hasselhorst, 1864

Whoever she was, she comes to us like this:
      lips parted, long hair spilling from the table

like water from a pitcher, nipples drawn out
      for inspection. Perhaps to foreshadow

the object she'll become: a skeleton on a pedestal,
      a row of skulls on a shelf. To make a study

of the ideal female body, four men gather around her.
      She is young and beautiful and drowned—

a Venus de' Medici, risen from the sea, sleeping.
      As if we could mistake this work for sacrilege,

the artist entombs her body in a pyramid
      of light, a temple of science over which

the anatomist presides. In the service of beauty—
      to know it—he lifts a flap of skin

beneath her breast as one might draw back a sheet.
      We will not see his step-by-step parsing,

a translation: *Mary* or *Katherine* or *Elizabeth*
      to *corpus, areola, vulva.* In his hands

instruments of the empirical—scalpel, pincers—
    cold as the room must be cold: all the men

in coats, trimmed in velvet or fur—soft as the down
    of her pubis. Now one man is smoking, another

tilts his head to get a better look. Yet another,
    at the head of the table, peers down as if

enthralled, his fist on a stack of books.
    In the drawing this is only the first cut,

a delicate wounding: and yet how easily
    the anatomist's blade opens a place in me,

like a curtain drawn upon a room in which
    each learned man is my father

and I hear, again, his words—*I study*
    my crossbreed child—misnomer

and taxonomy, the language of zoology. Here,
    he is all of them: the preoccupied man—

an artist, collector of experience; the skeptic angling
    his head, his thought tilting toward

what I cannot know; the marshaller of knowledge,
    knuckling down a stack of books; even

the dissector—his scalpel in hand like a pen
    poised above me, aimed straight for my heart.

You know, Mark Doty in an essay talks about how "your metaphors go
on ahead of you" and how one of the ways he begins writing a poem—

this essay's about a particular poem called "The Display of Mackerel"—is by looking at the thing that struck him, that got his attention, and just describing it in the most subjective terms possible, before he allows himself to make figurative comparisons that of course begin to reveal something about how he feels about the image, which then leads to a type of insight about it. So when I saw this image, I didn't particularly know why I was drawn to it, but I knew that I had to start describing it and hope that the description of it would lead me to understand what it meant.

But then, as I began doing it, I got stuck because I felt like . . . you know, one never likes to repeat oneself, and to me it felt like I was writing a poem I wrote in *Bellocq's Ophelia*—it had something similar to that for me. So I had lunch with Elizabeth Alexander, the poet, and I told her that I had this problem. She said to me that whenever that happens to her, she "decides to let the seam show," meaning that in the middle of the poem she'll say, "Why am I writing the same poem again?" as if that will become a line in the poem. Once I took that with me and sat down again, the turn in the poem happens, in which I begin to see that everything in that room has always been speaking to me about the nature of my relationship with my father, and about perceived and received knowledge across time and space, particularly that of the Enlightenment.

CD: Which is so historically patriarchal in both its artistic and scientific manifestations.

NT: Yes, and knowledge . . .

CD: "Knuckling down the stack of books. . . ."

NT: I have this lovely relationship with my father, but it's always also a very difficult one. I think that plenty of daughters also have relationships like this with their fathers, but I have the added bonus of my father also being my white parent, so it's not only a gendered complexity but a racialized one as well. So my father could begin to represent this kind of "whiteness Enlightenment knowledge," and I began to represent the "dark Other." My father could say that his idea of truth was knowledge, and mine was the more subjective knowledge, that my knowledge was the more "ideological" knowledge and his was the "truth," but he couldn't see that even that position was an ideological one.

CD: Not able to see it because his eyes are too fixed on the subject or on the object?

NT: Perhaps that's why I use the word "myopic" and "myopia" so much in this book.

CD: Yes, you write about it in your poem about a Juárez painting—the portrait of his wife and child. We'll turn to that in a minute.

NT: Well, you know, one of the other things that comes into play is that my father and I used to give readings together a lot, and in those readings we would stand together and read poems that spoke to each other. So we would read back and forth, some twenty minutes of me and then him. I remember that whenever he would get to the moment in his poem "Her Swing," which is a lovely poem—it's very sweet, and it makes me very happy—there would be that moment when he got to the line "I study my crossbreed child"—the line in my poem is actually a quote from that poem—I would always feel, standing there next to him, something like the Hottentot Venus on display, that all of a sudden I became that creature that was sort of turning around in her otherness and difference. So the sentence to me had two problems: one is that it had a very sort of eighteenth-century classification aspect—the need to categorize and fix everything that you study—but then another is the word *crossbreed*. A human being can't be a crossbreed, so it is a sort of misnomer, and it suggests that in the mixture one of the partners is a little less human than the other.

CD: In your poem about your visit to Monticello with your father, titled "Enlightenment," you joke with him at that climactic point on the tour when you recall arriving at Jefferson's slave quarters.

NT: Well, my father took me to Monticello for the first time about twenty years ago. "Enlightenment" was the last poem I wrote for the book, and I had to take him back there, I think, to finish the book and to write that poem. Just to tour the house again—many things have changed in the past twenty years. Now the official position of the Jefferson Foundation is that Jefferson fathered some of Sally Hemings's children.

CD: Six of them.

NT: The docent will say that when you go there now. It was never discussed before, and it seemed impertinent if someone dared to ask the docent a question about it. So in the twenty years that have gone by, because they've acknowledged that, because they're trying to sort of resurrect the slave quarters on Mulberry Row, because they do not necessarily call the slave quarters the "servants' quarters" anymore but use more precise language, the conversations that you hear have changed. My father and I walked around there and overheard people saying things like, "Well, she was mostly white," or "How white was she?" It's as if once it was official that he had done that, there had to be something else that made it so. That's because, well, she was "different," without saying she was "different"—that's what they were saying.

CD: You quote these specific lines in particular in the poem from Jefferson: "The improvement of the blacks in body / and mind in the first instance of their mixture / with the white."

NT: I'm quoting Jefferson there from *Notes on the State of Virginia.*

CD: But at that point in the tour, you say to your father, "This is where we part."

NT: "I'll head around to the back."

CD: And I guess he laughed.

NT: It was one of those moments where, you know, it just becomes necessary to have a little bit of levity. But it's also wicked of me at the same time. I think because I suppose I can just stand there while the docent says, "Imagine stepping back into the past," instead of thinking, *Really, do you want me to imagine that? Do I really want to imag-*

ine that? Things would not have been so good for me! So I make a joke out of it. It is my grandest attempt to make sure that this poem, which is very difficult on my father, as is the poem "Knowledge" that I just read, shows that we have a deeply loving relationship. It's complicated—it really is—and that moment has to do the work of communicating this complexity in the poem. So I'm glad I really said it.

CD: Would you mind reading the entire poem?

NT: "Enlightenment":

Enlightenment

In the portrait of Jefferson that hangs
    at Monticello, he is rendered two-toned:
his forehead white with illumination—

a lit bulb—the rest of his face in shadow,
    darkened as if the artist meant to contrast
his bright knowledge, its dark subtext.

By 1805, when Jefferson sat for the portrait,
    he was already linked to an affair
with his slave. Against a backdrop, blue

and ethereal, a wash of paint that seems
    to hold him in relief, Jefferson gazes out
across the centuries, his lips fixed as if

he's just uttered some final word.
    The first time I saw the painting, I listened
as my father explained the contradictions:

how Jefferson hated slavery, though—*out
    of necessity*, my father said—had to own
slaves; that his moral philosophy meant

he could not have fathered those children:
    would have been impossible, my father said.
For years we debated the distance between

word and deed. I'd follow my father from book
    to book, gathering citations, listen
as he named—like a field guide to Virginia—

each flower and tree and bird as if to prove
    a man's pursuit of knowledge is greater
than his shortcomings, the limits of his vision.

I did not know then the subtext
    of our story, that my father could imagine
Jefferson's words made flesh in my flesh—

the improvement of the blacks in body
    and mind, in the first instance of their mixture
with the whites—or that my father could believe

he'd made me *better*. When I think of this now,
    I see how the past holds us captive
its beautiful ruin etched on the mind's eye:

my young father, a rough outline of the old man
    he's become, needing to show me
the better measure of his heart, an equation

writ large at Monticello. That was years ago.
    Now, we take in how much has changed:
talk of Sally Hemings, someone asking,

How white was she?—parsing the fractions
    as if to name what made her worthy
of Jefferson's attentions: a near-white,

quadroon mistress, not a plain black slave.
Imagine stepping back into the past,
our guide tells us then—and I can't resist

whispering to my father: *This is where*
we split up. I'll head around to the back.
When he laughs, I know he's grateful

I've made a joke of it, this history
that links us—white father, black daughter—
even as it renders us other to each other.

CD: Such an ambitious, bold, and tender poem. On the dedication page of *Thrall*, you write, "To My Father." Then in the first poem of the book you write a proem titled "Elegy," dedicated "For my father." The last line of that proem is fascinating, but I'm not sure I completely understand it. I think I do, but would you mind elaborating on it? It has a powerful, mythical ending: "I step again into the small boat / that carried us out, and watch the bank receding—/ my back to where I know we are headed."

NT: The few words that you didn't say were, "Some nights dreaming, / I step again into the small boat." I will just say that to the audience because it is about recollecting that particular fishing trip again and again. So in a literal sense, it could simply mean the boat's headed that way, but I know I'm facing the other direction, and we've already been there in real life, so my back is headed toward the place we are going. But it's about going to that place, which I think is a place of knowledge, a place of finally coming to recognize something that has been germane to our relationship the whole time—that gets played out there. So it is a way of thinking about having to go down that path again—to see again everything that has brought us to the moment where we are.

The "moment we are" is the difficult moment when I am the ruthless daughter who, rather than experience fully the moment of fishing with my father, is already thinking of how it will be a poem when he's gone. When I say in the poem, "Your daughter, I was that ruthless. What does it matter if I tell you I learned to be?"—the "learning to be" comes, of course, from my father, and my father was a poet. And all my life with my father, we would be having a conversation, and then he would just "check out" for a little while, pull out the notebook he kept in his pocket, and write something down. I was always certain I had said something that made him need to stop and record it for a poem he would write. So I never quite felt that he was always there. And yet there in the poem, in the fishing trip, I've learned to do the same thing, and I'm going to make use of it. I know that there is something not wholly savory about that, but for me it's Yeats's "of the quarrel with others we make rhetoric, but of the quarrel with ourselves, poetry." So I have to acknowledge my own culpability and willingness to also make use of him.

CD: The poems in *Thrall* represent a leap for you into what you call the "ruthless" or truth-telling voice that pervades this book. You acknowledge your ambivalence toward your father in "Elegy"—the book's proem—but then seem to acknowledge him in your poem "On Happiness," near the end of *Thrall*, as the person who bequeathed the "permit" of poetry to you.

NT: That's interesting to think of—I think you're right, certainly.

CD: You write, "I would give you happiness if I could"—that unattainable fish, the salmon, that always slips out of your hands before you can let it go—and then conclude,

> . . . and then is to recall the permit
> he paid for that morning, see it
> creased in my back pocket—how
> he'd handed it to me
> and I'd tucked it there, as if
> a guarantee.

NT: You know, I'm really glad you brought that up. Because I am focused on writing about the literal image and because I write from experience, I try to capture something precise about the experience, the literal aspect of it. We actually had to buy our fishing permits that morning, and we got salmon licenses. We did not get trout licenses, which is why in the previous poem I had to throw the trout back—we didn't have a license for trout. But what happens is that, figuratively, it really does mean something else, doesn't it?

CD: I didn't want to read too much into it.

NT: But after everything I've been saying, how could you not?

CD: You've moved from the "unattainable salmon" to the literal "permit."

NT: Well, all I can say is that it really happened. But I know enough—and you would tell your students this—to know that it's not simply that it happened: it is what else you can make of it. And I believe that if we're precise enough about what really happened, we can find what is figuratively true and emotionally true in another way. I just saw an interview with Stanley Plumly in which he says, "Why not just say what happened?" Sometimes saying what happened can lead us to . . .

CD: That's actually a line from Robert Lowell's "Epilogue": "Why not say what happened?" It's an enormous temptation, is it not? I love the way the permit is folded sort of casually in your back pocket, and you end the poem with that. In contrast to those poems about your father and the Enlightenment and patriarchy and knowledge, you write a moving poem about your mother called "Mano Prieta," which is more imagistic, and I wonder if you could read that as a contrast to what we've just been talking about.

NT: Sure. I want to come back to what you're saying, because of course the book is very much about inheritance and where certain things come from, which is sort of why we started with "Calling."

Mano Prieta

The green drapery is like a sheet of water
        behind us—a cascade in the backdrop
of the photograph, a rushing current

that would scatter us, carry us each
        away. This is 1969 and I am three–
still light enough to be nearly the color

of my father. His armchair is a throne
        and I am leaning into him, propped
against his knees—his hand draped

across my shoulder. On the chair's arm
        my mother looms above me,
perched at the edge as though

she would fall off. The camera records
        her single gesture. Perhaps to still me,
she presses my arm with a forefinger,

makes visible a hypothesis of blood,
        its empire of words: the imprint
on my body of her lovely dark hand.

So one of the things I was thinking about is the backstory here. In recent years, it has occurred to me that the more I gained a reputation as a poet, the more people wanted to attribute any success or talent that I've had as a poet to my father because my father is a poet. It's a natural impulse for people to do that, but it's very complicated for me because, as I mentioned earlier, it's gendered and it's raced for us. When I was growing up in the Deep South, if I did anything well, white people would say, "Oh, that's your white side," as if nothing good came out of the part of me that was black.

CD: Well, that's right out of Enlightenment thinking.

NT: Yes, and it drove me crazy. In recent years, it's gotten even more pointed in that the thinking seems to be because my father's my white parent, he's also my poet parent, so surely all this comes from him and has nothing to do with the "imprint" of my mother's "dark hand" on me. So one of the things in my mind when I was working on this book, which I'm not sure if people see or not, is in a poem like "Calling." What I'm trying to suggest is that it may be *literally* true that my father's a poet, but what drives me, what calls me to be a poet—that utter necessity—may have come from the other side.

CD: I think that's in "Calling."

NT: Yes, and I think my mother is being erased as a part of what made me—she's been dead a long time now, so she's been erased in that sense. And attributing my calling to be a poet only to my father is another kind of erasure. If you notice, in all the *casta* paintings, whenever there is the black African mother she is either so black that she has no face or otherwise is erased, and the gestures of the father always seem like dominion. A hand draped casually—that's ownership, or something like that. I didn't know that was what I was seeing in the paintings at first and what I had been feeling about what was happening to my mother. You don't know until you start writing the poems.

CD: How would you respond to those who feel you characterize the Enlightenment in poems like "Enlightenment" as a male-dominated epoch that, for all its intellectual and scientific advances, was also racist?

NT: You know, I think I've never actually said that the Enlightenment was male or racist. I think that that's sort of the perception that might have come, but when I introduce those poems and talk about the Enlightenment, what I talk about is how good the Enlightenment was and how much it gave us, but there is complexity in that it also began to codify for us the ideas of racial difference. What's interesting to me about the Enlightenment is that it did both of those things together at the same time. So what I'm interested in in *Thrall* are the ideas that come to us from the Enlightenment about racial difference—these deeply engrained and unexamined notions of "white supremacy" and the twin "black inferiority" that we see manifest around us all the time and that come to us from the language of the Enlightenment. How can something so wonderful do something so not-wonderful at the same time? It's like, how can my beloved father also harbor notions of my "difference"—that is, a difference that is also less than? How do those two things go together? My father loves me, but does he also maybe think that the "improvement of the blacks in body and mind comes in the first instance of their mixture with the whites"? Is it possible to hold two ideas like that at once? Absolutely. When I'm called a "crossbreed," it's a parsing of me as well, and it is rooted in the grammar and syntax of the body and of ideas about race, about difference across time and space.

CD: In one of these *casta* paintings you write about, *De Español y Negra; Mulata*, by Miguel Cabrera, the woman's face is so black that it eclipses the light.

NT: That inheritance and where it comes from is what created the "Calling." This is a book very much about parsing as well, which is why "Knowledge" becomes such an important poem—the woman on the table is literally being parsed, being minutely examined, dissected. There's also the parsing of Sally Hemings when visitors to Monticello, in the poem "Enlightenment," are trying to figure out the proportions of whiteness. Then there's Dr. Samuel Adolphus Cartwright, who is dissecting a white-skinned Negro to prove the "essence of black inferiority" that he is sure is there.

CD: You write about that "dark imprint," as well as the "dark pantry" of your mind. The word *darkness* occurs in about every other poem of yours. I find that it works as an effective echo in your work. In addition to the "dark imprint" and "dark pantry of the mind," there's also the "dark subtext," the "dark Madonna," and the "dark earth."

NT: Well, I like to think that's true because it's *different* every time.

CD: You also write obsessively about the past as a "witness." You quote Hegel in *Beyond Katrina:* "The past is a ruin." But you add that it lives in images. You write that it returns as an iconic "red feather" because we can't ever get it right exactly. It's fictive yet also real. There's the fictive metanarrative about the past juxtaposed with the true narrative of the past. As a "witness," you talk about the importance of including what the official document omits from the lost narrative. One of your tasks as a poet is to fill in those omissions. You use the words *palimpsest* and *scrim* repeatedly as if you have to look through a curtain in order to see the past—the "Pentimento" you often call it. "What is home but a cradle of the past?," you write in your poem "Prodigal." Memory and forgetting are intertwined. You acknowledge that we live with forgetting and remembering, while feeling at the same time the compulsion to "get it right," to tell the true narrative of what's happening on Route 49 in North Gulfport. You bear witness to what's lost and erased, resigning yourself to that one moment, but also *trying* to remember, feeling *compelled* to remember, because if something vital and invaluable is lost, like home or a parent or a community, then there's an integral part of you, the witness, but also us, your reader, that's lost, in both real and vicarious ways.

NT: Right. I think that my relationship to the past is one in which I want to restore those narratives—those things that have been forgotten and erased. Sometimes it's more like what Robert Hayden wanted to do, which was to correct some of the misapprehensions about history, African American history in particular. When people don't know the fuller versions of history, they can make all kinds of assumptions about people and their nature. It was remarkable to me, in researching the Civil War for my book *Native Guard*, how many people had no idea that nearly two hundred thousand African Americans fought in the Civil War. I was told once—by someone people would have expected to be well read and knowledgeable—that the biggest problem with blacks in America is that "they've never had to fight for anything that they've received." As if they had only been passive recipients of white benevolence—not people who had fought and died to help advance this country to a fuller realization of its creed. I hear these things all the time. So part of what I'm trying to do is to tell fuller versions of history, which Americans can and should be proud of because it is our *shared* history.

In a more personal dealing with the past, with the necessity of making sense of it and remaking it again and again as we do, I think it goes back a little bit to watching my father pull out those notebooks. I think that what he was writing, in his thinking, became part of the official document. I've seen my father struggling with memory over the years, without him knowing how much he's lost, and one of the things he'll say to me is, "Tasha remembers everything, whether it happened or not." I've sort of struggled against that—I've struggled against this great umbrella of tradition and knowledge that he seemed to have that could always somehow undermine any story or experience that I had, as if I couldn't have perceived my own experience accurately. That someone else could and I could not. So to write it is also to create a little bit of a historical record. And as I try to write nonfiction about my own past, one of the things that occurs to me is that what is truest is perhaps not my re-creation of the past, not an autobiography of my past, but an autobiography of my mind at this moment needing to make sense of whatever I recall and how I recall it. That's probably the truest thing, and that takes us back to what is true and the questions I ask in the poem "Calling": "Why not make a fiction / of the mind's fictions?" We know that the mind works instinctively to forget; we couldn't survive if there weren't things that we forgot. Then there are things that we try to forget but can't, as well as the things that we rewrite without knowing that we've rewritten them, and they allow us to have another truth. So if my father's guilty of that, certainly I am too. What is truest is perhaps not my re-creation of the past, not an autobiography of my past, but an autobiography of my mind at this moment needing to make sense of whatever I recall and how I recall it.

CD: But you're really taking a close look at these paintings, which are both fictional and mimetic.

NT: Well, I think you try to do that by thinking about what Mark Doty said, again: that just beginning to describe before making those figurative comparisons will show you how you feel about things. Many people will never see the images, except for what is on the cover. The risk is that if someone were to look them up, she might say, "Well, wait a minute. I don't see it like that at all." The fact that I describe a man who's "knuckling down a stack of books" has everything to do with how I see it.

CD: The "knuckle"...

NT: Yes, as in: Who owns history? Who owns knowledge? The one who can knuckle it down like that.

CD: There are key moments in your poems, as well as in *Beyond Katrina*, where you decide just to "be quiet." You know that what someone has said is offensive or untrue or outrageous, and yet you, maybe for reasons that you weren't aware of at the time, decide to say nothing. Would you mind reading "Southern History"?

NT: Sure, as an example of my silence.

CD: Yes. We could also talk about the waiter who felt that Katrina "cleansed" the coast.

NT: That was the narrative we heard a lot.

CD: And you weren't able to say anything at the time.

NT: No, I didn't because I didn't want to shut him down. I wanted him to keep talking so I could hear his story, his version of things.

Southern History

Before the war, they were happy, he said,
quoting our textbook. (This was senior-year

history class.) *The slaves were clothed, fed,
and better off under a master's care.*

I watched the words blur on the page. No one
raised a hand, disagreed. Not even me.

It was late; we still had Reconstruction
to cover before the test, and—luckily—

three hours of watching *Gone with the Wind.*
History, the teacher said, *of the old South—*

a true account of how things were back then.
On screen a slave stood big as life: big mouth,

bucked eyes, our textbook's grinning proof—a lie
my teacher guarded. Silent, so did I.

My husband's a historian, and the one thing that bothers him about
that poem is that I take a measure of blame for keeping silent. He
recognizes that when you're a pupil in a classroom you may not have
the power to speak up and contradict authority. Still, I'm trying to
accept responsibility for the silence I maintained, even as there were
reasons I felt I couldn't speak up in that space. I think it's better to put
at least some of the blame on myself, which goes back to my thinking
about Yeats.

CD: And that waiter's comment—you write that you weren't quite
sure what he meant, giving him the benefit of the doubt.

NT: Well, I think it was a combination of those things. I think it was
an act of kindness as well as giving him the benefit of the doubt. What
I encountered when I was there was that so many people wanted to
talk about what had happened, and I found that what I wanted to be
was a listening ear. I wanted to hear people's experiences of the storm
and its aftermath without judging them or arguing with them, so that
I could make sense of all the different things that they might've felt.
. . . I think, in some ways, that's one of the things you have to do to be
a decent documentarian—to not necessarily interfere in that moment.
I wanted to hear what he had to say, and I didn't want to do anything

that would ruin what we'd built up over the time that he had been waiting on me and my brother. As it was, he felt comfortable talking to us, and I think he felt comfortable enough to say what he really thought.

CD: Speaking of your brother, Joe, you write about the silence you kept with him as well for a while, not intentionally in not writing to him, but getting these wonderful letters from him, not always know how to write back but realizing that he needed to hear from you. You confess movingly to yourself and him, "How can I live when my heart's in prison?"

NT: There were things I didn't want him to know, how frightened I was, how hard it was for me. What I tell myself—and I think I talk about this in the book—is that I did everything I could for my brother in terms of working to get him released as well as providing things he needed. I would send him what he asked for and would make sure there was money for the commissary. I would make sure that he had packages of books and articles to read, but I wrote him no letters, which I came to understand would have probably meant more to him than the objects—the things that I sent—socks and boot insoles. But I think that if I had written him, I couldn't have held back all the fears that I had about him being there—everything that worried me—and I wanted to present a face of strength and resolve so that maybe he could feel safer not having to know that I believed there was something to be worried about. So even when talking to him on the phone, I had to fill time with things that didn't go down a certain path.

CD: Did he understand?

NT: Oh, he did, yes. Writing the book made me realize all sorts of things—about myself, and my relationship to memory and to the past, and to nostalgia in particular. But in order to write it, I had to have conversations that broke those long silences with my brother. So now we don't have those silences anymore. I think they're dangerous.

CD: You talk about the "treachery of nostalgia" in your poem "Odysseus."

NT: That's right.

CD: You tell a wonderful story in *Beyond Katrina* about you and your grandmother while you're out shopping, She sees an old friend who doesn't know you and introduces you as "Nostalgia."

NT: The other woman introduces her granddaughter first, saying that it's her nickname but that her real name was something far more exotic and fancy. So my grandmother says, "Well, Tasha's real name is *Nostalgia*."

The metaphorical possibilities of this moment say something to me about my own relationship to the treachery of nostalgia—to want to go back to something that never existed at all, to have created it so fully in your imagination that you can't even see where you are or where you're going.

CD: She thought it was true?

NT: She knew that wasn't true! I don't know why! But the fact that she said it made me think, *Hmm, I'm upset because I just got called out!* It made me think, *Why would my grandmother say that?* But more importantly, the metaphorical possibilities of this moment say something to me about my own relationship to the treachery of nostalgia—to want to go back to something that never existed at all, to have created it so fully in your imagination that you can't even see where you are or where you're going.

CD: In closing, I would like to talk a little bit about your poem "Theories of Time and Space," which is kind of a credo for you in some ways.

NT: It is. Well, it's the opening of two of my books. I ended up starting *Beyond Katrina* with it as well. It's also the first poem I wrote for *Native Guard*. I was thinking of it figuratively when I wrote it—the idea that you can't go home again, you can't go back to the places you left behind, not because they're changed, but because you are. I was struck by Flannery O'Connor's words: "Where you came from is gone, where you thought you were going never was there, where you are is no good unless you can get away from it." When I turned in this book to my publisher in March 2005, I was still thinking figuratively, but by the end of August 2005 the poem had become quite literal to me because my hometown, Gulfport, Mississippi, had been wiped out by Hurricane Katrina.

Theories of Time and Space

You can get there from here, though
there's no going home.

Everywhere you go will be somewhere
you've never been. Try this:

head south on Mississippi 49, one-
by-one mile markers ticking off

another minute of your life. Follow this
to its natural conclusion—dead end

at the coast, the pier at Gulfport where
riggings of shrimp boats are loose stitches

in a sky threatening rain. Cross over
the man-made beach, 26 miles of sand

dumped on a mangrove swamp—buried
terrain of the past. Bring only

what you must carry—tome of memory
its random blank pages.

On the dock where you board the boat
for Ship Island, someone will take your picture:

the photograph—who you were—
will be waiting when you return.

That last image is literal. Before you get on the boat, there is a man taking pictures that he will develop while you are out spending a few hours on the island. You can buy the photograph when you disembark, but you're not the same person in the picture anymore because of those three hours. What remains is the evidence of constant change and inability to return to the past.

Galway Kinnell. Photo by Bobbie Bristol

2 / *Galway Kinnell*

G alway Kinnell was an award-winning poet best known for
poetry that connects the experiences of daily life to much
larger poetic, spiritual, and cultural forces. Often focusing
on the claims of nature and society on the individual, Kinnell's poems
explore psychological states in precise and sonorous free verse. Critic
Morris Dickstein called Kinnell "one of the true master poets of his
generation." Dickstein added, "there are few others writing today
in whose work we feel so strongly the full human presence." Robert
Langbaum observed in the *American Poetry Review* that "at a time
when so many poets are content to be skillful and trivial, [Kinnell]
speaks with a big voice about the whole of life." Marked by his early
experiences as a civil rights and antiwar activist, Kinnell's socially
engaged verse broadened in his later years to seek the essential in hu-
man nature, often by engaging the natural and animal worlds. With a
remarkable career spanning many decades, Kinnell won both the Pu-
litzer Prize and a National Book Award for his *Selected Poems* (1982).

Kinnell was born in 1927 in Providence, Rhode Island, and grew
up in Pawtucket. A self-described introvert as a child, he grew up
reading such reclusive American writers as Edgar Allan Poe and Em-
ily Dickinson. After two years of service in the U.S. Navy, he earned
a BA with highest honors from Princeton University—where he was
classmates with poet W. S. Merwin—in 1948. He earned an MA from
the University of Rochester a year later. Kinnell then spent many
years abroad, including a Fulbright Fellowship in Paris and extended
stays in Europe and the Middle East. Returning to the United States

in the 1960s, Kinnell joined the Congress for Racial Equality (CORE), registering African American voters in the South. Many of his experiences—world travel, city life, harassment as a member of CORE and an anti–Vietnam War demonstrator—eventually found expression in his poetry. One of the first voices to mark the change in American poetry from the cerebral wit of the fifties to the more liberated, political work of the sixties, Kinnell "is a poet of the landscape, a poet of soliloquy, a poet of the city's underside and a poet who speaks for thieves, pushcart vendors and lumberjacks with an unforced simulation of the vernacular," noted the *Hudson Review* contributor Vernon Young.

Of his first books, *What a Kingdom It Was* (1960), *Flower Herding on Mount Monadnock* (1964), and *Body Rags* (1968), *Body Rags* contains the bulk of Kinnell's most praised and anthologized poems. Using animal experiences to explore human consciousness, Kinnell poems such as "The Bear" feature frank and often unlovely images. Kinnell's embrace of the ugly is well considered, though. As the author told the *Los Angeles Times*, "I've tried to carry my poetry as far as I could, to dwell on the ugly as fully, as far, and as long, as I could stomach it. Probably more than most poets. I have included in my work the unpleasant because I think if you are ever going to find any kind of truth to poetry it has to be based on all of experience rather than on a narrow segment of cheerful events." Though his poetry is rife with earthy images like animals, fire, blood, stars and insects, Kinnell does not consider himself to be a nature poet. In an interview with Daniela Gioseffi for *Hayden's Ferry Review*, Kinnell noted, "I don't recognize the distinction between nature poetry and, what would be the other thing? Human civilization poetry? We are creatures of the earth who build our elaborate cities and beavers are creatures of the earth who build their elaborate lodges and canal operations and dams, just as we do.... Poems about other creatures may have political and social implications for us."

Though obsessed with a personal set of concerns and mythologies, Kinnell does draw on the tradition of both his contemporaries and predecessors. Studying the work of Theodore Roethke and Robert Lowell, Kinnell's innovations have "avoided studied ambiguity, and he has risked directness of address, precision of imagery, and experiments with surrealistic situations and images" according to a contributor for *Contemporary Poetry*. Critics most often compare Kinnell's work to that of Walt Whitman, however, because of its transcendental philosophy and personal intensity; Kinnell himself edited *The Essential Whitman* (1987). As Robert Langbaum observed in *American Poetry Review*, "like the romantic poets to whose tradition he belongs, Kinnell tries to pull an immortality out of our mortality."

Other well-known Kinnell works include *The Book of Nightmares* (1971) and *The Avenue Bearing the Initial of Christ into the New World: Poems, 1946–1964* (1974). The latter's eponymous poem explores life on Avenue C in New York City's Lower East Side, drawing inspiration from T. S. Eliot's "The Waste Land." A book-length poem that draws heavily on Rainer Maria Rilke's *Duino Elegies*, the ten parts of *The Book of Nightmares* revolve around two autobiographical moments—the births of Kinnell's daughter and son—while examining the relationship between society and community through a symbolic system that draws on cosmic metaphors. The book is one of Kinnell's most highly praised. Rilke was a particularly important poet for Kinnell and among his many acts as a translator, he would later cotranslate *The Essential Rilke* (1999), with Hannah Liebmann.

Selected Poems, for which Kinnell won the Pulitzer Prize and was cowinner of the National Book Award in 1983, contains works from every period in the poet's career and was released just shortly before he won a prestigious MacArthur Foundation grant. Almost twenty years after his *Selected Poems*, Kinnell released the retrospective collection *A New Selected Poems* (2001), focusing on his poetry of the 1960s and 1970s. His poetry from this period features a fierce surrealism that also grapples with large questions of the human, the social, and the natural. In the *Boston Review*, Richard Tillinghast commented that Kinnell's work "is proof that poems can still be written, and written movingly and convincingly, on those subjects that in any age fascinate, quicken, disturb, confound, and sadden the hearts of men and women: eros, the family, mortality, the life of the spirit, war, the life of nations. . . . [Kinnell] always meets existence head-on, without evasion or wishful thinking. When Kinnell is at the top of his form, there is no better poet writing in America."

Kinnell's last book, *Strong Is Your Hold* (2006) was released the year before his eightieth birthday. The book, which continues the more genial, meditative stance Kinnell has developed over the years, also includes the long poem "When the Towers Fell," written about September 11, 2001. In an interview with Elizabeth Lund for the *Christian Science Monitor Online*, Kinnell declared, "It's the poet's job to figure out what's happening within oneself, to figure out the connection between the self and the world, and to get it down in words that have a certain shape, that have a chance of lasting." Lund noted that "Kinnell never seems to lose his center, or his compassion. He can make almost any situation, any loss, resonate. Indeed, much of his work leaves the reader with a delicious ache, a sense of wanting to look once more at whatever scene is passing."

Kinnell lived in Vermont for many years, and he died in 2014 at the age of 87.

This interview took place on August 11, 2008, and October 10, 2009.

Chard deNiord (CD): In his elegy "In Memory of W. B. Yeats," W. H. Auden addresses the ghost of Yeats, "Mad Ireland hurt you into poetry." Can you, in thinking back on your career, remember what specifically hurt you into poetry?

Galway Kinnell (GK): I don't know. Perhaps the sense of stagnation I felt growing up in a decayed mill town in the Depression damaged me into poetry.

CD: You write about Pawtucket in several of your poems. One thing that struck me when you visited my creative writing class at Providence College last year was your comment that you were reluctant to call yourself a poet.

GK: A poet should not call himself a poet. Being a poet is so marvelous an accomplishment that it would be boasting to say it of oneself. I thought this well before I read that Robert Frost took the same view.

CD: Do you think it's dangerous to think of yourself as a poet?

GK: It's not dangerous. One may hope that one is a poet, or even believe it, but it's better all-around if someone else declares it.

CD: Would you say that Pawtucket hurt you into poetry?

GK: I grew up during the Depression years. My father became an absent person because he got up before any of us to work, and he was lucky to have a job that allowed him to come home for dinner. Then he went off again to work at night and then came home when we were asleep. So the only time I ever had any contact with my father was on Sundays, when after church I would go up on the porch of my prosperous neighbors who had enough money to have the *Sunday Providence Journal* delivered to their house, and they always left comics out for me. So I would get the comics and bring them home, and then I would sit on my father's knee and he would read the comics to me. It was a very important moment every week, but it hardly constituted a conversation session because he was talking in the voices of comic strip characters. He wasn't a very wonderful reader. He just read what was there. But being on his knee and seeing what he was seeing, hearing his voice, it was kind of wonderful.

CD: You capture this paternal affection in your new poems "Everyone Was in Love" and "It All Comes Back." You're back in your children's childhood years recalling key moments of their young lives and you're young yourself. Your recall of detail, affect, and even language is remarkable. There's a kind of Whitmanic embrace in these poems. You carry on Whitman's reverie from canto 6 of "Song of Myself" that begins, "A child went forth observing a spear of the grass," creating your own poetic definition of your childlike awe as well as your children's, but rather than writing metaphorically about an iconic child going forth, as Whitman does, you write specifically and literally. Maud and Fergus are real children going forth at your home in Sheffield, Vermont. So it's as if you're taking Whitman a step further in a very important modern, domestic way that's quite unusual for contemporary male poets.

GK: Well, that's nice to hear.

CD: In an essay you wrote titled, "I Seek the Death of Self in Poetry," you define the self that needs to die as the solipsistic self in order to give birth to a truer self that is more alive and natural. Malcolm Cowley wrote in his introduction to Whitman's 1855 edition of *Leaves of Grass* that Whitman created a transpersonal self, a self that crosses over from the speaker to something or someone else, as you often do with Maud and Fergus, as well as with bears, frogs, and sows. In light of this discovery you make about your transpersonal self in your poetry, I'm curious about the effect that some of the confessional poets had on you during the time you first discovered this crossover self in your poetry in the sixties.

GK: Confessional, or so-called confessional poets—I really don't like that term but that's what we call them—they mean a lot to me because they were among the first to realize that in poetry one can't really hold anything back. You've got to tell the worst, and then you can tell the best and the best will have a truth to it. Starting in the eighteenth century, there is so much false writing in English poetry, where everything's happy—sentimental depictions of the joy of childhood. Fortunately, someone like Blake comes along, who has the conviction and also the art to write searing poems about things as they are.

CD: You think that's the first place in English poetry where such candor emerges?

GK: No, well, I don't think so. I don't think you find that super sweetness in the seventeenth century or Shakespeare or Chaucer or in any of the higher poets. It was just part of the evolution of a civilization that had become satisfied with itself.

CD: You're the same generation as many of the confessional poets. I'm thinking specifically of Plath, Sexton, Snodgrass, Jarrell, Berryman, and Lowell. But you didn't buy into confessionalism completely. You were writing *Body Rags* and *The Book of Nightmares,* and you were spending time in the South working for CORE, taking a different, more socially conscious path.

GK: Yeah, I would never brand me with the confessional poets, as much as I admire them. I think I learned from them but didn't become one of them. There are many unpleasant revelations in my poetry, but they are not confessions but attempts to understand—or so I see them. The same could be said of the confessional poets as well. They just got swept into that unfortunate label that suggests that you want to rid yourself of your sins by telling everyone and being forgiven.

CD: Turning to the landscape in your work. The British historian Simon Schama wrote that "the landscape is the text on which we write our recurrent obsessions." It seems to me you have written your recurrent obsessions on the landscape of northern Vermont, finding this landscape irreducible as a natural source for your poems, just as Frost did before you. Could you talk a little about just what's so inspiring about the landscape of Vermont's Northeast Kingdom and elusive at the same time?

GK: Well, I'm not sure that I understand what Schama means. The house, the landscape, the weather are part of the environment when I write. The landscape provides silence, a variety of seasons. It provides a variety of animals and birds and trees. It provides a little cosmos of the best of the world. But I don't know if I'm writing more about myself here than I was, say, when I was living in New York City. Everything of yourself goes into everything you write. When I write, I could be anywhere—the obsessions arise from within.

CD: When did you move to Sheffield?

GK: I bought this old house in 1960. I've lived in it summers and parts of winters. It wasn't until 1995 that I succeeded in making it my permanent home. I liked living half in New York and half in Vermont. I think I might have felt something essential was missing in me if I had lived all the time only in the city or only in the country.

CD: You wrote about your Vermont house at the beginning of your career, and at the same time you also wrote such urban poems as "The Avenue Bearing the Initial of Christ into the New World" and "The

River that Is East." So you were equally influenced by both the land-scape that Frost wrote about and the urban landscape of New York City.

GK: I don't really live in Frost country. You know, Frost was born in California, and it was when he came to northern New England that he got the greatest ideas for his poems, seeing a world that he had never dreamed of there. He'd go down to the grocery store in the afternoon, and sit, listen, and talk with the men, the farmers as they came in, always secretly learning what it was to be there, and it was such an amazing place that he could do nothing but write about it. I had similar though less dramatic changes in my life. One was to move to the Lower East Side of New York and see the world of the Jewish poor, the immigrant poor of New York. And then I came up here, and I was shocked that this was not the New England of Robert Frost. That was a functioning, thriving farm country. This was a decaying farm country whose light was going out. There were two farms the year I arrived here. There's one now, and it's barely surviving. That first year was such a shock to me, and I wrote a lot of poems about it and a few poems about some of the people who were here—the storytellers and my best friend, Gus Newland, who was an old-time Vermonter. He came up here, and we worked on this house together for two full summers, ten hours a day we were talking together. I absorbed so much of just where I was that it allowed me to see—insofar as I had not—and to write poems about my life here.

CD: In your homage to Frost titled "For Robert Frost," you start off talking humorously about his gift for gab, asking, "Why do you talk so much / Robert Frost?" and you wrote that you were "worn out and aching in both ears." Did you find him a little boring?

GK: Boring? What he said thrilled me and also exhausted me. I love Frost's poems. I admire most his poem "Home Burial." To write it must have taken extraordinary self-knowledge and natural truth-fulness, as well as the power to enter into the feelings of another, a power not all poets possess. In this poem, I feel that Frost was determined to write the whole truth, and he did. Convincingly. He never surpassed this poem. It concentrates only on reality, and it is free of banter.

CD: "I'll come after you, I will" is such a brutal last line to that poem spoken by the husband.

GK: Edward Thomas objected to the harsh ending, but Frost stuck to his guns.

CD: Turning to your poems about your children, Maud and Fergus, I can't think of another American male poet who has written as affectionately and prolifically about his children as you have. You seem in paradise as a father in such poems as "Under the Maud Moon," "Little Sleep's-Head Sprouting Hair in the Moonlight," "Fergus Falling," "After Making Love We Hear Footsteps," "It All Comes Back," and "Everyone Was in Love," even though some of these poems address dark or frightening subjects—the Vietnam War, Fergus falling out of a tree.

GK: To me being a parent was entirely a joy. I never became angry with my children—and seldom even irked—except one time, when they were jumping around in the back of the car on one of those ten-hour journeys between Sheffield and New York. It's not as if I wrote only the good parts and left the bad parts out. For me it was all the good part. I may not have been a good father, in the sense that I traveled a lot during their childhood and adolescence, because that's how I made my living. It put a strain on my wife and on my marriage, and it wasn't good, but I had to do it and also, of course, I wanted to do it. They suffered. *Suffered* is possibly too strong a word, but they didn't like it. Whenever I was invited to go on a long trip somewhere, I explained to them at once what it would entail and asked if it would be okay with them if I did it, and they saw it was important to me and said, "Yes, do it." Of course, I realize that their wish to accommodate me prevented them from telling me how much really it would cost them for me to be away for so long.

CD: In almost every book since *The Book of Nightmares* you have included poems about your children. A recent poem from your last book, "It All Comes Back," is a favorite among my students.

GK: I'm glad to hear that.

CD: They love the way the son is father of the man in this poem.

GK: I wanted life to go on in this way forever. They were wonderful children. They didn't play the piano or sing or do anything elaborate; they just were great children. They seldom quarreled, and when they did, it was usually over some small thing and usually they settled it themselves. They had an interest in all sorts of things and liked playing together. And I liked the habit they had, right up to college, of using my knees as their favorite chairs, when company came.

CD: In addition to writing about your children, you also write about the past in general as both a kind of trope for memory, paradise, and loss. In your poem "The Past" from your 1985 book of the same title, you write:

> I wanted to sit at the table
> and look up and see the sea spray
> and beach grass happy together.
> I wanted to remember the details:
> the dingy, sprouted potatoes,
> the Portuguese bread, the Bokar's coffee,
> the dyed oranges far from home,
> the water tasting of decayed aluminum,
> the kerosene stench.

By recollecting random things from your past, you hold on to the past in the present, living twice as it were. This poem appears to be an important apology for the elegiac side of your view of the world, as you claim in the poem yourself:

> For of the four
> possibilities—from *me-and-it-*

still-here to *it-and-me-*
both-gone—this one, *me-here-*
it-gone, is second best,
and will do, for me, for now.

I'm curious why you omitted this poem from your last selected poems, especially since it expresses the actual logic of that elegiac side?

GK: Did I leave it out of my selected poems? Well, a "selected poems" does not necessarily consist of only the best poems. It is also a sampling of the range of the work. I trust readers, if they like the selected poems, to get other of my books and possibly discover in them poems they like as well. But if I had known that you liked "The Past" especially, I would have put it in the *New Selected.* For one thing, it is fully unencumbered by religious thinking.

CD: Do you feel that poetry remains an elusive process?

GK: I know that as time passes, some poems that seemed to me rather perfect cease to, and sometimes, maybe even after twenty years, I see what's wrong. So I mark the corrections in a copy of the book. In my library is a corner where the books are labeled "Marked Copy" in heavy ink on the covers.

CD: In the Whitman anthology you edited titled *The Essential Whitman,* you edited several of Whitman's poems by incorporating his most successful changes in the various editions of *Leaves of Grass,* thus creating new versions of his poems that consisted of his best revisions. Do you feel there are only a fraction of Whitman's complete poems that are, to use a term from Samuel Johnson, durable?

GK: If you gave a book of Whitman's final versions of his poems to someone who knew little about poetry but could recognize it, such a person could read and read and find the book extremely uneven. I came upon Whitman in college, but I soon stopped because, like many poets, he wrote so many awful poems and published all of them. Also, he revised his poems unwisely and made some of his early poems worse. He seems to have lost the capacity to criticize his own work and come to feel that whatever effused from his being was glorious. As I wandered through his poetry, I encountered so many of Whitman's rotten poems that I gave up—temporarily. Ten years later I studied his poetry in preparation for teaching a course on Whitman at the University of Grenoble. Suddenly I fell in love with his poems, and he has been my greatest influence ever since. I realized that if one starts by reading very closely Whitman's first book, the unrevised "Song of Myself," one would be obliged to see his genius at once. As far as *The Essential Whitman*, I tried to collect into that book only his best poems in their best versions.

CD: A consistently raw quality runs throughout your work, resounding with primordial energy. It's almost as if you write with dirt in your mouth, figuratively speaking, of course.

GK: That's pretty good.

CD: Does this make sense to you?

GK: I don't know, but I like it.

CD: But there's also an agonistic quality in your work that contains both antinomian and metaphysical elements, a quality that is on the one hand Frost-like in its affirmation of earth being "the right place for love," this visceral, mortal planet where your hunter in "The Bear" discovers "that sticky infusion, that rank flavor of blood, that poetry" by which he lives, and a metaphysical view on the other, a realm beyond this world as you describe it in "Under the Maud Moon" where there is "a sadness / stranger than ours, all of it / flowing from the other world."

GK: I wonder if either can exist without the other.

CD: There's a memorable line in your poem "Pure Balance" in *Strong Is Your Hold* about clarity. It reads as an epiphany, as something that just came to you suddenly after a whole life of thinking, or not thinking, about the craft of writing poetry. You write, "Clarity / turns out to be / an invisible form of sadness." This seems like such a profound conclusion to come to after a lifetime of writing. With both ecstasy and sadness in your writing. But for clarity to be only sadness in the end, as opposed to a mixture of happiness and sorrow, this seems particularly curious. Do you think this statement had more to do with the mood you were in that day than anything else?

GK: It think it's true, but I think when I wrote that I said to myself, I hope nobody ever asks me to explicate that. [laughs] Well, you know, it's not like a dictum to believe; it's an inside thing. Clarity makes something else true, but that's one thing—sadness—I think it is.

CD: Strong public speakers appear in much of your poetry as well, from *The Book of Nightmares* to your poem about 9/11, "When the Towers Fell." Other poets of your generation, Philip Levine, Adrienne Rich, W. S. Merwin, Maxine Kumin have also alternated back and forth between their public and private muses. With regard to your relatively recent poem "When the Towers Fell," you have credited Paul Celan's poem "Death Fugue" as an influence. Was Celan's poem a particularly strong influence behind "When the Towers Fell"?

GK: Well, he was never an influence, as far as I can see, but "Death Fugue" is a poem I've always very much admired. It is a poem to live by. I wanted to quote bits of it in my own poem.

CD: It's hugely ambitious, as are many of your other prophetic or public poems such as "The Fundamental Project of Technology," "The Avenue Bearing the Initial of Christ into the World," "The Dead Shall Be Raised Incorruptible," and "Vapor Trail Reflected in the Frog Pond." We live in a time when very few people seem to be listening to poets or at least taking them very seriously. Perhaps this has always been the case. Auden said, "Poetry makes nothing happen" in his elegy for Yeats. But what has compelled you to write your Amos-like jeremiads and lamentations?

GK: I don't think of my "public" poems as prophetic or exceptionally persuasive. I think of most of them mostly as outcries. The number of people who take poetry seriously probably varies with the number of serious poems there are. A poem often makes something happen, but as the reader may appear on the outside the same after it, you could conclude that nothing has happened. I hope the "nothings" that happened in the Iranian people from reading poetry—they are great poetry lovers—carry them into the streets to attempt their brave and probably brief revolution[*Interviewer note*: GK refers here to the protests that followed the Iranian presidential elections in the summer of 2009].

CD: You taught English and American literature in Iran for a year. Was that a fulfilling experience?

GK: Well, yes and no. That was an important period of my life. I spent over a year in Iran in 1959 and 1960. I met a great assortment of people. I became friends with well-known poets including Nader Naderpour and Forough Farrokhzad. Among my friends from other countries were a Japanese, two Frenchmen, an American who knew Iran well, and a Norwegian who spoke fluent Farsi. It's an amazing country—or at least was. Weekly readings in coffee houses by professional reciters of the great poems of the past; miracle plays, performed secretly out in the countryside, being forbidden by the shah; elaborate underground streams carrying fresh water through the desert; "strength houses" where ancient martial arts were performed; I could go on. For a long while I thought of writing a book called "The Iran I Loved" and including a lot of my photographs and prose, but it would have taken some doing, especially corralling and identifying the photographs. I didn't write much poetry while I was there. I don't know all the reasons, but one was that so much of it I didn't understand. I wrote a lot of very long letters about Iran. I was writing weekly articles for the English language edition of an Iranian newspaper, and I was ceaselessly traveling around Iran with my camera. At the same time, I was preparing for and teaching two courses at the University of Tehran.

CD: They published your photographs there?

GK: The newspaper published my photographs and descriptions of some aspect of Iran each week in the centerfold of the Sunday paper.

They gave me airline tickets for travel, but I didn't trust the upkeep of the airplanes and so drove everywhere in my little quatre chevaux. The time flew by. As for poetry, I ended up with a lot of descriptive fragments. Back in the states, I did write a novel set in Iran, called *Black Light.*

CD: Did you find the Persian culture inspiring?

GK: I loved the presence around me of an ancient world. The shah was trying to modernize Iran, but luckily everywhere the past showed through.

CD: Did you learn any Farsi?

GK: I learned about five hundred words but I couldn't speak or write it. I concluded that for a person like me, with a limited power to learn languages, one can't read Farsi unless one already can speak it. As opposed to Spanish, where the written language tells you exactly how to pronounce every word.

CD: In addition to living in Iran, you also lived in several other countries and states. Did you suffer from wanderlust?

GK: No, I take sustenance from wanderlust. To get me out of my rut, to see all I can of the world. When I was fourteen, I read Harry Franck's *A Vagabond Journey around the World.* I don't know if it was any good, but it was a bible to me when I first read it. And then Richard Halliburton's books, *The Royal Road to Romance* and *The Glorious Adventure.* Halliburton got this same wanderlust a generation before me and went to Princeton, also. Basically, perhaps, I just wanted, as an earthling, to know as much as I could of the earth. When I hiked for days and days at a time through some of the great western forests, I didn't always know where I was exactly. Some people might say I was lost. But I wasn't. I am an earthling. This is my home. I watched the positions of the sun. I read the stars. I studied the terrain. And I had a map and a compass in my pocket.

CD: Such purposeful wandering reminds me of the line in Frost's

"Directive" where his speaker's guide "has only his getting lost at heart." You know that line?

GK: Actually, yeah. You know I was reckless. I was fearless in a way when I was young. I almost died more than a few times.

CD: You did?

GK: Not through my own doing, but from my, you know, sense that I couldn't be touched. That I was invincible, and yet if I weren't, so what?

CD: Where did you get this sense of invincibility?

GK: I didn't really think I was invincible, but the things I had to do were more important than worrying about my own safety, so I gave in to a kind of recklessness. One of the times, I was about to fall off a mountain, and my friends came looking for me in the dark with flashlights and found me hanging from a cliff.

CD: How long had you been hanging?

GK: Not very long, ten minutes.

CD: Long enough.

GK: But I was getting tired.

CD: And you couldn't climb up?

GK: I couldn't climb up. Another time occurred in Louisiana when I was working as a civil rights worker for CORE. I was almost killed by some local racists who stalked me. Through a series of accidental moves that I made, not knowing I was about to be ambushed, I went into a store owned by blacks to get some Dr. Pepper because I was thirsty—I had been talking all evening. I was rushed by about fifteen black men with rifles who told me that there was a car of white men waiting for me down the road in the darkness. The black men had come to protect me, and they offered me a ride. They told me I should make a decision. They could work their way through the woods, which they knew very well, and surround this car, and all step out at once with their rifles on the car and just hold the men there, and if they resisted they would shoot them. And the white men would know that they would shoot them. Or I could drive off in the other direction, and they would prevent the car from following me. I chose the second. I didn't want a blood bath. So I was in my little Volkswagen with the gas pedal already to the floor, and I looked behind me, right behind me. There was a car full of black men, with their rifles pointing backward.

CD: Your escorts.

GK: Yeah, and right behind them came this car of white men, and then right behind them came another car of black men. So the white men were surrounded, and they were slowed down.

CD: It could very easily have been a tragic scene.

GK: Very much like what occurred the next year when those three civil rights workers, Chaney, Goodman, and Schwerner, were killed in Mississippi. I was doing the same kind of work. In the next state, I would have been killed or shot and buried. There were a few other close calls in other places, but those were my closest calls. Anyway, oddly, I wasn't frightened, even afterwards. I was indifferent to it.

CD: There's a renegade spirit in your adventures as well as your writing. You inject such intense psychic and emotional energy in your poems. Your language emanates it. Do you find a large difference in the energy you expend in your daily living and your writing? You have maintained amazingly high poetic energy in all your books, upping the ante in your subject matter with each new collection.

GK: I don't know if I can up the ante again. My energy comes and goes. Without energy, words are flabby. Energy is their air. It is the kind of energy that allows someone like Stanley Kunitz, putting all his bodily capabilities on hold, using every scrap of energy he saved up, to write—until he was one hundred.

CD: The following lines by Dickinson describe the psychic tension in much of your work:

> For each ecstatic moment,
> we must in anguish pay,
> in keen and quivering ratio,
> to the ecstasy

The magic of your poems often lies in your courageous cold stare at death itself, as in "The Quick and the Dead."

GK: You know, I'm old, getting old, what they call old. I don't really feel old, but I am old and I've got lots of afflictions. So I am prepared to die—I'm not prepared to die, that's wrong. I can't say I don't mind dying. I would hate to die, but I know I can die without feeling miserable. Does that make sense?

CD: Yes.

GK: As for that Dickinson poem, that's a wonderfully intense poem. But you probably noticed too that her writing life was quite short, the poems of great intensity were probably all done in the in the space of four years.

CD: 1861 to 1865.

GK: Pretty much corresponding to the years of the Civil War. She had started writing poems about four or five years before that. She wrote her greatest poems when this country was wracked with war. I don't know of anybody who can write with such intensity about that most painful of subjects. And then they diminish. So that's what the cycle of her life's work was like for her; it was very short for her. She got more done in those four years than probably Whitman when he was writing *Leaves of Grass*. He was writing all the time, writing furiously, describing his vision of coming into a new world. A new understanding of New York was marvelous to him. I can't imagine a day went by where he didn't write something. He was living another life really. He was living the life of a seer as well as a liver. Rilke had only small clusters of years when he was really writing. The same thing is true of Keats. Keats, of course, had only a handful of years.

CD: It's terrifying to think about.

GK: I know. And then there's some people like Wordsworth who mostly wrote the pleasanter side of his life and very little of his inner experience.

CD: But not Coleridge.

GK: No, Coleridge had his great moments.

CD: Is his poem "Frost at Midnight" an important poem for you? It has a similar fatherly compassion as many of yours, especially the entreaty for his son at the end: "Therefore all seasons shall be sweet to thee."

GK: I love the poem.

CD: When did you write "The Quick and the Dead," which is in your most recent book? That poem has remarkable intensity.

GK: I hope it has that intensity. *Strong Is Your Hold* came out in 2006, so that's already two years ago when *Strong Is Your Hold* came out and two years of fiddling around with publication, and then there were probably about nine years of silence before these. So during those nine years I wrote many of these poems, and they may have intensity, but I wasn't an old man then. I was a young man and so it just came out. One poem, then another and another, over the course of the years, which brought on transformation into old age. I tried to do what I could to delay it, but I could never conquer it.

CD: In your elegies for your sister and your mother, you use the words *elsewhere* and *someplace else* to describe that realm they have crossed over to. In your poem "Promissory Note," you use the word *oblivion* to describe what follows death. These atheistic references remind me of Whitman's musing on death in "Out of the Cradle Endlessly Rocking," where he also resists using religious language to describe the after-nonworld.

GK: I must have been eighteen or nineteen when I realized that much of Christianity is made of wishes. When I graduated from college, my mother asked me if there was a heaven. I thought: Who am I to crush her hopes? I said, "I don't know." "What?" she replied rather indignantly, "You spent four years at Princeton and you didn't even learn if there is a heaven!" In retrospect, I don't think she was hoping that my answer would strengthen her faith but simply hoping to find the truth.

CD: In your book *What a Kingdom It Was* you use a lot of King James phraseology. I'm thinking in particular of such poems as 'The Avenue Bearing the Initial of Christ into the World," "The Supper after the Last" and "The Dead Shall Rise Incorruptible." But these poems aren't Christian at all or even religious. They are in fact rife with natural imagery and atheistic conclusions that echo Wallace Stevens's pagan credo at the conclusion of "Sunday Morning." So I'm wondering what your rationale was for incorporating Christian references and conceits into several of your own poems in *What a Kingdom It Was?*

GK: The music of *What a Kingdom It Was* might sound a Christian note but not a Christian belief.

CD: This poem, along with the others I mentioned, end with mortal and pastoral images: "I breathe the shape of your grave in the dirt," from "The Supper after the Last," and from "To Christ Our Lord" these last two lines, 'The swan spread her wings, cross of the cold north, / the pattern and mirror of the acts of earth." So rather than there being any mention of heaven or religion, these poems point earthward in their conclusions, away from religious transcendence.

GK: Little by little I stamped out the Christian applications.

CD: You've mentioned you held in some scorn poetry workshops and writing courses when you were at Princeton.

GK: Well, not really. There were only a few workshops, taught by R. P. Blackmur and John Berryman; it would be absurd to be scornful of their courses. The true reason I didn't enroll was that I didn't feel my poetry was developed enough. I didn't want to submit work that I already knew was badly flawed. But one of the professors in the English department, Charles Bell, saw something in my poems. I liked his poems too, and we developed a wonderful, lifelong poetry friendship, during which our meetings were sometimes very much like workshops.

CD: I don't know when you wrote "Meditation among the Tombs." It was pretty early.

GK: It was early, yes.

CD: A stanza such as this:

> But if the darkness finds the graves where we
> Were buried under sillions of our past
> Still pointing gloomy crosses at the east,
> And thinks that we were niggard with our bravery,
> Our ghosts if such we have, can say at least
> We were not misers of our misery.

This seems pretty good to me.

GK: I guess one could find passages of interesting poetry in some of those early poems, but most were awful all the way through. That's one of the poems I showed Charles Bell, that he liked, when I was a junior in college. So that's it. If I'd gone into Berryman's class and shown them that they would have all burst into chuckles.

CD: Really?

GK: Yeah, they would have.

CD: Well, you found your own way. You went to Rochester for a year, and then taught for two years at Alfred University, then the University of Chicago. You traveled after that throughout the world. You were active in the antiwar movement; you took part in the civil rights movement in the South. You seem to have been percolating the whole time.

GK: Yes, I was, most of the time. Rochester was very important to me. I don't think I wrote more than a handful poems that I've kept from that year, but I felt like I came out a different person than when I went in.

CD: You've mentioned your admiration for Emily Dickinson, particularly her intense output during the Civil War. But I wonder what you think about her vacillation between faith and skepticism, between her passion for nature and her terror at dying. One minute, death presages oblivion, as she states in "I Felt a Funeral, in My Brain" where she feels "wrecked, solitary, here," then seemingly faithful the next, as in her poem "Of Course—I prayed" where she carries on an intense one-way conversation with God about his absence. But like you, she often seems far too attached to the things of this world to entertain any real notion of heaven. "It is too difficult a Grace / to justify the Dream," she writes at the conclusion of 569, "I reckon—when I count at all—"

GK: I don't know that it's her attachment to things of this world so much as it's her clear-sightedness. She seems to have been soaked in Christianity in her youth. In her adulthood I'm sure that her Christian usages were mostly ways of speaking. Her sisters and brothers were Christians, but it seems to me—and many others—that Emily was a staunch skeptic.

CD: Like Dickinson, you use particular language in your poems about the agents of death, which are also the agents of life. I'm referring to the flies and maggots in such poems as "The Flies" and "The Quick and the Dead." You seem deeply intrigued by these creatures.

GK: Theirs is an impressive world.

CD: You have some beautiful lines about that specifically in "The Quick and the Dead," where you write,

> I know that if no fellow creatures
> can force their way in to do the underdigging
> and jiggling and earthing over and mating
> and egg-laying and birthing forth, then for us
> the most that can come to pass

will be a centuries-long withering down
to a gowpen of dead dust, and never
the crawling of new life out of the old
which is what we have for eternity on earth.

GK: I wonder if Emily would have appreciated this passage given the earthiness of the language.

CD: I wonder how one could presume to speak for Emily, but I would like to answer yes. If she liked Higginson's natural descriptions, which she did, going so far as to memorize them, I certainly think she would like yours. I'm curious to know where you find words like *plouters, pronotum, noggles, sloom, drouking, moils, gowpen,* and *dunch.* I can't find them in any dictionary.

GK: They're old words that have stuck to my brain as I read about that nether world, and sometimes peeked into it. They're actual words, except perhaps I made up *dunch. Moils* and *pronotum* are still words in good standing. Others, unfortunately, have passed out of usage. I hate losing them, so I use them. But I use them only when they pay their way, so to speak, when they seem to express things more accurately or more vividly than our contemporary vocabulary. Do you think that happens?

CD: Oh, yes, the word *noggles* describing the way a large beetle moves, I see it. In your poem about the wounded snake, "Burning the Brush Pile," the word *hirpled* describes the hitching motion of a hurt snake perfectly. But I did wonder if these words were neologisms?

GK: They are real words, some still used in certain parts of England.

CD: These are wonderfully descriptive words that you have brought back into the language. Not just one or two but dozens.

GK: Well, I wish I had in fact brought some of them back. I see no sign of it.

CD: They must have been used by somebody.

GK: There is a *Webster's* dictionary that includes a huge number of the words that have fallen off the back end of the language. Being old, it does not of course include many of the new words. The *OED* is quite good when it comes to old words. But this *Webster's* I just mentioned, *The Webster's International*, 1925 edition, may be even better.

CD: I have to say it looks fantastic.

GK: It looks like an ordinary old *Webster's* but it's considerably fatter.

CD: Looks like a sacred book.

GK: Yes, it *is* a sacred book. And when you open it, you find lovely pictures and illustrations. It has a weakness for snakes and skulls.

CD: Here's the word *cere* you use in your poem "Ode and Elegy" about the hawk. "The cere above the hawk's beak / flushes hard yellow from exertion." But this word may still be used to describe, as it says here on my web dictionary, "the fleshy, membranous covering of the base of the upper mandible of a bird, esp. a bird of prey or a parrot, through which the nostrils open."

GK: It is still used by birders. What I wanted to point out especially about the dictionary is that each page is divided horizontally into two, a top section for words in use, a bottom section, in smaller print, for words that are out of use.

CD: This is amazing, so much more satisfying than looking up words on Dictionary.com.

GK: I would be surprised if the computer, with its attention focused on the front end of the language, would reach for many of these disappearing words. Now, see *hirples*: "to walk with a cramp."

CD: I'm not sure how you first found this word, even in this dictionary.

GK: I must have stumbled across it somewhere.

CD: Where did you get this dictionary?

GK: In a bookstore. One that specialized in used dictionaries and encyclopedias. That kind of bookstore doesn't exist anymore.

CD: I'm going to get one. I could use one. We didn't talk about your translations.

GK: Well, you know we could sit here for the rest of our lives . . .

CD: But who would feed the chickens?

GK: And we would suddenly wake up twenty years from now and wonder . . .

CD: Which reminds me of these lines of yours:

> Then I will go back
> to that silent evening, where the past just managed
> to overlap the future, if only by a trace,
> and the light doubles and casts
> through the dark a sparkling that heavens the earth.

In the last poem of *Strong Is Your Hold,* a poem titled "Why Regret," you write, "Doesn't it outdo the pleasures of the brilliant concert / to wake in the night and find ourselves holding hands in our sleep." These are actually the last two lines of the poem. They make the valiant claim about what means most to you, not the brilliant concert or perhaps poem also by implication, but waking in the middle of the night to find yourself holding hands with your beloved.

GK: Is it a valiant claim, or is it a wonderful, surprising realization? Isn't to find in a moment that we, who chose years ago to live as a couple, are still thrilled to be with each other, isn't that about the most blessed thing of all?

CD: Yes, and especially heartening to hear from someone who has achieved as much as you as a poet.

GK: Art is wonderful, but the moment love is smashed, darkness falls, deafness falls, nothing survives as it was.

Carolyn Forche. Photo by Don J. Usner

3 / *Carolyn Forché*

B orn in Detroit, Michigan, in 1950, poet, teacher, and activist
Carolyn Forché has witnessed, thought about, and put into
poetry some of the most devastating events of twentieth-
century world history. According to Joyce Carol Oates in the *New
York Times Book Review*, Forché's ability to wed the political with the
personal places her in the company of such poets as Pablo Neruda,
Philip Levine, and Denise Levertov.

An articulate defender of her own aims as well as the larger goals
of poetry, Forché is perhaps best known for coining the term "poetry
of witness." In her groundbreaking anthology *Against Forgetting:
Twentieth-Century Poetry of Witness* (1993), Forché described the
difficulties of politically engaged poetry: "We are accustomed to
rather easy categories: we distinguish between 'personal' and 'polit-
ical' poems. . . . The distinction . . . gives the political realm too much
and too little scope; at the same time, it renders the personal too
important and not important enough. If we give up the dimension of
the personal, we risk relinquishing one of the most powerful sites of
resistance. The celebration of the personal, however, can indicate a
myopia, an inability to see how larger structures of the economy and
the state circumscribe, if not determine, the fragile realm of the indi-
vidual." Calling for a new poetry invested in the social, Forché's an-
thology presented poets who had written under extreme conditions,
including war, exile, and imprisonment. The anthology solidified her
place as one of America's most important and aware poetic voices.

Forché's first book of poetry, *Gathering the Tribes* (1975), however, is resolutely personal, recounting experiences of her adolescence and young adult life. Published when she was just twenty-four, the book won the 1975 Yale Series of Younger Poets Award. Judge Stanley Kunitz described the work as centering on kinship and noted that Forché "tries to understand the bonds of family, race, and sex." Highly praised as a young poet of "uncommon vigor and assurance," again according to Oates, Forché received a Guggenheim Fellowship and traveled to El Salvador as part of Amnesty International, in time to witness the unfolding civil war. While there she viewed inadequate health facilities that had never received the foreign aid designated for them, saw young girls who had been sexually mutilated, and learned of torture victims who had been beaten, starved, and otherwise abused. Her experiences found expression in *The Country between Us* (1981). As reviewer Katha Pollitt observed in the *Nation*, Forché "insists more than once on the transforming power of what she has seen, on the gulf it has created between herself and those who have seen less and dared less." The poet herself admitted to the compelling nature of her Central American experience. "I tried not to write about El Salvador in poetry, because I thought it might be better to do so in journalistic articles," she told Jonathan Cott of *Rolling Stone*. "But I couldn't—the poems just came." In these poems Forché "addresses herself unflinchingly to the exterior, historical world," Oates explained. She did so at a time when most of her contemporaries were writing poetry in which there is no room for politics—poetry, Pollitt stated, "of wistful longings, of failed connections, of inevitable personal loss, expressed in a set of poetic strategies that suit such themes."

The Country between Us was named the 1981 Lamont Poetry Selection and became that most-rare publication: a poetry bestseller. In a critique for the *Los Angeles Times Book Review*, Art Seidenbaum maintained that the poems of the second volume "chronicle the awakening of a political consciousness and are themselves acts of commitment: to concepts and persons, to responsibility, to action." A *Ms.* reviewer called the book "a poetry of dissent from a poet outraged." More than one critic singled out her poem "The Colonel," centering on her now-famous encounter with a Salvadoran colonel who, as he made light of human rights, emptied a bag of human ears before Forché. Pollitt remarked that "at their best, Forché's poems have the immediacy of war correspondence, postcards from the volcano of twentieth-century barbarism." Forché herself told Cott: "The voice in my first book doesn't know what it thinks, it doesn't make any judgments. All it can do is perceive and describe and use language to make some sort of re-creation of moments in time. But I noticed that the person in the second book makes an utterance."

A dozen years passed between the publication of *The Country between Us* and Forché's editing of *Against Forgetting: Twentieth-Century Poetry of Witness.* Matthew Rothschild in the *Progressive* called the poems in the anthology "some of the most dramatic antiwar and anti-torture poetry written in this benighted century." They provide, Gail Wronsky pointed out in the *Antioch Review,* "irrefutable and copious evidence of the human ability to record, to write, to speak in the face of those atrocities." Building on the tradition of social protest and the antiwar poems of the late 1960s, Forché presents a range of approaches: "Many of the poems here are eyes-open, horrifyingly graphic portrayals of human brutality," observed Rothschild. "But others are of defiance, demonstrating resolve and extracting hope even in the most extreme circumstances."

In an article in the *Mason Gazette,* Forché commented that "the poetry of witness reclaims the social from the political and in so doing defends the individual against illegitimate forms of coercion." The year following the publication of *Against Forgetting* saw Forché bring out her own book of witness, *The Angel of History* (1994), which won the 1994 *Los Angeles Times* Book Award for poetry. The book is divided into five sections dealing with the atrocities of war in France, Japan, and Germany and with references to the poet's own experiences in Beirut and El Salvador. The title figure, the Angel of History—a figure imagined by Walter Benjamin—can record the miseries of humanity yet is unable either to prevent these miseries from happening or to prevent the suffering associated with them. Kevin Walker, in the *Detroit Free Press,* called the book "a meditation on destruction, survival and memory." Don Bogen, in the *Nation,* saw this as a logical development, since Forché's work with *Against Forgetting* was "instrumental in moving her poetry beyond the politics of personal encounter. *The Angel of History* is rather an extended poetic mediation on the broader contexts—historical, aesthetic, philosophical—which include [the twentieth] . . . century's atrocities." And Steven Ratiner, reviewing the work for the *Christian Science Monitor*, called it one that "addresses the terror and inhumanity that have become standard elements in the twentieth-century political landscape—and yet affirms as well the even greater reservoir of the human spirit."

Forché's next collection, *Blue Hour* (2003), took its title from the translated French phrase for dawn. According to a review in *Publisher's Weekly*, the book draws on personal memories, "ethereal images of twentieth-century horror," and is "dosed with a mysticism derived from Heidegger and Buber." Placing Forché squarely in line with the "visionary abstraction" of fellow poets Michael Palmer and Jorie Graham, the reviewer found sections of the book "lovely and mysterious," and praised the tour-de-force at its center, "On Earth," for the adroit foregrounding of its own "lyric complications." Her new books include the collection *In the Lateness of the World* (2017), which was a finalist for the Neustadt International Prize for Literature.

Carolyn Forché is also a noted translator and teacher. Her translations of poets as various as Claribel Alegría, Georg Trakl, Robert Desnos, and Mahmoud Darwish have won great critical acclaim. She has won numerous grants and awards, including fellowships from the Lannan Foundation, the National Endowment for the Arts, and the Academy of American Poets. In 1997 she was presented with the Edita and Ira Morris Hiroshima Foundation Award for using her poetry as a "means to attain understanding, reconciliation, and peace within communities and between communities." Hope J. Smith commented in the *Madison Gazette* that "Forché's work is unusual in that it straddles the realms of the political and the poetic, addressing political and social issues in poetry when many poets have abandoned these subjects altogether. In recognizing the link Forché has made between these worlds, the Hiroshima Foundation recognizes her human rights work as much as it does her writing." Forché is currently university professor at Georgetown University, where she directs the Lannan Center for Poetics and Social Practice.

This is the third part of a longer interview I conducted with Caro-
lyn Forché on October 17, 2015, that appeared in the January 2017 is-
sue of *World Literature Today* under the title "Voices from the Debris
Fields."

Chard deNiord (CD): I'm curious about what Stanley Kunitz might
have said to you about your turn away from the lyrical narrative.

Carolyn Forché (CF): You mean after *Gathering the Tribes*?

CD: Yes.

CF: Because of Stanley's historical experience and his wariness of
ideological, doctrinaire leftist politics and what happened in the
thirties—the Hitler-Stalin pact and Stalin's imposition of a command
economy, collectivization, and the Gulag—he was justifiably skeptical
and wary. He did not perceive a path that didn't run straight through
that doctrinaire leftism. He liked *The Country between Us*, but he also
said, "But that's enough of that now."

CD: He respected your move away from your early first-person aes-
thetic of lyricized experience and a subjective first-person speaker to
a newfound ambition of witnessing disinterestedly to the atrocities
in El Salvador? What did he say to you about this?

CF: He said something like, "You know you cannot be an activist and
stay engaged overseas. This is not the life of a poet. And your work
must make a turn away from this because it's a trap, it will destroy
you, and it will destroy your work." I think he was worried that I
would become subject-driven and message-driven and that my en-
gagement in human rights and social justice issues would overtake
my freedom as an artist. I think he thought that. And that's certainly
fair enough. I understood what he was trying to tell me. I just didn't
follow the advice, partly because I knew at the time that I was still
writing as I always had, without preconceptions, without, as Keats

would have it, "designs upon the reader." But Stanley was patient and kind toward me always.

CD: Kunitz once remarked in an interview with Mark Wunderlich about poets in America, "To live as a poet in this culture is the aesthetic equivalent of a major political statement." But I get the sense that he believed in you, despite the political turn you took after *Gathering the Tribes.*

CF: Yes, we were friends. We spent time together in Oxford, and he knew what he had done for me in choosing me for the Yale Prize. He understood in depth how he had transformed my life. I remember being on one of the London double-decker buses with him—I think we were in London, in fact—and he leaned over and said, "Isn't it amazing, you know, what happened to your life?" Because he knew where I had grown up and that my father was a tool and die maker. And it's true, he said, "I bet when you were a little girl, you never imagined that you would be riding on one of these double-decker buses through London." I said, "You're right, I didn't."

When we first started corresponding, he asked me about my influences because he was writing an introduction for the *Gathering the Tribes* book and wanted to know a little bit more about me. I was so naïve and so young. I didn't understand what he meant by *influences.* What he had meant, of course, were my poetic influences: who did I read, who had I studied, my formation—he wanted to know about my formation. And I thought he wanted to know about the influences upon my life. So I wrote him about my parents and grandparents and most particularly about Anna, my paternal grandmother who had lived with us when I was young. I talked about that childhood and about a Buddhist monk I had later met in New Mexico. I talked about hiking through the western American wilderness—I was listing all of these as my influences. And they were really the wellsprings for most of the poems in *Gathering the Tribes.*

He later told me he was amused and touched, and he found my answer endearing because it had nothing to do with poetry or I didn't mention any poets. So he made do and wrote the introduction using

Stanley Kunitz and Carolyn Forché

what I had provided. He was very kind. Every Christmas I would visit him for some hours in New York, and I would take him a tin of caviar, he would make a martini for me, and we would talk. He loved his caviar too, but he always put it away. He never opened it. He always put it in the fridge and came back with the martini, so we never shared the caviar. Good for him. It was a gift. I remember the last time I saw him in New York for one of those Christmas meetings, which had become a little bit of a tradition for us. We talked, that last time, about the ultimate dispersal of the human spirit following death. We talked about death, and I asked him what he believed and what he believed would happen after we die.

CD: Do you remember what he said?

CF: Yes. He said: dispersal. Our energy, all of the energy, the molecules that constitute our being, disperse into the universe to be reconstituted in some other way. And he said, "If you think about that deeply it will be a very consoling idea." And I never forgot this. That became a two-martini meeting because we were talking about death. Anyway, he died not long after that. I asked him about being . . . he was in his late nineties then. "I'm the same as I was at around thirty years of age inside. I'm living in a body that is much, much older, and is worn out, and this is difficult to bear. But," he said, "I want you to know that for the rest of your life you will be yourself. Unless you have Alzheimer's or something, you will be yourself, and you will always feel somewhat the same age spiritually, mentally, and psychologically, but not physically."

CD: The two of you remained very close until he died in 2006.

CF: I loved Stanley.

CD: His affection for and belief in you transcended any difficulty he might have had following your shift toward a more political muse after your return from El Salvador in the early 1980s.

CF: He did read *The Angel of History.* He also believed that I had to turn away from Holocaust writing and meditations of that kind. He felt that I was contemplating—that I was dwelling—too much on history and particularly the darkest episodes of the history of the twentieth century. And he wanted me somehow to escape from that.

CD: Because he must have confronted the same thing.

CF: He wanted to spare me, I think. But I said that there's no way out; I have to pass through this. And he understood.

CD: And you're still passing through it.

CF: He understood. What I really loved doing with Stanley was walking around in England looking at gardens. He loved that too. He knew the names of every shrub, tree, and flower.

CD: His garden in Provincetown was famous.

CF: It was beautiful. He also had an indoor garden on Twelfth Street, a little atrium filled with very special plants. I have never seen such an exquisite indoor garden, in a window that went to the outside. A small conservatory. He knew the names of everything, and almost no one else I have encountered does. He would delight in English gardens, and we would just traipse up and down the streets. It was very difficult to keep up with him. He was already in his late eighties or nineties when we were in England, and he could hike up and down hills and look at gardens and never tire. I once asked him what accounted for his longevity—did he have any recommendations? I asked if he thought I should take up running, and he said, "Oh, heavens no. A martini a day is what I believe in."

CD: One and one.

CF: Well, he always said, "one for me," but he gave me two the night we talked about death. He was radiantly tranquil and lucid. And, with the martini, almost more impish. His humor expanded a bit. It was wonderful. He seemed to know and to have read everyone, and he would tell wonderful stories about Cal [Robert] Lowell and others. And he didn't mince words about certain people. Those stories are not to be repeated, but you know if I brought someone up that he didn't care for, he'd say, "Well, that person did this or that," and I was always surprised. He wasn't afraid of voicing his opinions about things. But he was fiercely loyal to the people he loved and believed in. Robert Hass. Louise Glück, who was like his daughter. He had been her mentor, I think. And that might be one reason why—because we had shared Stanley—Louise has always been so open and generously kind toward me.

CD: Such a heartening story to hear about a group of poets' enduring affection and loyalty toward each other. Certainly not always the case.

CF: Louise has been really supportive. She defended me in her book of essays, *Proofs and Theories*, and for that I'm deeply grateful. But she is also scrupulously honest with me. At first she did not like *The Angel of History*. She did not like it and told me so, or said that she had misgivings, and when she heard me read from it at Williams College, she read it again and wrote me a note that read: "I've changed my mind about that book." I felt taken seriously by her.

―――――――――――

CD: If I could turn to a historical matter in your two anthologies, *Against Forgetting* and *Poetry of Witness*, in which you expound at length in your introductions of each volume, for the first time, really, in American literature, on the idea of the poetry of witness and extremity in the context primarily of Europe and Latin America. I notice that you don't discuss those American poets such as Pound, Eliot, and Frost who did travel to Europe in the early twentieth century and then those later on—Robert Bly, James Wright, W. S. Merwin, and Galway Kinnell—who also lived in Europe. There is an arc, broken as it is in places, to that American agon, connecting with international poetry. Like you, these poets also felt they had to become more international.

CF: And to connect with their peers.

CD: Yes.

CF: Yes. Mostly during the fifties and sixties.

CD: Bly included so many important translations of such poets as Machado, Vallejo, Trakl, Neruda, Hesse, and others in his journal *The Fifties* and then *The Sixties*.

CF: And he's promoting Spanish and French and surrealism and also Scandinavian poetry as if it were surreal.

CD: Exactly. He called it "letting the dogs in."

CF: Then you have the split. Donald Allen's anthology and the whole split between the academic poets and the other tributary of the river: what Lowell called "the raw," the countercurrent of the Beats, Black Mountain, and others.

CD: Right, the *New American Poetry*.

CF: Yes.

CD: Your two anthologies on the poetry of witness, along with your last three books of poetry, *The Country between Us, The Angel of History*, and *Blue Hour*, reflect an international ambition similar to Robert Bly's, but with a more particular focus on the poetry of witness. You were the first to write about "The Poetry of Witness," an essay published in *American Poetry Review* in 1981. Czesław Miłosz published a book entitled *The Witness of Poetry* in 1984, but you're really the first poet and critic to categorize a certain kind of poetry written in extremity as "poetry of witness." It's a little ironic, I think, given the amount of poems written in extremity throughout Europe and Central America in the past century, that an American poet would be the first to identify and then anthologize the best of these poems, and then, in your second volume with Duncan Wu, expand your project to include poems of witness from the entire tradition of English poetry. It's fascinating that the poetry of witness was conceived by a young American woman in the late 1980s following more than a century of poets writing poems of witness without calling them that or anything else with a political or religious connotation to distinguish them from other kinds of poetry. Do you think poets outside of America have an aversion to labeling poetry written in extremity, as well as other kinds of poetry, such as feminist poetry, confessional poetry, Beat poetry, et cetera?

CF: I'm not sure there's an aversion to labeling in other traditions, if we mean by that the formation and coalescing of schools and movements. I can think of several—the Misty poets of China, who wrote in resistance to the Cultural Revolution, and in Germany, twentieth-century expressionism, New Objectivity, and Dada, then something pejoratively called *Trümmerliteratur* or "rubble literature," written in the West in the aftermath of the war out of the misery of life as it was then. In the East, there was Social Realism. Interestingly, in the 1970s when U.S. poets were avoiding anything that might be regarded as political, the Germans were also turning inward with a movement called the New Subjectivity. Ingeborg Bachmann, the prose writer Peter Handke. The New Subjectivity didn't take over everything. There were also Hans Magnus Enzensberger, Günter Grass, and Heinrich Böll. After the Berlin Wall came down and the Stasi files were opened, there emerged an East German group called Prenzlauer Berg poets after the Berlin neighborhood where they lived. It was later discovered that they had been informers to the Stasi.

There are also other examples: the Hungry Generation in West Bengal (poets who revolted against colonialism), and in 1940s Britain The New Apocalyptics, who resisted political realism. I don't know of any school or movement that explicitly defines itself in relation to the experience of extremity. I suspect that "rubble literature" was more a dismissive critical response than a proclamation of identity. For me poetry of witness does not announce a school, movement, or species of poetry. It is simply a way of reading works that perhaps might be dismissed as "political" in a narrow sense, particularly in the United States during the late twentieth century.

CD: Have you encountered any criticism about signifying poetry written in extremity as poetry of witness in Europe or Latin America?

CF: There seems to be great interest in the thought of witness, in this mode of reading and consideration. I have found this particularly true in Mexico, Armenia, Vietnam, England, Libya, Finland, Sweden, Zimbabwe, South Africa—mostly places where I have had opportunity to discuss these ideas.

CD: The arc of American poets' agon over the past century has been such a start-and-stop affair, from Ezra Pound and T. S. Eliot's post–World War I poetry and essays, to Robert Bly's "letting the dogs in," as he liked to refer to his inclusion of Latin American poets and European modernists in his journal *The Fifties* and *The Sixties*, to Charles Simic and Mark Strand's beautiful anthology, *Another Republic* (1976), to your first anthology, *Against Forgetting* (1993), to J. D. McClatchy's *Vintage Book of Contemporary World Poetry* (1996), to Ilya Kaminsky and Susan Harris's *Ecco Anthology of International*

Poetry (2010), and finally to your most recent anthology, *Poetry of Witness: The Tradition in English, 1500–2001* (2014). How exactly do you see your anthologies and poems as an integral link in this arc of American poets' desultory struggle over the past century to connect internationally, particularly in your focus on the poetry of witness?

CF: Bly was devoted to translation, and rightly so, as we had translated so little up to that point and neglected most of the rest of the world. I really think that the nadir of this was during the 1950s in the aftermath of the House Un-American Activities Committee and at the height of the Cold War. From about 1948 to 1961, when those first translations began to appear—that period was somewhat introspective and quite xenophobic, and there's another factor: we were triumphant after the Second World War, and we saw ourselves as the center of the world and certainly the reigning world power. Ours was the default ideology. In other words, what we perceived mattered in a way that the perceptions of the rest of the world did not.

CD: Yes, exactly, and sort of the incipient notion of American exceptionalism, although it wasn't called that then.

CF: When you think about what happened in the 1960s, which really didn't happen until the late 1960s, following the civil rights movement, and the antiwar movement of the late 1960s and the seventies, what did the establishment fear? They feared the political engagement of the 1930s. They had no other model for this than Stalinism. U.S. citizens in opposition could not be other than "fellow travelers."

CD: Right. In the book by Eric Bennett I mention above, *Workshops of Empire*, he chronicles the history of the Iowa Writers' Workshop, particularly in light of the pedagogy that Paul Engle developed at the workshop in response to the communist threat of downplaying the role of the individual in the creation of complex literature. The University of Iowa has publicized it as a testimony to the idea that "vivid renderings of personal experience would preserve the liberal democratic soul—a soul menaced by the gathering leftwing totalitarianism of the USSR and the memory of fascism in Italy and Germany."

CF: As I mentioned, my colleague at Georgetown wrote a book on that same subject, and there's new information now being studied about U.S. government manipulation of literary culture, which might suggest that literature has been taken far more seriously than might be supposed.

CD: Like luring the Eastern European intelligentsia away from behind the Iron Curtain.

CF: They were manipulating and funding literary magazines, promoting certain literary careers as opposed to others. They operated within the United States, too, in a manner that was actually illegal at the time. The Congress for Cultural Freedom, funded by the CIA, had offices through the world, funding symposia, magazines, and scholarly endeavors. The organization also mounted campaigns against individuals—Pablo Neruda is one example. The magazines included *Encounter* in the UK, *Quadrant* in Australia, *Quest* in India, and *Forvm* in Austria. There were many others, some which at that time accepted money without clear expectation, such as *Partisan Review* and *Kenyon Review*. The CIA itself considered this intervention "its most daring and effective Cold War instrument." There are books to recommend on this subject, in addition to Rubin's, including Frances Stonor Saunders's *The Cultural Cold War: The CIA and the World of Arts and Letters.*

CD: Averell Harriman and the CIA supported Paul Engle with a small donation of $10,000.

CF: So that was still happening by the time we reached the possibility of intervention in Central America.

CD: And in a way that affected pedagogy in MFA programs as well.

CF: It was not only politics that they opposed but political engagement of any kind and, by extension, interest in the rest of the world, unless the objective was literary translation of certain acceptable poets and authors.

CD: So this literary reaction formation to the communist threat was absolutely fascinating. It created a pedagogy that championed the Emersonian ideal of man on the farm or man thinking, as opposed to the mere farmer or anonymous worker. In literary terms, the heroic writer. Paul Engle was actually fired from the MFA program he founded at Iowa, known as the Writers' Workshop, only to then found the International Writing Program, which has had even more of an international impact. Writers such as Mo Yan, Bei Dao, Etgar Keret, Dubravka Ugrešić, and Janusz Głowacki are among its alumni.

CF: The domestic Iowa Writers' Workshop was the mother ship for the other programs, which replicated its ideology until quite recently, and this still holds at many programs. Not all, of course. But there are faculties that still counsel students to avoid politics.

CD: This goes back to the early days of the CIA when it was called the National Intelligence Authority in the early 1940s.

CF: When I went back to research the biographies of all possible poets to include in *Against Forgetting*, I began to notice patterns. These sent me back to the library, to the files, and to the newspapers, further and further until I found the Congress for Cultural Freedom and the other government efforts toward cultural intervention and control, and I thought, "Wait a minute, there's much more going on here than I had imagined," and so then, years later, when I had found out about the committee within the intelligence agencies formed to monitor, undermine, counter, and oppose journalists and others involved with Central America, it wasn't as surprising to me. Disturbing, unnerving, but not surprising.

CD: Yes.

CF: You need to read Rubin's book for one piece of this.

CD: Do you mean in the United States?

CF: No, in Africa and elsewhere. In the United States they didn't really have to do very much. The periodicals once funded by the Congress for Cultural Freedom have distanced themselves, folded, or disavowed this support since then. But historically there's plenty of research that's been brought to light. When I began to wonder why I was being accused of being political when I didn't feel myself to be, in the strictest sense, political, as I hadn't joined a group or affiliated with a party, I began to sense that something else was behind the accusation, a strong current, an undertow. Rather than argue about the relation between politics and poetry or the poet and the state, I decided that it might be wiser to open another space for this discussion, one that had to do with ethics and morality and the social space of conscience, the dissemination of information, the fifth estate, and so on. There was a space for debate and argument and a viable and thriving critical culture, so I thought to propose this rather than argue in Cold War, Manichaean terms.

I would propose an alternative. I didn't feel particularly drawn toward political engagement, as I understood it. I bristled at the censorship—what I considered censorship—of art, censorship of poetry, censorship of testimonial writing, and the impulse to tell poets what to write about and what not to write about. This went against everything I believed about art in a free republic. "Witness" was initially misread as just another way of talking about politics. I didn't want to have that argument but rather to talk about the validity of this other space. Probably I should've had the argument, but I didn't feel up to it at the time. I never defended myself and never answered the attacks on the concept of the poetry of witness. As for interference by the intelligence agencies in our literary culture, well, that is a matter of record and now must be confronted and taken into account in any understanding of the postwar period.

CD: Well, it's fascinating, isn't it? How it affected the pedagogy of creative writing programs.

CF: I think that it affected the fiction—the prose—more than poetry. I could be wrong.

CD: Eric Bennett discusses writers who were celebrated during the Cold War, particularly Hemingway and Dos Passos.

CF: Dos Passos wasn't celebrated; he was buried. So, too, any writer whose work seemed to have a political dimension—and who was celebrated? A number of others. The pedagogy leaned toward producing a form of low-mimetic realism. This whole notion of "writing what you know" was interpreted to mean that one must write exclusively or primarily from within the sphere of American domestic life.

CD: Yes, there was a stealth agenda.

CF: And if you do situate your writing in, God forbid, another country, you do so as the location of personal drama. One writes from the position of a visitor or a tourist but not from any other position. The place served as backdrop for the unfolding of something deeply personal, the breakup of a marriage, perhaps, or a search for identity.

CD: Right. So this kind of pedagogy must have inhibited the readership of a few giants like Milan Kundera who were writing behind the Iron Curtain for a long time.

CF: To the degree that these writers were dissidents, they were considered acceptable and even interesting. Kundera was not a dissident and never claimed to be. Brodsky was a dissident. Miłosz was, after a time, a dissident, but he also had been a diplomat for communist Poland.

CD: And so there was this delay.

CF: The dissidents received substantial and quiet support, and they were embraced and accorded academic and critical legitimacy.

CD: Especially the Russian poets.

CF: Especially the Russians. But there was a lot of literature that never got published.

CD: That you, in fact, actually published in *Against Forgetting.*

CF: Well, for example, Wisława Szymborska. She was not known nor embraced here at that time, nor really was Zbigniew Herbert. I don't think that Szymborska's books were available here when *Against Forgetting* appeared. I wasn't looking for politically acceptable writers. I was looking for who was there.

CD: And who had been censored.

CF: Yes, and who was there and had suffered in certain ways. When you go to Poland, as I went to Poland fairly soon after the collapse of the Warsaw Pact and the Soviet bloc, there were writers who weren't forgiven or accepted because they had not openly been dissidents. There's a stage when a sort of cleansing goes on, a test of political purity, and you dare not ask to consider the times they lived through and their situations. Perhaps they weren't, in fact, political, perhaps they were having their—

CD: Well, sometimes they were just trying to survive.

CF: Well, you know what happens with reputation and readership. It's partly the work itself, of course, but it is also a question of who promotes the works and how much, who translates it, and who has the power to make it visible in the English-speaking world and beyond.

CD: And that's what you've done in your anthologies.

CF: For some of them, yes, but it was heartbreaking to leave people out because I knew that if I could include them, there would be a chance that other people would discover them, so there's a little bit more life for their work. But those I had to leave out—they're going back into the deep library of oblivion, and someone else will have to rescue them in the future. I had to edit the anthology to one-quarter of what I had assembled for that volume. There are three-quarters left in various boxes in my house.

CD: You've talked about this, the cost of the book.

CF: That's right, and they didn't want—they couldn't sell it at a higher price.

CD: It ended up being twice the size you had proposed originally, and they did sell it.

CF: They did sell it. They told me something funny, since it's still in print twenty-three years later. Dear beautiful Carol Houck Smith, who was its editor at Norton, told me that she was "afraid that it isn't going to stay in print; it's not going to sell." I said, "I'm not doing it for that reason, but I do think it will because poets have long shelf lives." I said, "You don't just go out and buy the latest poet. If this book is valuable, they will keep reading it." She was used to editing fiction, where, apparently, the new matters.

CD: Yes. But then she started editing books of poetry too.

CF: She did, but she knew how to sell and promote fiction, and so she thought my book had to meet some of those same requirements.

———————

CD: Well, this is interesting in light of your own work because in *Blue Hour*, for instance, you give yourself over to the selfless voice of the other in which the earth itself witnesses to oppression and injustice. You're channeling, but it's interesting what you said about the poets you had to put back into the drawer. It's as if you're saying, "Well, there is a kind of uber-witnessing."

CF: The figure of the angel Metatron, the archangel in Judaism known as the Recording Angel.

CD: So we have to resign ourselves to the earth itself witnessing to hidden or forgotten injustices.

CF: The earth takes us all back one way or another. We stay here, dispersing here, and the earth itself will disperse.

CD: And that involves a kind of faith in a way, but I don't want to call it religious necessarily. What would you call it?

CF: It's a faith in meaning, in the sufficiency of life itself. And the dispersal that we will experience is a dispersal that our earth will experience, our sun, our planetary system, and our galaxy. Everything is unique and once. Unique and once. One can mourn that but also celebrate it. I wanted to say something about the Recording Angel, the Metatron, who appears in *The Angel of History*. I didn't name the Metatron in that work but instead simply referred to it as "the recording angel." The celestial scribe.

Wim Wenders broke this figure into individual human-like angels in his film *Wings of Desire*. He had them especially interested in libraries—these angels in their long dark coats would stand in the libraries, looking over the shoulders of those who were bent in study over books. They also rode trains and subway cars, and they would simply listen, much of the time feeling sad while overhearing human thought. They liked libraries, I think, because they could listen to the thoughts of those who were reading human thoughts in books: the testimony of human life itself, for which the libraries serve as repositories. All those books standing, binding to binding, in the dust, waiting.

CD: What are they waiting for?

CF: They're waiting for the opening of the book. Edmond Jabès talks about this in a very beautiful way. And writing in that way, the sacred becomes a way of preserving—

CD: And that idea seems to infuse a lot of your recent poetry.

CF: It gives me hope. It merges my sense of the spiritual with my sense of art. I absorb writings of others and I write myself, recording and opening. Jabès works with two figures: the reading of the book and the writing. If you've read his four-volume *Book of Questions*—there are other books, but that is where one would begin, and then *The Book of Margins, The Little Book of Unsuspected Subversion, The Book of Shares*. Rosemarie Waldrop is his translator and best interlocutor and an extraordinary poet herself. I also recommend *Questioning Edmond Jabès*, both the title of the book and the act itself.

Witness is the legibility of the mark of extremity and the wounding and the passing through fire.

CD: Like the Elvis Costello song, "Everyday I Write the Book."

CF: That's right. And Emmanuel Levinas. If you think about his work, and Buber's I-Thou, and you think about Levinas's idea of our infinite and inexhaustible responsibility for the other—what if the other is encountered in the book?—in words, in language: witness is the legibility of the mark of extremity and the wounding and the passing through fire. It's legible in the book, saved in the book, and the Levinasian responsibility to the other is the responsibility of the reader to the book and to what is read and known there. Do you see what I mean?

CD: Yes.

CF: So that is how this all fits together, although it isn't something that I have been able to articulate in one place.

CD: Well, I think that's what's waiting. I mean it's the natural culmination in many ways of these two volumes.

CF: You have seen the Q&A I did with Christian Wiman in *Poetry* magazine, right?

CD: Yes.

CF: He asked questions that began helping me tease this out. He's asked me to speak at Yale in the fall. Maybe this is what I should write, speak...

CD: I think that it's a natural next step in your thinking.

CF: I have to go to Yale in a couple of weeks—this is more stressful because it's for an annual lecture before an international human rights symposium.

CD: So you are going to the divinity school *and* the law school?

CF: Yes. This is the law school and it's for human rights, from the point of view of international human rights—law at the intersection of other disciplines, this year particularly in the arts.

CD: Does this make sense?

CF: Yes! It does. But it's a bit daunting. The reason I withdrew a bit from the poetry world, why I backed off the whole discussion of how literature and poetry were suppressed and manipulated by political powers in the United States—I didn't want to engage it. I was fearful, I think, that I would be dismissed or, worse, vilified. I have witnessed attacks upon scholars in the academy. Such attacks are difficult to counter because they mask as something else.

CD: What does it mask as?

CF: Disinterested scholarly or critical appraisal.

CD: It's interesting—how the idea of New Criticism figures into this.

CF: Well, then you have to go back to the Agrarians, how and when they were formed, how they were promoted and rewarded, the masters of the beautiful art of close reading.

CD: I'm glad you brought that up because it also has to do with the fugitive poets who were Agrarian. They figure into this very profoundly.

CF: I admire and practice the art of close reading and teach it to my students. But if it's done in order to isolate the literary work from its context, for example, in political engagement, then the practice has itself been politicized and deployed against the freedom of art. To the degree that this was an instrument of that endeavor, I reject New Criticism while embracing the practice of close reading. When I entered the MFA world, I have to say that, especially when I briefly taught at the University of Arkansas, there was considerable commitment to the New Criticism.

CD: There's a detached purity to it that's appealing to the New Critics for its emphasis on the ultimate expendability of the author in his or her creation of literature, as Eliot argues in his famous essay "Tradition and the Individual Talent."

CF: You don't have to consider anything other than the text on the page. It's self-enclosed, self-referential. The focus is entirely upon the organic unity of the poem, severed from the hand that wrote and the time in which the poet lived, from the surroundings. New Historicism arose to counteract that, most notably in the work of Stephen Greenblatt. And I think *Poetry of Witness,* to some extent, that is why it was resented: for reinscribing the importance of the life and the historical context, that we look at the life and the experience. I think it's a wonderful practice to read closely and then to understand something of the life and the times, and, if possible, to tease out the trace or mark of that experience.

CD: I think your example of Miklós Radnóti is a very powerful response.

CF: What is one going to do with that? One can read closely in Hungarian, can think about the complexities of the translation, but if one doesn't know where those eclogues came from—

CD: It doesn't matter that he was buried for six months?

CF: No, it doesn't matter that he was forced to march, it doesn't matter that he was one of twenty-two survivors out of two thousand—and so who can ignore those things? And forget that Paul Celan was a poet who lived through the Holocaust. This doesn't matter? That seems to me absurd.

CD: Yes.

CF: I remember reading an essay in the *New York Review of Books* by Helen Vendler, a very thoughtful essay on Czesław Miłosz, and I think that she became aware that he was, in this work, taking into account his life and times, but she seemed to insist that in his case it was different: this is Poland. In other words, the political concerns and commitments and decisions matter if you are from Poland, but she also seemed to suggest that we, as U.S. citizens, weren't supposed to have such concerns or commitments. We were supposed to remain unaware of the larger world and also of our own country's crimes and complicities.

CD: And this is where you've suffered.

CF: Well, you know I don't worry about—

CD: I know you don't. But what the backlash did to you.

CF: The backlash came from somewhere. It had a gestation and a formation. As Trump supporters didn't come from nowhere, it was something cultivated, yes. And you can take the pieces and assemble them. The confessional poets emerged in a period of great interest in psychoanalysis and examination of the mind, and that was a nice distraction to have during the 1950s.

CD: The evolution from the Agrarian and the New Critical to the confessional was inevitable.

CF: Yes, and it all worked well. And in a way, the generation that published translations around 1961—Strand, Bly, Wright, Merwin—all published translations almost simultaneously. They threw a spanner into the works a bit. There was resistance to these poets at first, not as a group, but individually.

CD: Because?

CF: Because they had translated poets from other countries and all at once. They also had broken with formal, academic poetry and begun writing free verse. They had broken with the past and all at once. They were all lions, of course, as well as Adrienne Rich, who didn't translate but who also broke with the academic formalists.

CD: Well, she was writing poems about Elvira Shatayev, the Russian climber who died on Lenin Peak.

CF: Yes. With that subject matter, she also departed from the expectations of academic formalists. These poets went in search of another poetry. They went in search of poetry from other countries and for a reason. There was frustration. There was a pent-up sense of a rigid lack of possibility.

CD: There seems to be a long-term resentment that Europeans harbor toward the American MFA culture.

CF: The Europeans understand the political dimensions of the manipulation, but I think they also feel there's a measure of legitimacy to this, that American writing is oblivious to the rest of the world and could be accused of solipsism.

CD: That's an easy generalization to make, but you just mentioned seven giants who—

CF: Who rebelled against it? Yes. But you asked about MFA culture, not literary culture. I think the Europeans, and some others, perceive the former as suffering from that deliberate resistance to social awareness we spoke about earlier. But there are extraordinary moments, in literary culture, of resistance: Charles Simic and Mark Strand and their anthology, *Another Republic: Seventeen European and South American Writers.*

CD: Great book.

CF: A brilliant anthology—a precursor for me.

CD: Where did one go just twenty-five years ago to read Francis Ponge or Carlos Drummond de Andrade or Yehuda Amichai or Yannis Ritsos?

CF: We didn't have a substantial international anthology in print at that time. When I taught at the University of Arkansas, I developed a course called World Poetry. That was really controversial at the time. My colleagues, all men, really resented this course and spoke against it, even though Miller Williams was himself committed to translation. So the initial gathering of poems that became *Against Forget-*

ting were from the World Poetry class at the University of Arkansas. And why? Only because I couldn't find any books that had contemporary works in translation. There were no anthologies. Eventually, I thought I should make an anthology that I can use in class because I kept photocopying poems. *I can't keep doing this, I can't.* I had to feed dimes in the copy machine. They changed the fair use laws, and such copying became problematic.

My mother had seven children, all born within ten years of each other. My mother would always call out to us, "Would somebody answer that door? Somebody pick up the baby? Somebody?" And I was standing at the copy machine and one day said to myself, "I wish somebody would make an anthology so I wouldn't have to do this anymore." And I heard my mother: "Would somebody please be somebody?"

I had this big phonebook-sized, photocopied stack of poems, and I was invited to take the ID badge of somebody else to go into the American Booksellers Association convention, held in D.C. that year. And someone was in town, I can't remember who it was, who said, "Why don't you come with me?" Someone else couldn't make it, and I could wear her badge. I had the anthology with me for some weird reason, and I ran into a man I had known in the El Salvador anti-intervention network. I was shocked to see him in the American Booksellers convention. He asked how I was, what I was doing, and if I had another book coming out. This was well after *The Country between Us.* I said, "No, no other book; I can't write poetry right now."

But I didn't want to say I wasn't doing anything. So I told him that I was editing an anthology of poets in translation from various parts of the world. He thought it might be something that his company might be interested in. As it turned out, he was now the sales manager for W. W. Norton. He took my contact information and said, "I'll be in touch." And then about a week or two later, he wrote and said, "Come up to New York; I have arranged a meeting, and we'll talk about your project." I took the train to New York and went to the Norton offices. There was a young receptionist who greeted me with, "Oh yes, yes, Ms. Forché sit down, and we'll be right with you. Would you like some coffee?" and I answered, "Yes, I would love some coffee." She reminded me that we had ten minutes before my presentation starts.

CD: You didn't know that you had to make a presentation? The guy didn't tell you?

CF: Well, no, he didn't. I said, "Presentation? I didn't know about a presentation." And she said, "It's going to be in the board room with the senior editors." I told her that I hadn't known this and didn't have a presentation. And she said, "What do you take in your coffee?" I told her I took milk. She disappeared and never returned. I'm led into the room with all these men and one woman, Carol Houck Smith, and I thought: *I'm dead. I don't have a presentation. What am I going to do?* The nuns always trained us to confess, so I said, "Ladies and gentlemen, I didn't realize that I was expected to give a presentation, and I don't have one, so I thought what I would do is speak extemporaneously about this project and then I could answer your questions." I talked for about half an hour.

There was this silence, they were listening, and an older man raised his hand and he said, "Ms. Forché, what exactly is a poet of witness? And how is one different, for example, from Robert Frost?" And I thought, *Uh oh. Probably this doesn't make any sense.* I offered to tell them a story about one of the poets that I included, and I told the Radnóti story. There was silence, and one of the younger men asked how long it would take me to finish. I answered, perhaps foolishly, "A year!" *One year,* I thought, *I could do it in a year.* "Oh, really?" they said. I said yes. They asked more questions, and then I left. A week later I had a contract to deliver the anthology in a year. And of course I had no idea how to procure permissions. I didn't even know where most of the poems came from because I had photocopied them randomly from library books. I didn't have the citations regarding who had published them or translated them. I had to start over from the beginning.

CD: How did you manage to gather all these poems together?

CF: It took three years. A friend living in Minnesota offered to write for the permissions. She became the angel of permissions. Andrea Gilats.

CD: Then you got some help, right?

CF: People started sending me poetry and recommendations. But I didn't really have any help. Daniel Simko and I did a lot of the work together—

CD: And Peter helped you also.

CF: Yes, Peter Balakian and also David Kaufmann and others. I asked advice from many poets and translators, but the publishers would not allow me, for financial reasons, to commission new translations. I was limited to already published, available translations. I was asked to write an introduction, headnotes for each of the sections, and of course biographical notes. I also decided to include a selected bibliography. The publisher required me to have my headnotes vetted by historians, so we did that. All of them came back approved. It was quite a task: World War II in two pages. But the challenge for me was very real. I had, for example, written a section on the Middle East and hoped to write in such a way that my own sentiments would not be apparent. The happiest moment I had was when both Israelis and Palestinians responded that they liked their headnote and thought I saw things from their respective points of view.

CD: Is that when you got to know Mahmoud Darwish?

CF: No, I got to know him later. I had admired him but didn't know him yet. I got to know him through the editor Munir Akash and his wife, Amira El-Zein, a poet, scholar, and translator. Perhaps you know them?

CD: No.

CF: He is the Syrian editor and publisher of *Jusoor*, an Arabic literature journal.

CD: Did you get to know Yehuda Amichai?

CF: Yes, I knew him from when he was teaching at NYU, and he also brought me to Israel in the mid-nineties to read at a festival in Jerusalem that he organized.

CD: So just a huge amount happened afterward, after this came out.

CF: After *The Country between Us* came out, a lot happened. After Norton contracted to publish *Against Forgetting*, the work took another three years. It came out in 1993. So it took from 1981, when *The Country between Us* was published, until 1990 to gather the poems and decide to make an anthology.

CD: It was really a teaching tool more than anything else.

CF: All of us used to photocopy a lot, in those days. It was about sharing work with students and getting them to read in translation or at least to read outside American literature. I just wanted the students to know more. And I also wondered why they weren't reading Tomas Tranströmer and other important poets from other traditions, the living and the dead.

CD: What's interesting, as far as your own experiences, is that you wrote poems in El Salvador that were poems of witness, and so you must have identified with other poets—in other words, you weren't approaching this from purely an academic—

CF: It was when my work was attacked by other poets, and there were more than a few such attacks, that I began to look toward the work of others. It was a bit like developing a disease and needing to find out how others had coped with it. And the only way I could find out was to discover other poets who had gone through wars and later written poetry. Most of the poets I found were from other countries.

CD: Strangely, you were criticized by several of your American colleagues and fellow poets for doing this.

CF: Yes, that's true. There was some praise and interest, and there were some lovely things that happened, especially when I began to realize that some readers of *The Country between Us* weren't poets, and that was gratifying. I received letters from people from many walks of life, also from people in prison. I accumulated a trunkful of poetry books, mostly translations, in my car, those I had with me when I visited Terrence Des Pres. We started thinking about our question, your original question, which concerned education, and the political formation, the formation of consciousness, within the academy.

With respect to the formation of writers and poets, much has been said about undergraduate and graduate programs in creative writing. There is much that is positive that needs be said. Before the great democratization of higher education made possible by the GI Bill, most people couldn't go to college. Before the proliferation of MFAs, most people couldn't become writers. So that, I think, is a very positive thing. And I think there are many ways of looking at the elephant of MFA programs from different points of view, including the political. Some of the criticism comes from an elitist, reactionary position. Some of the criticism is legitimate and concerns the pedagogical inheritance from Iowa: the depoliticized writer and poet, the apolitical poet. So are we coming back to something? I don't know.

CD: Well, back to Terrence just for a second.

CF: Okay.

CD: You know, his belief in sharing painful experiences radicalizes the poet, I think in a transformative way, returning him to an emphasis on community rather than individual ego.

CF: Terrence had a tendency to view things in an interesting way.

CD: In what way?

CF: He tended to generalize from particular instances. He hoped that the confrontation with evil would radicalize and activate the empathic imagination. However, in some people this confrontation does not have that outcome. You see, he used the term *human* (to make us more human) as a positive term.

CD: And that word *community* becomes very interesting as far as the figurative community, the literary community, *the* community. And so he started examining what that community is.

CF: What is it? Or what does it mean to say to become more "human"? Because humans are capable of horrible things, and that is true of all of us. He always valorized the term. And I always wanted to ask him about this, but I didn't have the language to ask him, and then he died. I formulated the question after his death. I've never been able to interrogate that because—you know what I'm talking about—Terrence was my mentor, but I did introduce him to poets from other traditions. He wrote his dissertation on Shelley, but he hadn't read a lot of contemporary poetry. He had known Mona Van Duyn at Washington University, and he also knew Helen Vendler at Harvard when he was in the Society of Fellows, so he had some contacts with people who were poets or who wrote about poetry. But he didn't really read that much of it—if you looked at his shelves, there wasn't. And then he opened up and just began to devour that work. This became his project after *The Survivor*.

I think in a certain way he set me on the track of the anthology as well. We always talked about these poets, and he'd come up with a beautiful essay and publish it somewhere; eventually these essays became his next book. I think that our conversations led him to *Praises and Dispraises* and me to *Against Forgetting*. And the notion of witness evolved in part from our conversations about bearing witness. I remember telling him that I thought that many poems could be read as "witness," and he suggested that I think about it. We talked our way toward this. I tell my students, "It's not a *thing*, 'poetry of witness'—I made it up. You can't go around talking about it like you talk about Romanticism or something."

CD: Whitman has this wonderful sentence, "The proof of a poet is that his country absorbs him as affectionately as he has absorbed it." Which isn't really Romantic—

CF: In Whitman's case, we definitely have absorbed him.

CD: Thinking of all the schools of poetry today, all the backlash you have experienced, of the small readership of poetry now, 6 percent of the public reads poetry and literary fiction—

CF: Six percent? That seems high to me.

CD: I agree.

CF: I mean, just over 2 percent of Americans are in the prison system. And 6 percent read poetry!

CD: There's a larger community, it seems to me, that transcends what Whitman's talking about here.

CF: He lived in a time of formation of nation-states and the birth of a republic. And now we live in a time when we must become a world community. If we are to survive, we writers must go in the direction of creating a world community of poets or a world republic of letters. It doesn't have to do anymore with nation-states or with national identities.

To return to Mahmoud Darwish for a moment: Munir wanted me to collaborate on a translation he and Amira were making. They sent Mahmoud some of my books, and he told them he wanted me to do the English, to make these English poems. He said, "My translations have been frustrating for me in the past because they're accurate from the Arabic, but they're not yet poems in English." So he asked me if I would do it, and we spent the summer translating *Unfortunately, It Was Paradise*. It was a spectacular summer, and then I met Mahmoud when he came to the states to read one magnificent evening at Swarthmore College, an evening that included an introduction by Edward Said and music by Marcel Khalife, the Lebanese master of the oud.

Men and women came from all over the eastern seaboard. They were all in there, in hijab, without hijab. And when Marcel, who had set some of Mahmoud's poetry to music, started to play one of those pieces, the whole auditorium erupted, singing along in Arabic and from memory. It sounded like a choir from heaven. It was late April and my fifty-third birthday, as I remember, and Mahmoud later took us all to a steak house for a birthday celebration. This is among my most cherished memories.

CD: Well, you know, Carolyn, you must feel, at this point, embraced by the world. More so than by your own country.

CF: I've been very lucky.

CD: Don't you feel that?

CF: I do.

CD: And what you said about living in Paris for the first time, being in Paris that year: you said you love the Parisians and the French because they didn't care if a poet had been published or not. A poet was a poet.

CF: If you said you were a poet, the first question they asked was not, "Oh, have you published?"

CD: They were just interested in what you were thinking.

CF: Or they would say, "Oh, I'd love to read your poems!"

CD: Which is so un-American.

CF: I feel badly that Americans feel that they have somehow to prove themselves.

CD: That really is counter to your whole project in many ways, right? I mean like those poems in Radnóti's pocket.

CF: He wrote them hoping that someday, somewhere, someone might read them. It was like Celan's message in a bottle: somewhere, some-day, *on the shores of the heart.*

CD: So those are the interesting, earthly books we were talking about. Where they exist on earth.

CF: I miss Mahmoud Darwish and Czesław Miłosz and Tomaž Šalamun and Tomas Tranströmer, all of them gone now. I feel incredibly fortunate to have known these poets, and that I was able to meet Wisława Szymborska. I have a book signed by her, and I treasure it. I feel blessed. My goodness, it makes up for, well, I don't need things to be made up for. You know what? It teaches you things, it tests you, and that's fine. Most people on earth go through horrible experiences. Humans suffer and starve. What I feel about those times now, those years, is simply a kind of curiosity, a desire to know, as we were discussing earlier. Why the thinking was what it was. And how that has changed, and I think it has changed profoundly, not only since 9/11 but because of the aftermath wars, the endless wars we have prosecuted following that attack.

CD: But we'd be mistaken in thinking any of these voices will save us.

CF: No, such saving is always radically uncertain.

CD: So yes, radically uncertain, and yet there is nonetheless a noble purpose and cause in preserving these voices at the same time. As well as extrapolating them into snowflakes.

CF: And if you think about Whitman, he was writing about our period. He thought he was writing about the birth of a republic in the contiguous, continental states. He thought he was looking at the birth of a nation. And because he was praising the multitudes, all who had gathered from all around the world and their great numbers, he really was present with regards to time. He saw our century, too, and the birth of humanity.

CD: And then once you realize that was true . . .

CF: Then it doesn't matter.

CD: It doesn't matter. And that is a great—what was it? You put words to it...

CF: Well, you're free, which Stanley Kunitz always believed. The other thing that I think was good was that it all happened to me when I was very young. I was thirty-one when *The Country between Us* was published, so I was impressionable enough. I got that part over with early.

CD: Well, many never get beyond their need for fame.

CF: Fame is evanescent. You are yourself, regardless of whether you are known by a multitude of others.

CD: Yes.

CF: You have to walk around in your body. That does not change. But I think that being known by people you don't know is a very difficult experience.

CD: In the sense, being known by people you don't know—

CF: Yes, because of the level of exposure. You're exposed, and you can easily develop a false sense of selfhood and of reality that doesn't correspond to actual reality. The world is no longer reflected back to you undistorted. Poets mostly never have to worry about this because they are almost never that famous in the larger world.

CD: There are a few delusional people who think that it does matter.

CF: To provide some context on what does and does not matter: my husband took this photograph [opens to a photograph in El Salvador: Work of Thirty Photographers]. He was in a vehicle on a road in El Salvador, and he saw figures moving up ahead. And they were moving around on the road, so he slowed down, and he decided he wanted to see who it was and what was happening. He stopped the car, parked it, got out of the car, and walked toward the figures, and he saw that they—he showed them his camera, put his hands up, they were military—and he saw that there were bodies in the road and that the soldiers had machetes. He put his hands up and walked slowly, slowly, toward them taking pictures, and they saw that he was taking pictures. It was a period in the war when the military was proud. They stood and posed behind each of those corpses, and he took the last picture with them standing behind the corpses, as if actually wanting to be photographed. And then he got in the car and drove slowly off. But this is the picture he took, and they had just mutilated the bodies. They were soldiers—soldiers who became, in this image, anonymously and briefly famous.

CD: They had guns too.

CF: Yes, but they used the machetes to cut the bodies up.

CD: It's like the colonel being proud of the ears.

CF: That's right. Harry [Mattison] was working for *Time* then, but this photograph was published in *Newsweek*. And they captioned it: "Soldiers on Macabre Guard Duty." So the soldiers were presented as simply "guarding."

CD: But they did do it.

CF: Yes. They were doing it as Harry encountered them.

CD: So the U.S.—

CF: *Newsweek* changed the caption to "Macabre Guard Duty," and Harry said that's when he realized—

CD: What was going on.

CF: But this was very difficult. When I look at these pictures now, they look as if they were taken in the far past, in another time. [turns another page of the book] Those are the guerillas. Look at them. They're just kids here. They're poor. They rose up and fought and died years ago. Knowing them changed everything for me.

CD: And you were there, at that time.

CF: Yes, I left just before the war was thought to have officially begun. I was there during the time of the death squads.

CD: And you saw a lot of that.

CF: Corpses, yes. Many. But the war itself, meaning the military engagement between the U.S.-supported Salvadoran military forces and the guerillas, mostly happened after I left. I was never in the fighting. I witnessed the death squads' brutalities and butchery. I didn't see the fighting. But I did go back when the fighting was over and the truce was made.

CD: So this gets back to my point that you weren't interested in the poetry of witness—

CF: No, that idea hadn't been born yet.

CD: Right, right. But it was instilled in you, it was born in you as a result of your own firsthand experience before you even began writing about it. As opposed to reading a news story or hearing about it.

CF: In the beginning, I was translating a woman poet.

CD: Claribel Alegría.

CF: Who was deeply affected by things she had witnessed as a child, and I had to work through that in her poetry, and I became—

CD: In El Salvador, right?

CF: Yes. But something happened.

CD: Something happened. You know that's interesting, because you know how the book *The Prophets* always talks about "something happened." For a prophet to be a prophet, Heschel talks about this in his two books, that one of the key things he mentions is that something happened.

CF: You can't say what.

Claribel Alegría and Carolyn Forché (left) in Mallorca in 1977

CD: Exactly, but that *something* happened to you.

CF: It's an explosive moment, and it turns you in another direction.

CD: For the rest of your life.

CF: Yes. You can't go back. I didn't know that at the time, but I would choose it again.

CD: Something happened to Amos, something happened to Hosea, something happened to Isaiah.

CF: And you can never go back. I'm calling the memoir *What You Have Heard Is True*, the first sentence of "The Colonel" poem. It has an epigraph from James Baldwin: "For the strangest people in the world are those people recognized, beneath one's senses, by one's soul—the people, utterly indispensable for one's journey." Leonel Gómez is that person for me. My book is not about the war itself, but about what happened before the war.

CD: You were a good friend of Daniel Berrigan, who recently died. You both come from a Catholic background and had intense discussions about witnessing and other matters. Could you talk a little about the nature of your friendship as well as some of the ongoing conversations you had with him? Do you think your religious background as a Catholic ended up having a strong influence on you as a poet who has followed in the prophetic tradition of witnessing, as Berrigan did?

CF: I think the answer is yes, my poetry is influenced by the crucible of Catholic formation. My friendship with Daniel began upon my return from El Salvador, when I was involved with the antiwar, anti-intervention, sanctuary, and witness for peace movements. Daniel was also deeply committed to this work, and our paths sometimes crossed. We had long conversations and one recurring argument concerning the right of the oppressed to defend themselves and overthrow their oppressors by force after all peaceful means have been exhausted. Daniel, the radical pacifist, did not support the use of violence under any circumstances. In the immediate aftermath of my experience in El Salvador, I was persuaded of the right of the oppressed to armed revolution under certain conditions. Now, I no longer believe that change comes about through force of arms. I wish

I hadn't wasted what time I had with Daniel on this particular argument. The rest of the time we talked about the theology of liberation, poetry, and other such worthy subjects. We taught a few workshops together, one in a monastery in upstate New York, presenting poetry of witness. He was an extraordinary human being, a dedicated and deeply spiritual priest. It is a great honor to have known him.

CD: In your various interviews you show a familiarity with a large number of philosophers and critics, like Emmanuel Levinas, Walter Benjamin, Jean-François Lyotard, Hannah Arendt, and Hans Magnus Enzensberger—to name just some of them. Are these authors ones you've largely read on your own? Leaving aside Benjamin, whose presence in *The Angel of History* is clear, how important are these writers for understanding your work?

CF: As an undergraduate I studied existential phenomenology, but since then I have read largely on my own, often guided by friends with scholarly expertise in continental philosophy and twentieth-century European thought. We've talked about some of them: Sandor Goodhart, Geoffrey Hartman, Tony Brinkley.

CD: Near the end of your 2000 interview with David Wright, you comment: "Poetry is what maintains our capacity for contemplation and difficulty. Poetry is where that contemplation and difficulty converses with itself. Poetry is a very important endeavor. It's so important, it's so sacred a practice that the way in which it's been commodified is an angering problem for me. I don't want it to be that way. I'll continue to write it out of joy and longing to do so." How would you modify, augment, or intensify that comment today, some sixteen years later?

CF: I still believe that writing and reading poetry and other forms of serious literary art preserve our capacity for meditative attention and contemplation; I still believe strongly in the necessity of poetry, of imaginative art. I would no longer say that poetry has been commodified, and I'm not sure what I meant by that at the time. I have always considered poetry to be an artistic practice that most resisted commodification.

I still believe that writing and reading poetry and other forms of serious literary art preserve our capacity for meditative attention and contemplation; I still believe strongly in the necessity of poetry, of imaginative art.

CD: Besides people like Terence Diggory, are there any other critics whose work you value? Whether of your own poetry or that of other poets you admire?

CF: Calvin Bedient, Robert Boyers, James Longenbach, Dan Chiasson, Juliana Spahr, David Orr, Alicia Ostriker, and others.

CD: Besides Ilya Kaminsky, what other living poets' work do you admire, find compelling, moving?

CF: There are many, and may I be forgiven for omitting? I think I would like to mention some younger poets, if I may, such as Ishion Hutchinson, Tarfia Faizullah, Jericho Brown, Jamaal May, Natalie Diaz, Sherwin Bitsui, Don Mee Choi, Valzhyna Mort, Tracy K. Smith, Mai Der Vang, Nikola Madzirov—

CD: You have written and said so many memorable things about the poetry of witness over the years. I would like to conclude by asking you to respond briefly to a few questions about some of your most incisive comments and insights with regard to your maturation from a lyrical poet at the start of your career to a poet of witness who has sacrificed her subjective muse for a more selfless voice that, in your own words, "lays open to the other [in] an unending address, a call to the other, which manifests that-which-happened."

I'd like to start with this provocative quote you made several years ago: "One can say I'm political but not say I'm ethical? I remember the poet June Jordan once said to me, 'I don't know what my politics are, but I know what I want to help have happen.' I always liked that phrase." What's more appealing to you specifically about saying "I know what I want to help have happen" than talking about your politics?

CF: I lean toward ethics rather than politics, toward intersubjective awareness, the practice and cultivation of imaginative empathy, a sense of interdependence within the biosphere.

CD: You have often quoted this claim about language by Paul Celan: "One thing remained attainable, close and unlost amidst all the losses: language. Language was not lost, in spite of all that happened. But it had to go through its own responselessness, go through horrible silences, go through the thousand darknesses of death-bringing speech." Now that you have edited two large volumes of the poetry of witness, *Against Forgetting* and *The Poetry of Witness: The Tradition in English, 1500–2001,* could you talk a little about just what it is about "language" that survives extremity? Just how poetry finds the last word within the "horrible silences" and "thousand darknesses"? Are there any poets in particular in either of your anthologies that you feel address this mystery directly?

CF: Czesław Miłosz acknowledges that in some poets a peculiar fusion of the personal and historical appears, and in such poets, we may also observe a certain reticence; they are poets of silence as much as of the word; they have deeply assimilated personal and collective experience and have surrendered themselves to the work of poetic transmission. They are often perceived as hermetic and obscure while imagining themselves to be striving for utmost clarity. If I had to choose two poets who most exemplify this fusion, they would be Paul Celan and Ingeborg Bachmann.

CD: You write this trenchant definition of the poetry of witness in your essay "Reading the Living Archives: The Witness of Literary Art":

> Witness, then, is neither martyrdom nor the saying of a juridical truth, but the owning of one's infinite responsibility for the *other one* (*l'autrui*). It is not to be mistaken for politicized confessionalism. The confessional is the mode of the subjective, and the representational that of the objective. . . . In the poetry of witness, the poem makes

present to us the experience of the other, the poem *is* the experience, rather than a symbolic representation. When we read the poem as witness, we are marked by it and become ourselves witnesses to what it has made present before us. Language incises the page, wounding it with testimonial presence, and the reader is marked by encounter with that presence. Witness begets witness. The text we read becomes a living archive.

Your idea of the text becoming a living archive posits language with a sacred function but not necessarily in the religious sense. William Blake wrote that the "most sublime act is to set another before you," which gets at your notion of "humans coming into being through relation." Where do you draw the line in your thinking, if you do draw a line, between the religious and human connotations of the poetry of witness as a living archive that wounds with testimonial presence?

CF: There is a certain sacred radiance to the language of witness. After all, the term itself, *witness*, derives from the Greek μάρτυρας (*mártyras*). In my own apprehension, both sacred and secular connotations are available; the language suggests constellations of thought and awareness, human and divine.

CD: Would you mind elaborating a bit more on this quote from your essay "Twentieth Century Poetry of Witness," especially what you mean by "poem as trace, poem as evidence"? It seems like a poem of witness in your description of it here takes on a metaphysical validity all of its own, one that must involve both the poet's sovereign imagination and the reader's faith in the poem.

By situating poetry in this social space, we can avoid some of our residual prejudices. A poem that calls us from the other side of a situation of extremity cannot be judged by simplistic notions of "accuracy" or "truth to life." It will have to be judged, as Ludwig Wittgenstein said of confession, by its consequences, not by our ability to verify its truth. In fact, the poem might be our only evidence that an event has occurred: it exists for us as the sole trace of an occurrence.

As such, there is nothing for us to base the poem on, no independent account that will tell us whether or not we can see a given text as being "objectively" true. Poem as trace, poem as evidence.

CF: Language here is regarded not as representational but as evidentiary; the word is indexical, pointing toward that which happened. One is moved or marked by the poem in the act of reading: by the vortices of the imagery, metaphorical resonances, metonymic play, by the music, the compression of utterance. Language written in the aftermath of extremity bears the imprint of that experience, regardless of its content; it is that which is written out of that which was endured. In many respects, this is ineffable. The words come not from recollection in tranquility but from wanderings in a debris field.

Language written in the aftermath of extremity bears the imprint of that experience, regardless of its content; it is that which is written out of that which was endured. In many respects, this is ineffable. The words come not from recollection in tranquility but from wanderings in a debris field.

Editorial note: The following addendum was added in November 2016.

CD: The country is reeling in the wake of the recent election. What are your thoughts?

CF: In times like these, and from what I know of the world, one must marshal inner strength; must be courageous and resolute, calm and vigilant; must connect with others of like mind; must not compromise with racism, bigotry, and hatred; but must also be quietly prepared for the consequences of every confrontation (physical harm, imprisonment, death)—must do so anyway, must go to every length to protect others. Not many humans can do this. Many will live as many lived in Eastern Europe and in Russia under totalitarianism. They will mind their own business, get what they can to survive, and go about their daily lives. That's all right for them. We should not be judgmental of them. But there were dissidents too, and they worked together, and after decades of work, the system came down. In this moment, because of environmental death, because the next five years so matter (are crucial to human survival), we do not have "decades." Harry and I have lived in countries under oppressive regimes, with governments supported by the United States. We have not often been the good guys. Most people in the United States paid no attention to this. They lived their lives. While all this was going on, while the wars were going on, they had fun, studied, worked, had kids, took the boat out on weekends. But in those countries, people suffered greatly, disappeared by the tens of thousands, were tortured and mutilated, and still people fought back. They lived in clandestinity. I knew some of them. They saw the world clearly. They found a peace within themselves. A friend said to me once: "I don't fear death. When I made my commitment, I was already in the grave." We are going, now, to wait. We're going to be courageous and resolute, stoic and clear-eyed. We're going to watch carefully and keep our intuition on high alert. We'll know what steps to take when the time comes. I believe that the president-elect will sit in the White House and everything will be done by others, most especially the legislators. They will change some laws, but he will not be able to deliver on his promises to the people who elected him. There will come a time when his supporters will realize that they have been betrayed. Then we'll see. Those are my thoughts this morning.

Jane Hirshfield. Photo by Michael Lionstar

4 / *Jane Hirshfield*

ward-winning poet, essayist, and translator Jane Hirshfield is the author of several collections of verse, including *The Beauty* (2015), a finalist for the National Book Award; *Come, Thief* (2011); *After* (2006), shortlisted for the T. S. Eliot prize; and *Given Sugar, Given Salt* (2001), a finalist for the National Book Critics Award, among others. Hirshfield has also translated the work of early women poets in collections such as *The Ink Dark Moon: Poems by Ono no Komachi and Izumi Shikibu, Women of the Ancient Court of Japan* (1990) and *Women in Praise of the Sacred: Forty-Three Centuries of Spiritual Poetry by Women* (1994). Inspired by both Eastern and Western traditions, Hirshfield's work encompasses a huge range of influences. "Greek and Roman lyrics, the English sonnet, those foundation stones of American poetry Walt Whitman and Emily Dickinson, 'modern' poets from T. S. Eliot to Anna Akhmatova to C. P. Cavafy to Pablo Neruda—all have added something to my knowledge of what is possible in poetry," Hirshfield explained to *Contemporary Authors*. Equally influential have been classical Chinese poets Tu Fu, Li Po, Wang Wei, and Han Shan; classical Japanese Heian-Era poets Komachi and Shikibu; and such lesser-known traditions as Eskimo and Nahuatl poetry.

Hirshfield published her first poem in 1973, shortly after graduating from Princeton as a member of the university's first graduating class to include women. She put aside her writing for nearly eight years, however, to study at the San Francisco Zen Center. "I felt that

I'd never make much of a poet if I didn't know more than I knew at that time about what it means to be a human being," Hirshfield once said. "I don't think poetry is based just on poetry; it is based on a thoroughly lived life. And so I couldn't just decide I was going to write no matter what; I first had to find out what it means to *live*."

Hirshfield's poetry works with short forms, spare lines, and careful imagery of natural and domestic settings. Her poems frequently hinge on a turning point or moment of insight. Her early work, including *Of Gravity and Angels* (1988), focused more intently on natural settings. By the time she wrote *The October Palace* (1994), she was exploring themes for which she would become well known, such as awareness, consciousness, and the vicissitudes of perception. In her latest work, Hirshfield has continued to investigate the nature of the self and "ethical awareness," in the words of poet Rosanna Warren. Warren noted that Hirshfield's language, "in its cleanliness and transparency, poses riddles of a quietly metaphysical nature." Hirshfield's ability to marry philosophical meditation with domestic observation has been widely remarked upon. In the *Georgia Review*, Judith Kitchen said of *Given Sugar, Given Salt*: "It's about how to negotiate the difficulties of living while, at the same time, paying homage to what life has to offer. The poems are penetrating; they reveal a quick intelligence and an even quicker intuition." Hirshfield's intuition is matched by the formal assurance of her craft. *Publisher's Weekly* described the world in her poems as "allegorical scenes like bare stage sets," noting how Hirshfield yet manages to "introduce elegant observations in conversational free verse, in words drawn from common American speech" into seeming emptiness. Steven Ratiner, in the *Washington Post*, noted of Hirshfield's technique in *Come, Thief*: "The reader's attention rests comfortably on a few spare images, while the mind is allowed to wrestle with what's unseen, unsaid."

Hirshfield has also published two important anthologies of poetry by women. In the late 1980s she began collecting sacred verse by women after the poet and translator Stephen Mitchell asked for her help in compiling his anthology of sacred verse. "I had a feeling that women had always written about these things and that it was just a matter of finding them," she explained to Joan Smith of the *San Fran-*

cisco Examiner. "It was like a treasure hunt." The result of Hirshfield's research, *Women in Praise of the Sacred: Forty-Three Centuries of Spiritual Poetry by Women,* spans the centuries from 2300 BC to the early 1900s and includes the work of seventy poets from many cultures, spiritual traditions, and social classes. *"The Ink Dark Moon* and *Women in Praise of the Sacred* were each done in the effort to make more widely known the work of historical women poets whose words I found both memorable and moving, able to enlarge our understanding of what it is to be human," Hirshfield explained to *Contemporary Authors.* "They were also done to help counteract the lingering myth that there were no historical women writers of significance."

In addition to poetry and anthologies, Hirshfield has also published a collection of essays, *Nine Gates: Entering the Mind of Poetry* (1997). Based on lectures or adapted from previously published essays, Hirshfield's prose touches upon such subjects as originality, the nature of metaphoric mind, translation, and the psychological shadow. The nine essays cite numerous examples from familiar works written in English, as well as from Japanese works in translation. "With her feet firmly planted in both the Western and Eastern canons, Hirshfield delivers a thorough and timely collection on our relationships to poetry, our relationship to the world, and everything in between," stated a *Publishers Weekly* reviewer in praise of *Nine Gates.* Hirshfield's second collection of essays, *Ten Windows: How Great Poems Transform the World* (2015), explores the transformative power of poems by poets including Emily Dickinson, C. P. Cavafy, Elizabeth Bishop, and others.

Hirshfield's many awards include fellowships from the National Endowment for the Arts, the Rockefeller Foundation, and the Guggenheim Foundation. She has received honors including the Poetry Center Book Award, Columbia University's Translation Center Award, the Bay Area Book Reviewer's Award, the Commonwealth Club of California Poetry Medal, and the Hall-Kenyon Award. In 2004 she was awarded the Academy Fellowship from the Academy of American Poets. She was elected a chancellor of the Academy of American Poets in 2012.

Hirshfield once told *Contemporary Authors*: "My primary interest has always been the attempt to understand and deepen experience by bringing it into words. Poetry, for me, is an instrument of investigation and a mode of perception, a way of knowing and feeling both self and world.... I am interested in poems that find a clarity without simplicity; in a way of thinking and speaking that does not exclude complexity but also does not obscure; in poems that know the world in many ways at once—heart, mind, voice, and body."

This interview took place at the public library in Concord, New Hampshire, on October 10, 2012, when Hirshfield received the Jane Kenyon Award.

––––––––––––

Chard deNiord (CD): Thank you for meeting with me today. You graduated from Princeton in 1973 at the age of twenty, worked on a farm for almost a year, then began your apprenticeship at the Zen Center in San Francisco. You once said, "I don't think poetry is based on just poetry. It is based on a thoroughly lived life. So I couldn't just decide I was going to write no matter what. I first had to find out what it meant to live." How do you see your apprenticeship in Zen in its connection to writing poetry?

Jane Hirshfield (JH): Any life is overwhelming. From the time I learned to write, words offered, for me, a way to swim a flood. Writing was a way to craft a self, to saturate myself more deeply in experience, to discover my own inner life and to find in it a more elastic set of responses, away from the expectations of others. I was looking for a way to organize chaos into meaning. Putting words into music, shape, and statements that came from a less blunt, less habitual world made that feel possible. Zen practice, when I found my way to it, was another form of that attempt and inquiry. The intentions of meditation are not, as some seem to think, the erasure of self but its discovery and expression at a different, and somehow freeing, level.

CD: How did you happen to make your way to Zen? It seems an unpredictable turn.

JH: As an undergraduate in college, I read Japanese and Chinese classical literature in translation, and Buddhist ideas were woven into those works. Also, Gary Snyder came to campus and gave, along with a poetry reading, a talk about the Yamabushi mountain-climbing monks of Japan. He was the first American Zen practitioner I'd seen. He had an earring, a ponytail, a sense of the comic; he wrote poems in his own voice and of our own time. That showed me that Zen that could be lived out in the world I knew. That mattered; it unlocked something I hadn't known at the time was even a door.

After graduating and a year working on a farm, I thought I was getting into my red Dodge van—which had yellow tie-dyed curtains, green wall-to-wall carpet, a library, a typewriter, and a homemade built-in bed—to look for some place where I might be happy to live and work as a waitress and write poems. It was the early 1970s; this seemed the obvious thing to do. But I knew there was at that time one Zen monastery in America, Tassajara Zen Mountain Center, in the wilderness inland from Big Sur. When I arrived in California, I went there, and because it was summer—a less strict time of year—I was allowed to go in. I stayed for a week as what's known as a guest student. By week's end I knew I was interested in doing this more. But still, I thought, "I'll go to the San Francisco center, stay a few months, then I'll know all about Zen and carry on with my life." After three months, what you know is that you know nothing. I realized I was going to be there for a while.

CD: You remained a formal Zen practitioner for close to eight years. What happened to your relationship to poetry during that time?

JH: I had no idea really if I would ever go back to poetry or who I would be when I'd finished the traditional one thousand days of monastic training—during that monastic time, you were supposed to do nothing outside the strict practice of Zen, and I wrote just one poem in those three years. I felt only that I was doing what I needed to do with my life, learning what I felt needed learning, and I trusted that whatever happened afterward would be the right thing.

CD: Can you say anything more about what you now feel that time brought you?

JH: Stepping out of any ordinary relationship to time and purpose was an immense gift. In the simplicity of a monastery (and simplicity is the hallmark of any monastic tradition, not just Zen), you can begin to feel the world around you in a nonutilitarian way and to feel what happens when your own inner longings aren't always the center of your life. It's difficult but also profoundly intimate. You're living in a way you know people have lived for ten thousand years, maybe longer. You're running an experiment on your own views and intentions, and on what kind of person you might become and how you might then live in this world if they are decentered. In steep simplicity you can begin to feel inside your own skin the interconnectedness of your own life and the larger lives of others—other people, birds, fish, the plain white bowl in your hand, the trees, deep time, the unstable and flammable earth.

From the outside, monastic life can look useless, unhelpful, extraneous, passive. It can look purely selfish to people whose understanding of activism takes some less quiet form. Yet it isn't at all. The same paradox appears in making art. It looks private—it is private—and yet a work of art made in personal desperation can change not just the writer but a culture, how we see and treat one another. Any true perception is activism. Randall Jarrell's "Death of a Ball-Turret Gunner"—a person is not the same after reading that poem. War-making may continue, but you are not the same.

The other thing I learned—or attempted to begin to learn—at Tassajara, was some courage to stand face-to-face with whatever comes. To stay inside an experience without withdrawal, flinching, or embarrassment and not be so quick to flee the darker parts of a life. Skittishness doesn't serve a poet—or a person. I wanted to learn how to move toward what's hard instead of away. And you know, what's difficult isn't only what's obviously painful. The exposures of love, the exposures of being seen at all, the exposure of being open to seeing—these, for me, were hard. Rilke's "every angel is terrifying" was a feeling I recognized well.

CD: After such a long time not writing, what brought you back to poems?

JH: When I left Tassajara, I spent some time away. I was—I know this sounds unlikely—eventually driving an eighteen-wheel lumber truck, with a partner, to save up some money. I started writing again, and we were based in Fresno, one of the alive centers of American poetry at the time. I never met Philip Levine there; I was far too shy to go knock on anybody's door. For a time I was also in Missoula, Montana, and I didn't knock on Richard Hugo's door either. But I did meet one of Phil's former Fresno State students, Roberta Spear, whose first book Phil had chosen for the first National Poetry Series contest. Roberta—who died, too young, of leukemia—looked at my poems and said, "Oh, yes, there's something here, keep going." That bit of encouragement made a difference I can't now measure. I gradually found my way back into the world of poems, even after going back into formal practice in the Bay Area for a few years more but in a practice place where writing wasn't forbidden. Philip Whalen, one of the original Beat poets, was at that time a priest in the same Zen community, and poems are a part of traditional Buddhist teaching. In retrospect, to have stopped writing for three years was a fine part of my training in poetry. A poet needs to be as friendly with silence as with words.

CD: Tell me more about what happened when you were eight years old. It seems something awakened in you emotionally, spiritually, at a young age, compelling you to begin to write. Did you experience an inchoate sense of an inner life, a kind of budding consciousness about the world and your place in it? The kind of childhood awakening Elizabeth Bishop describes in her poem "In the Waiting Room" in which she realizes she's "an I ... an Elizabeth ... one of them too"?

JH: I have no memory of such a gorgeously transformative moment. I've always assumed that the teacher who taught me to write must have said or done something. My parents did read but not passionately, and not poetry. I've come to wonder if people aren't simply constituted a certain way, just as dogs are shy or bold from birth. The first book I bought with my own allowance—that was when I was eight— was a book of Japanese haiku. I was growing up on the Lower East Side of New York City. I can't guess what pulled me to haiku. But the choice foreshadowed a great deal of my life.

CD: You didn't actually start publishing until the early eighties. Your first book, *Alaya*, was published in 1982. And then *Of Gravity and Angels*, six years later.

JH: I did publish one poem earlier, in 1973, with the dazzlingly original title "Love Poem." I was one of the four winners of what a year later became the Discovery Award. That involved giving a reading at the Poetry Society of America . . . a terrifying occasion. Then I walked away from that public world for a good long spell. *Alaya* is pretty undeveloped work. It has the flavor of the seventies about it, and it simply doesn't sound like me to me. When my British publisher asked if they could do a selected poems drawing from my first five books, I suggested we use no more than three poems from *Alaya*; he talked me up to six.

CD: I can recognize the poetic seeds of your later work in your early books—an intense yet deeply composed perspicacity permeates all your work. Still, many of your poems from the eighties use a more pastoral language than the runic language increasingly prevalent in the later books. By *runic* I mean inquisitive, imaginative, courageous—less governed by the formula of a clear lyrical narrative leading to epiphany than an evocative, koan-like style.

Rosanna Warren describes your mature voice well in the citation she wrote in 2004, when you received the Academy of American Poets Fellowship. She noted your work's ethical awareness and wrote that your poems' "language in its cleanliness and transparency poses riddles of a quietly metaphysical nature." What do you think happened to you intellectually and spiritually between 1988 and the later books that precipitated this linguistic leap?

JH: My work has always, at least thus far, evolved over time. A person changes, the culture changes, the art form changes. Each of these things seem to be happening more quickly now than they did in the past, and I suspect that's connected. It's only fifty years ago that Rachel Carson wrote *Silent Spring*; people were still throwing empty potato chip bags and soda cans out their car windows onto the highways. When I went to college, the words *deconstruction* and *postmodern* never came up; now they're close to passé.

Reading Celan, Lorca, Tranströmer, Brecht, Pessoa, Miłosz's more difficult poems and the work of the more experimental poets of the Bay Area in the 1980s and early nineties expanded my comfort with less-spelled-out domains. Reading the Scandinavian, Eastern European, and South American poets also expanded my interest in a more surreal imagination on one side and on the other in the kind of poem I think of as holding small, particular chips of experience.

There's also the simple matter of aging. Age increases uncertainty-tolerance; curiosity grows more objective and broad. As Novalis said, a person spends the first half of a life looking inward, the second half looking outward. My later poems are still subjective—any good poem requires the poet have something staked on it, something in some way a matter of life and death. But what is subjective expands into what was formerly objective, perhaps. Stones, philosophical concepts, history—when these begin to be felt as personal, poetry becomes possible. I do hope that doesn't sound exactly the opposite of how I mean it.

CD: Just as it took you eight years to complete your formal studies in Zen, it took you another significant period of time—twelve years—between the publication of what you call your "apprentice volume" in 1982 and the publication of *The October Palace* in 1994, the book I'd say marks a clear aesthetic break from your early, more accessible poems to your more runic, leaping style barely hinted at in the interim 1988 book *Of Gravity and Angels.* It feels to me something more than simply a matter of aging or widened reading. Your work is marked by a sense of patience and invitation, of doors left standing open, but was there also some precipitating event that caused this sudden change?

JH: I don't think anyone's account of her own development can be wholly trusted. But yes, there was a distinct moment of stock-taking and realization. When *Of Gravity and Angels* was coming out from Wesleyan University Press, two things happened. First, the editors asked for a four-line excerpt for the catalog. You'd think that would be simple, but my poems worked on the level of the whole poem and weren't making excerptable, memorable phrases or statements. The quick brush stroke of singular perception was missing, and I felt that as both an inadequacy in the art and a lack of courage. Think of Wisława Szymborska's "the happiness of skating on thin ice"—what a magnificent, original, and calligraphic perception! I knew my poems weren't doing that and I wanted them to.

The other, related realization I felt as I looked at the book as a whole was—I almost don't know how to put this—that the poems were perhaps too lyrical. You said just now "pastoral." That quality isn't just a matter of rural imagery—my imagery continues to draw greatly on the natural world—it's a matter of not applying sufficient pressure of feeling and mind. Again, I felt this a problem of courage. I wanted more oddity, more surprise. There are some very unusual imaginative occurrences in that early work, yet they felt somehow smoothed. And so I asked the muse to open the gates of the strange, to do things in my poems that might trouble, might frighten.

One other thing must have also contributed to leaving things in a poem more unabridged—translating the two great women poets from classical-age Japan, Ono no Komachi and Izumi Shikibu, for *The Ink Dark Moon*. This meant years bringing into English poems in which statement lies next to statement, image lies next to image, without any filling in of the connections between them. I've never wanted to directly imitate Japanese poetic forms, I wanted my own hybrid voice, my own seeing and speaking. But still, practicing new scales changes the ear, the eyes, the hands.

CD: One of my favorite poems in *The October Palace* is "Inspiration," which begins:

> Think of those Chinese monks' tales:
> years of struggling
> in the zendo, then the clink,
> while sweeping up of stone on stone . . .
> It's Emily's wisdom: Truth in circuit lies.

This seems to me a voice making a dramatic turn away from the co-herent, lyrical, often metaphorical narratives that dominate your first two books—such poems as "Heat," "Ripeness," "October 20th, 1983," "Completing the Weave"—to bold leaps that intone the rigors and mysteries of enlightenment. It sounds from what you just said as if you shifted, somewhat deliberately, in the early nineties from mining familiar circumstances and subjects to writing more by faith about the strange and even weird, wrecking yourself "solitary here," as Emily Dickinson described her state of unknowing in her poem "I Felt a Funeral, in My Brain."

JH: Might I say first that I do feel that some things in my work are continuous? "October 20th, 1983," was about the now-forgotten invasion of Grenada, and *Of Gravity and Angels* has many poems that emerged from what Rosanna Warren named "ethical awareness." "Justice without Passion" was written out of bewilderment over the Robert Bork Supreme Court nomination hearings. The poem emerged from noticing a pun—the two possible meanings of *even-handed*. That awareness caused me to think harder about what *even-handed* justice might mean, about how the metaphor of a blindfolded woman holding scales plays out in our shared social discourse—and I concluded that while sometimes a blindfold is needed, sometimes it is blinding. Another poem, "The Women of Poland," envisions the food ration lines of Poland then in the news; I wrote about that long before discovering how important the Polish poets (some of whom must have stood in those lines) would become for me. Questions of justice, violence, and fate are in every book . . . the first Gulf War, Indira Gandhi's assassination, the genocide in Rwanda, the Velvet Revolutions, September 11. *Come, Thief* is haunted by the Iraq and Afghanistan wars, by Abu Ghraib. They knock at the poems in sometimes visible, sometimes hidden ways.

But to go back to your question, it's rare for me to take such a conscious hand to what I do; mostly, I'm not able to write poems on willpower or by conscious decision. But yes, I threw a request to the muse, and my work since then has been in some way a continuation of that request for a poetry more permeable to strangeness. In writing, in revising, some part of me continually asks, "What else? What different? What more?" I've long loved Czesław Miłosz's statement that he has "always hungered for a more spacious form," for a more spacious poem. The title of the poem that line appears in—"Ars Poetica?"—has a marvelous question mark at its end. Until the end of his life, Miłosz questioned, experimented, surprised. One of my small favorites is a late poem in which he describes himself as waking in the middle of the night and saying to himself, "strange, strange, o how strange, how strange, O how funny and strange."

CD: Would you say that Miłosz's spaciousness-hunger has played out in some way in your own work?

JH: Spaciousness can take many directions. To ask of each poem what it hasn't done yet, hasn't found yet, is a search for increase. Indeterminacy's openness and authority's clarities are each expansions beyond baseline lyricism, and each in different ways can feel, for me, a risk. Some of the poems people respond to most strongly are poems I've almost thrown away, whether because I thought they were too peculiar or because I feared they were sentimental. I knew, for instance, when I wrote so very many poems about the *heart*, that some readers would bristle at the word. But I needed to look at the heart, at my own and others,' and in those years—the mid-nineties—I may not have been alone in finding the inner life and the life of feeling neglected, suppressed. A recent poem's last line seems to be relevant here and is itself a line that seems to have struck some chord in others: "Think assailable thoughts, or be lonely."

CD: And what about the "form" in Miłosz's statement?

JH: Well, more of my work uses what I think of as "wandering rhyme" than people seem to realize, and over time I've worked also in what I think of as less, perhaps, forms than modes. An ode, for instance, is more a mode—a mood that evokes a certain kind of approach and voice—than it is a form in the stricter sense that a sonnet is. These modes in my work are most often self-defined—the short pebble poems, the longer associative-meditative assays, are ways of writing I first stumbled into, then began to feel consciously as a shape and tone in which certain things could happen. In the most recent book, *Come,*

Thief, there's also one haibun, a few prose poems, a villanelle, a poem I think of as loosely a ballad. At the heart of the idea of form, I find, is this—what you are able to think will vary with the tone and music of your thinking. Similarly, what you care about will shape what you see and say. Somewhere between those two things, a poem's voice begins.

CD: Your most recent two books, *Come, Thief* and *After*, include a number of the verse and prose poems subtitled "assays." These poems undertake intriguing, oblique, and often figurative analyses of wildly varied subjects, both abstract and material: shadows, termites, gravel, possibility, the words *to, ah, and*, and *once*, envy, hesitation, the garden of Ryoanji, tears, translucence, Edgar Allen Poe, articulation, hope, and judgment. Could you talk a little about your yen for both precise, even empirical investigation of a subject and your perception of the simplest things as runes that contain liberating secrets? The puzzling language in these poems seems much more influenced by ancient sacred texts from the East than nondeterminate postmodern language from the West. I'm still puzzling over these lines from "'To': An Assay": "Being means and not end, you are mostly modest, / obedient as railroad track to what comes or does not."

JH: I made my way into the assays over some years. Earlier poems worked near that voice and that set of strategies, but it didn't become conscious as a distinctive mode until I wrote the poem about Poe. I'd written about him the year before in a regular essay, and when the poem came, the beast was so shaggy, so near prose in its rhythms and procedures, that I thought the reader needed some help catching the way I myself heard it speaking. Looking for a facilitating title, I stumbled into the idea of "assay"—"Poe: An Assay." The word was in my mind not so much from any literary use as from the scientific journals that come to the house—I live with a scientist. On the back, at that time, would be ads for half-million dollar "assaying" machines. I did know the word is a cognate of *essay*, from the French *assayer*, "to try," and the association with prose-thought is why I chose it for the Poe poem, but the assayings of molecular chemistry were equally intended.

I'd thought that a one-time subtitle, but then other poems began to arrive in the same mode. Breaking some contemplated subject into its component parts and associations, some outer, some inner, using the sense of imaginative molecular labeling—these approaches felt a good tool for breaking ideas and objects open, and for breaking myself open in new ways as well.

I do have to say, for me this mode is quite the opposite of anything Eastern, sacred, or vatic. I can guess what may have led you to see that—something about the long sentences and the willingness to be authoritative. But no.

The imagination of the assays is centripetal, pulling against the literal or objectively physical in these poems, but their center of gravity is always the thing itself. The poem tests the strength of its own gravitational orbit and sees what it finds. The assay on gravel found the question of part and whole, then death. The assay on *to* found precipitous time, then death. The assay on *tears* found misunderstanding. The assay on *hesitation* found the earliest moments of love. The assay on *judgment* found, well, judgment, and my own extraordinarily mixed relationship to its place in our lives.

The assays open subjects I probably would not have found my way into by any other voice. Prose poems function the same way—and as you've noted, some of the assays are also prose poems. Others are also odes. For me, it's a supple and compounding invention. As for those lines you asked about, from the one on the preposition *to* . . . well, *to* has to go where it's pointed, does it not? Its assay is full of the word itself, used many different ways. It began playfully, it started with an image straight out of Sunday morning children's cartoons. That it ended up being about death was a surprise. But death is the place the railroad track of existence leads to.

CD: In the four books of poetry following *The October Palace* (*The Lives of the Heart* in 1997, *Given Sugar, Given Salt* in 2001, *After* in 2006, and *Come, Thief* in 2011), you continue to explore in your own poems, I believe, what you've referred to in *Nine Gates* as the liminal—the "threshold state of ambiguity, openness and indeterminacy" by which a writer crosses the boundary of the separate self into broader identification with others. Are you finding it easier or more difficult here, now, to conjure new poems in this threshold state?

JH: What a good question. For me finding a new poem is always unknowable and difficult. At times a poem may just begin to say itself in me. Other times I feel like a fly fisherman going out to a river and hoping that something will be there. I never take for granted that I'll be able to write. There's no acorn stash of ideas in my desk drawer. There's only the wish to know my life through writing, a wish felt sometimes as desire, sometimes as desperation. What reservoir the words come from remains a mystery to me. And over the course of my life, there have been many pauses. The times of stopping seem to allow old habits of being or thinking or saying to fall away. When I start again, something is different.

CD: You've complemented your books of poetry with several anthologies, translations, and a collection of essays, *Nine Gates: Entering the Mind of Poetry,* in 1997. That came out the same year as *The Lives of the Heart,* and your anthology *Women in Praise of the Sacred: Forty-Three Centuries of Spiritual Poetry by Women* was published in 1994, the same year as *The October Palace.*

JH: Yes. I've rather liked having twins. It's very efficient. And entirely surprising to me, since I don't think of myself as at all efficient or as prolific. Yet this somehow keeps happening. I'm just now trying to figure out whether the next book of essays and next book of poems may or may not coincide.

CD: Then there's also your e-book on Basho, *The Heart of the Haiku,* which appeared in 2011, a few months before *Come, Thief,* and *The Ink Dark Moon: Poems by Ono No Komachi and Izumu Shikibu, Women of the Ancient Court of Japan,* which first came out in cloth in 1988, alongside *Of Gravity and Angels,* and then in an expanded paperback edition in 1990. You started your research for *The Ink Dark Moon* while you were still at Princeton, correct?

JH: Yes, I learned of these women poets' existence at a seminar table in East Asian studies. But there were only six or so of their poems in English, along with the Noh plays about Ono no Komachi. I waited fifteen years for some scholar to translate more. When that didn't happen, and I was given a year's support from the Guggenheim Foundation for my own work in 1985–1986 and coincidentally introduced to Mariko Aratani, who became my cotranslator, I ended up working on two books that year instead of one.

The anthologies and translations I've done have always been more accidental than planned. *The Ink Dark Moon* was the first accident. Once I'd done that book, though, and it was so very welcomed by readers and scholars, a door opened, and I've kept walking, each time unexpectedly, through it.

CD: This reminds me of the conclusion of your poem "Inspiration": "'Enlightenment,' wrote one master, / 'is an accident, though certain accidents make you accident prone.'"

JH: Just so.

CD: Do you think that working so closely as you have with the work of other poets has expanded your own poetry writing?

JH: Yes and no. Some part of me shies away from working in others' fingerprints. After a life immersed in Japanese literature, I've written one haiku, one haibun, and a single tanka that doesn't even appear in a book of my own. (Astonishingly, that tanka is circulating on the internet.) My desire has been to learn from others but then to make, when I write, something simply my own. There are ways to allude and include. Early Sanskrit erotic poetry, for instance, is an extraordinary body of work, in many ways reminiscent of the poems of the Japanese court women. One recent poem, "Cellophane: An Assay," ends with a quoted image from that source.

CD: You say something very interesting on the subject of sounding like others in the chapter on originality in *Nine Gates*, in a passage speaking of traditional Japanese poetics: "Individuality of feeling mattered immensely, but individuality of expression would have been found bizarre by these writers. Over the thousand years between the late eighth century's Manyōshū anthology and the appearance of Basho, poetic diction and strategies changed little, yet the poems themselves changed deeply. There are problems inherent in such a conservative aesthetic—problems of staleness and repetitive feeling, of an almost mechanical juggling of familiar imagery—though any set of artistic values can produce bad writing." You go on to say, "Good poems leap over the pitfalls."

JH: Yes, in that way it's like the English sonnet—you think of how many terrible sonnets have been written—

CD: Yes.

JH: And then, Keats comes along and ...

CD: Transforms it.

JH: And all that reification of language just falls apart, without abandoning the form. And then Marilyn Hacker comes and does it again. So yes, of course it can be done. Richard Wright's thousands of haiku are superb haiku and also superb poems of our own time and world. But for me there's just some feeling of taboo. It may be that I'm too susceptible to the pulls of what I love—the way a magnet will get pulled into another if it gets too close.

CD: That's fascinating. When I interviewed Ruth Stone I asked her what contemporary poets she read, and she responded, "I don't read them." And I said, "Why not?" And she said, "Because I'm afraid they would influence me so strongly that I wouldn't be able to write my own poetry."

JH: I can understand that. I, though, take the opposite strategy. I read as many other poets as I can, current and past, in English or in translation. That's the other way to avoid possible over-influence—reading widely.

CD: Opening broadly is clearly important to you. Your poem, "The

Envoy," which Robert Bly has described as "one of the greatest poems of the past fifty years"—no small praise, although such high praise has been known to enervate the muse—captures what you've called "the threshold state" so economically and simply while also emanating a wise, spiritually venturous expression. Could you talk about it a little? Here's the poem:

The Envoy

One day in that room, a small rat.
Two days later, a snake.

Who, seeing me enter,
whipped the long stripe of his
body under the bed,
then curled like a docile house-pet.

I don't know how either came or left.
Later, the flashlight found nothing.

For a year I watched
as something—terror? happiness? grief?—
entered and then left my body.

Not knowing how it came in,
Not knowing how it went out.

It hung where words could not reach it.
It slept where light could not go.
Its scent was neither snake nor rat,
neither sensualist nor ascetic.

There are openings in our lives
of which we know nothing.

Through them
the belled herds travel at will,
long-legged and thirsty, covered with foreign dust.

— from *Given Sugar, Given Salt* (HarperCollins, 2001)

JH: One task life demands of us each is to come to some relationship with not knowing. Childhood's chorus is "Why?" "Why?" "But why?" It's a useful question. But adulthood is, in part, acknowledging that there will be many times it can't be answered. This is part of what Keats had in mind in his now-famous description of "negative capability," and the Greek gods are an invention of the inscrutable.

At the center of this particular poem lies the inscrutability of the emotional life, of how it lives in us and we in and with it. It arrives. It stays. It vanishes. An earlier poem, "The Gods Are Not Large," is somehow related. We might construct some story, but we can never understand fully what has happened to us in our lives. The most powerful shakings of the psyche, joyous or ruinous, are felt as a matter for awe, in the old sense of that word. We're unmade by them. Again, there's Rilke: "Every angel is terrifying."

I hope it doesn't diminish the poem if I say that rat, snake, and room actually existed. My poems often begin with the facts of my life—the seen, the heard, the tasted, the observed. The psyche chooses, from the stream of any day, what might magnetize some deeper understanding. So this poem started with a quite concrete, literal experience but then moved toward the inner experience the outer one summoned. Something difficult was going on in my life, and the poem was written amid that, but it also looks at what for me is a continuous puzzle: why does it feel so essentially necessary and yet so ambivalently wanted to have the fixed shapes of my life unfixed?

CD: Are there any other things you might say about this poem?

JH: Well, snakes and rats, even actual ones, have their train of what a Jungian might call their royal meanings. Both awaken an immediate jolt of fear, but there's more than that. In the West, a snake is a revelation of the pure, ungloved and unhidden phallic; it is dangerous, poisonous in both the actual and biblical garden, and frightening. In Asian cultures, though, the snake is a wisdom creature, bringing the under-earth's hidden truths and tunnels. Rats are everywhere resourceful and Tricksterish and also pariah-survivors we pull back from. I've developed some affection for rats in my poems—but not in my house.

Just yesterday, someone brought me a copy of *Given Sugar, Given Salt* to sign. In the German still-life on the cover, there are many edible things, a beautiful small parrot, an insect. There's also a little rat or mouse eating one of the sixteenth-century sweets on the table. The man told me his wife couldn't believe he'd bought the book—he is wildly rat-phobic. But isn't it exactly our phobias we need poems to work through and with? The terrors woven into the fabric of our lives require poems—not to answer them, but to meet them. And doing just that underpins "The Envoy." Writing it didn't answer my unanswerable circumstance. The poem doesn't choose between terror, happiness, or grief. Such labels can't catch the actual reality of what we feel when some huge change comes through a life and undoes it, leaves it to be somehow remade again. We don't know if the snake ate the rat or if both escaped or if both are still there. But an image lets you begin to take something in, to absorb it without either dissection or encysting. In the end, all I could do in "The Envoy" was allow its images to speak through me, to say that my life felt to me like belled herds unseen in the night; that events come incomprehensibly, from elsewhere, thirsty and dusty; that the sound of our lives wakes us and we listen and become that listening, become the herds.

CD: Your poems not infrequently use animals—animals presumably real and seen in the world—to explore both the animals themselves and other subjects. "Sheep," from the new book *Come, Thief*, is one poem in which you address the mystery of animal encounter.

> It is the work of feeling
> to undo expectation.

A black-faced sheep
looks back at you as you pass
and your heart is startled
as if by the shadow
of someone once loved.

Neither comforted by this
nor made lonely.

Only remembering
that a self in exile is still a self,
as a bell unstruck for years is still a bell.

Would you mind talking about this encounter, particularly in regard
to how the animal's gaze redounds on human consciousness?

JH: Yes, of course. Sheep are prey animals, which means they will
always look at you whenever you're near. For me, there is something
powerful in any gaze shared across species, and sheep's eyes and
faces are especially alien, as goats' eyes and faces are alien. We have
sheep in children's stories and give children stuffed-animal lambs,
but in that moment of actual, shared looking between living crea-
tures, the difference between us steps forward. The sheep is nervous,
wondering what are you going to do—walk by, feed it, eat it? We are
not part of their children's stories, and the look is not neutral; it's full
of intensity, immediacy, and feeling. For the sheep, that gaze is a mat-
ter of life and death.

And so the looking of those black-faced sheep—I saw them while
crossing northern Scotland on the way to read on the Isle of Skye—
felt significant, something more than itself. It's Emily Dickinson's
"Haunted House," isn't it, the way certain moments simply begin to
feel inhabited by something more freighted? Later, writing the poem,
I began also to think about feeling itself. I'd been learning some of the
neuroscience of emotion for an essay about poetry and surprise. "It is
the work of feeling to undo expectation" is a neurochemically accurate
statement—a new emotion always signals some change in the status

quo. And this, as I've been saying, is something I want. To be shaken, undone, disrupted. (Or some part of me wants it, the braver part.) We are most alive in the moment the ladder is tipping.

A poem is in many ways just that, a tipping and catching: "X happened, and I felt A, then I felt Q." That Q is the undoing and remaking of ordinary expectation. If you simply felt B, you wouldn't need a poem. I've come to feel that the emotions are, as Gary Snyder once defined poetry, "very high quality information." They are as deeply a part of our capacity to navigate the world as the more cognitive intellect is. "I'm frightened," "I want," "I'm worried"—these sensations are information that allows us to respond to our this-moment circumstance. To return to the poem and your question, animals' intelligence is seated in their emotional lives. Sheep are quite brilliant at being sheep, but what they know, they know by desire, fear, curiosity, hunger, courtship.

CD: Could you say something more about the poem's ending? You don't sweep up all the dust at the end of this poem, or in your poems in general.

JH: Thank you. Yes, I'd like not to slam the door on mystery at a poem's finish. Mystery is what you are trying to let in, if you enter the realm of poems at all. Think of Dickinson's complaint: "They shut me up in prose."

I wonder, though, are you curious about the ending's exiled self, or its bell? I'll choose the bell; there are quite a few bells in recent poems. I think for me it is somehow an image of a life's resonant possibilities, or perhaps of a fate. A fate is sometimes lived out fully, sometimes not. Many things that are possible for a person do not happen. Missed loves, as in this poem's earlier image, but not just that. Untaken choices, I think, remain part of your life, just as a bell is a bell, whether or not it is ringing. Your life is your longings as much as any set of events.

There are things that come up for a person, things you continue wrestling with for years. Fate and its accidents is one of those for me. Another is how we enter and engage with our most powerful feelings, especially the ones we'd prefer not to have. Let me add—mostly I try to forget whatever I may know about my own obsessions, about my poems. I think it unhealthy for a poet to know very much about what or why he or she writes—you might then stay in only that one small paddock. And yet you're forced to notice. An interviewer asking questions is one way that happens. So I'll repeat, having already long fallen down that rabbit hole in this conversation, that another thing my poems have been haunted by is the hunt for permeability, for finding a way to say yes to what I'd rather say no to, for allowing the difficult thing to come in.

CD: Can you think of a poem of yours that captures this quality of "allowing difficult things in"?

JH: "The Weighing" is the one I'd usually offer, but a newer poem comes to mind, "My Weather."

> Wakeful, sleepy, hungry, anxious,
> restless, stunned, relieved.
>
> Does a tree also feel them?
> A mountain?
>
> A cup holds
> sugar, flour, three large rabbit-breaths of air.
>
> I hold these.

I hope this poem's heard as a little comic. Seeing the air in a measuring cup as a volume of rabbit-breaths; anxiety equated with sugar, relief with flour; wondering what the inner life is of trees and mountains. . . . I think it's funny, anyhow.

Yet it's also about something serious—all these emotions pass through us, and what are we to do about it? Anxiety, for me, is almost intolerable. Yet it also is good information. Anxiety tells you not just that something is wrong but that there's something you haven't done and need to; the higher the amplitude of anxiety, the more desperate you are to do something to end it. And sometimes you can't; sometimes there's nothing to do. What then? Well, then you wait. It's unlikely, though not impossible, that on your deathbed, this very anxiety will be what's with you. In the meanwhile, though, it helps to realize that you, your emotions, your whole excruciating inner landscape, are just that—landscape, one of the shapes of existence. And perhaps some freedom can be gained by the recognition of that universality, some proportionate return to humor. Are trees anxious? Well, no, I don't think they are. Yet they must have their own forms of suffering, and every existing person or thing will carry exactly what they're given to bear. Sometimes it's terror; sometimes it's flour. Whatever it is, you have to let it in. The top of a measuring cup is lidless.

CD: You've sometimes quoted a poem by Izumi Shikibu that seems related to these matters:

> Although the wind
> blows terribly here,
> the moonlight
> also leaks between the roof planks
> of this ruined house.

JH: It took a very long time to translate that poem, when I was working with Mariko on *The Ink Dark Moon*. I had the words, I had the grammar, I knew something important was in it, but I literally couldn't understand it. When I finally did understand—if you wall your house up so tightly that no wind can get in, no moonlight will get in either—that changed my relationship to my life, to pain. It changed my poems. It changed everything. And this is what I want from a great poem, to be left a different human being, with a different capacity and a different comprehension.

CD: You've been thinking about permeability for a long time, both in your poems and in your essays. A great deal of the final chapter of *Nine Gates*, "Writing and the Threshold Life," is about the necessity for a permeable boundary in great art.

JH: Increase of openness, increase of freedom, fearlessness to try anything, to be anything, a right sense of justice . . . all these things are somehow related also to empathy, permeability, and compassion. And poetry is built, I think, on various devices of compassion. We wouldn't understand any image in any poem if it weren't felt as if from within our own skin.

CD: *Nine Gates* advocates the importance of emptiness as a vessel for compassion. Emptiness as a Buddhist understanding is quite similar, again, to Keats's notion of negative capability, in which the poet empties herself of her own personality and ego in order to identify with others. You start the chapter on threshold with a long excerpt from a Noh play about a more subtle understanding of self and other, sacred and secular, and quote Pablo Neruda's "Poetry," in which he says,

> Poetry arrived
> in search of me. I don't know. I don't know where
> it came from, from winter or a river . . .
> abruptly from others,
> among violent fires
> or returning alone,
> there I was without a face
> and it touched me.

How similar that unknowing also seems to the Buddhist koan, "Show me your face before your parents were born." You write later in that chapter about Walt Whitman as a figure of threshold and transpersonal self—that is, the self that crosses over from speaker to other. Is it necessary to distinguish between Buddhist tenets and the language of poetry?

JH: It's ironic for me that so much of this conversation has been about Buddhism, when my own definition of Zen is that Zen is nothing more than the taste of your own tongue in your own mouth. I'd much prefer my poetry not wear a spiritual label. Ideas and images and concepts found in Zen are found in Neruda, in Whitman, in Wordsworth, in the Roman Epicurian and Stoic poets, in the Nahuatl poems of Mesoamerica. . . . The recognition of transience, suffering, connection are basic human experiences.

Zen is simply what happens if you don't hold other ideas in your mind and open your eyes. That's what I want poems to do as well. To press on the edge of what's possible to say, on the edge of what's possible to know. You don't need a poem to hold obvious, easy information. If you want to learn how to bake a cake, there might be some marvelous poem about cake baking, but you'll probably reach for a cookbook. What poems require are experiences that face in more than one direction at once, that can't be held in any other vessel except the language of poetry.

CD: Very nicely put. I just want to read this passage by Lewis Hyde, from his *Trickster Makes This World*, since we've been talking a lot about the notion of the Trickster. Hyde makes the point that the Trickster is an amoral—not immoral, but amoral—figure who, according to the eminent anthropologist Paul Radin, "is at one and the same time creator and destroyer, giver and negator, he who dupes others and who is always duped himself. He knows neither good nor evil yet he is responsible for both. He possesses no values, moral or social, yet through his actions all values come into being."

JH: Yes, yes, that's a marvelous account of Trickster's inhabitance of the threshold. I love Lew's book. Trickster-reality really is one fundamental aspect of how the world works. Hermes, it's worth remembering, is the god who faces both directions when placed at a crossroad, and Trickster's domain is in so much we've been discussing. His language is disruptive and mercurial. Word play is Trickster, the slyness of rhetoric is Trickster, jokes, irony, the doubled readings that come out of poetic music and line breaks. In every literate culture that has writing, Trickster invents it, then uses it to foment revolutions of mind ever after. Whatever the current order or current understanding of things is, Trickster says, "Let's try it another way."

CD: That's wonderful. As we're close to closing, I wonder if you'd say a few words about the title of your newest book, *Come, Thief.*

JH: I had in mind many things, but especially an old Chinese teaching story. An old hermit returns at night from gathering wild greens for his supper, comes back to his small hut that has almost nothing in it, and discovers he's been robbed. But the thief didn't take the cast-iron cauldron, it was too heavy. The hermit picks up the pot and goes running down the road, yelling, "Wait, wait, you forgot this!" I want to invite that thief also into my life. The thief is the Trickster figure, is love, is loss, is time, is aging, is whatever comes in, whether you think you want it or not, and leaves everything changed.

CD: And one last question: In thinking about the range and the scope of your work, I'm wondering if when you look back on your early work, even as far back as *Alaya* and *Of Gravity and Angels*, do you, as Frost wrote in his poem, "Into My Own," find that you "have grown more sure of all you thought was true" or less sure but more comfortable with what you don't know you don't know?

JH: Very much the second—less sure. But more glad of my unsureness.

James Wright. Photo by LaVerne H. Clark

5 / *Anne Wright*

A nne Wright is James Wright's widow and editor of *A Wild Perfection: The Selected Letters of James Wright* and *Selected Poems: James Wright*.

This interview took place on May 5, 2012, at Anne Wright's cottage in Westerly, Rhode Island.

Chard deNiord (CD): What was it like being married to James Wright?

Anne Wright (AW): An adventure. We had fun together.

CD: The romance endured.

AW: The romance endured, absolutely.

CD: You were a poetry lover and had written poetry yourself before meeting James. You obviously loved his work, so that was part of the romance, but there must have been something about his work in particular you loved, along with his manner.

AW: His manner, his sense of play, his humor.

CD: He was, from what I've heard, very funny.

AW: Very, very funny.

CD: Someone once compared him to the comedian Jonathan Winters.

AW: He loved to imitate him.

CD: James did his dissertation on the comedy of Charles Dickens.

AW: I mean, of all things for him to choose, you know? So he had a wonderful sense of humor. He had a photographic memory. He was vulnerable. He was romantic. Of course he was also deeply haunted. That was fascinating too—his part mystery and his part very-much-there. He loved children, and I worked with children. He would come over to the West Side Community Nursery School at snack time. I mean there were just so many endearing things about him, and he was lovely to my nieces and nephews. He treated them as his own children.

CD: He'd had a difficult first marriage.

AW: *Difficult*, I think, is the word.

CD: Can you comment on his mother's behavior toward him?

AW: She was discontent with life in general, I think. She was very proud of her boys. And they all did amazingly well. Both Jack, James's brother, and James went to college.

CD: But their life wasn't her life.

AW: No.

CD: As a keenly intelligent and literate woman, she must have felt that life had treated her harshly, burdened by her job as a laundress.

AW: She guarded her family, the nuclear family—I can't stand that phrase, but you know what I'm talking about—and she only really let her own family members into her house. She quarreled constantly with neighbors and her husband's sister, Lillian.

CD: Protective in what sense?

AW: She was overprotective. She had the attitude of us against the world. When I first went to the James Wright festivals, James's aunt Lillian said to me, "I come to these festivals to get to know you, Annie, and to get to know my nephew James Wright, because Jessie excluded us. She pushed us away." Jessie was James's mother's name.

CD: Do you think this overprotectiveness was a personality trait, or was there a practical reason?

AW: I don't think there was a practical reason, no, because Lillian was a wonderful person. She would have been a good friend for Jessie, I think.

CD: What do you think she was protecting? Why isolate the family?

AW: I don't really know. I never understood that. Jessie didn't even like James to visit his grandmother, Elizabeth Lyons, Jessie's own mother. Nevertheless, he did anyway. He stopped by her house every day after school. In an autobiographical sketch written in high school, he wrote that he had a mother, whose name was Jessie, at the farm in Warnock, Ohio, to talk to. She was witty with a sometimes sharp, sometimes harsh side to her. She was always welcoming to me but found it hard to express warm emotions or affection. I have the impression she didn't hug her children or kid around them in a playful manner. In later years she picked on Dudley, her husband, bossed him around, ran him down verbally, which upset James. I think she wanted to be a loving person but didn't know how. She was very bright and loved to read but left school when she was only fourteen to help out her family.

CD: James had a nervous breakdown his senior year of high school.

AW: Yes, he did.

CD: Do you think that had anything to do with Jessie's overprotectiveness?

AW: It could have. I wasn't around his family when he was growing up, of course, but James once said to me, "It was my mother that should have gotten help, but I was the one who had the breakdown." He was very sensitive.

CD: He must have identified so closely with her. Her name was Jessie, and Jennie is the name of the dead girl in the poem "To the Muse," but no critic or friend of James seems to know who Jennie was.

AW: No. I don't know either. Jennie was just a muse to James. I don't mean *just* a muse, but . . .

CD: Why would he pick the name Jennie?

AW: He loved that poem "Jenny Kiss'd Me" by James Henry Leigh Hunt. I always thought that might have something to do with it.

CD: I have it here.

> Jenny kiss'd me when we met,
> Jumping from the chair she sat in;
> Time, you thief, who love to get
> Sweets into your list, put that in!
> Say I'm weary, say I'm sad,
> Say that health and wealth have miss'd me,
> Say I'm growing old, but add,
> Jenny kiss'd me.

AW: Yes, that's the poem James loved.

CD: So maybe he fell in love with the idea of a girl named Jenny who he first envisioned as this woman in James Henry Leigh Hunt's poem. Perhaps she represents poetry itself to him, or his anima, which is also his elusive muse. If that was the case, then Jenny was more a part of James's psyche than an actual other or beloved, that lost self he called by a feminine name in "To the Muse" who he so desperately wanted to raise from the depths of the Powhatan pit. Just my speculation, but does this at all seem plausible to you?

AW: Yes.

CD: Not an actual other woman to be concerned about but perhaps real enough as an "interior paramour," as Wallace Stevens would say.

AW: Yes, I think also she was his ideal of the woman he kept hoping he would meet.

CD: His Galatea who materialized as a revenant or bardo figure. Critics and biographers have speculated whether a flesh-and-blood Jenny attended James's high school.

AW: I don't think she did. No. He never mentioned one if she did.

CD: She also appears in several other poems: "The Idea of the Good" in the *Collected Poems*, "Jenny Sycamore that is now the one wing / the only wing" in the poem "Son of Judas," and "Jenny cold, Jenny darkness" in the poem "October Ghosts." In a brilliant essay he wrote in the early eighties on the arc of James's poetry, from *The Green Wall* to *This Journey*, Robert Hass defines Jenny this multifarious way: "Jenny . . . is beauty, loneliness, death, the muse, the idea of the good, a sexual shadow, a whore, the grandmother of the dead, the lecherous slut of the Ohio, an abandoner of her child, a 'savage woman with two heads . . . the one / Face broken and savage, the other, the face dead,' the name carved under a tree in childhood close to the quick, a sycamore tree, a lover, the first time he ever rose."

AW: And he dedicated *Shall We Gather at the River* to her. There were certain things he just couldn't tell anyone.

CD: You and James were married in 1967.

AW: Yes. His poem "The Lights in the Hallway" is about me and where I lived. That was one of the newest poems he included in *Shall We Gather at the River.*

CD: Yes, a beautiful love poem to you. What a leap he makes in this poem from the "lights in the hallway," your hallway, to what he feels in his "clasp" of you:

> Terrified by the roundness of the earth,
> And its apples and its voluptuous rings
> Of poplar trees, the secret Africas
> The children they gave us.

There is also a fascinating poem in *Two Citizens* called "Voices between Waking and Sleeping in the Mountains" in which he turns away from his interior muse, Jenny, to you, his actual beloved—

> that body I long for
> The Gabon poets gaze for hours
> Between boughs toward heaven, their noble faces
> Too secret to weep.

AW: Yes.

CD: In "Voices between Waking and Sleeping in the Mountains" he openly discusses your secret and his secret:

> If only I knew how to tell you.
> Someday I might know how.
>
> Meantime your hand gathered me awake
> Out of my good dream and I pray to gather
> My hands into your hands in your good dream.
>
> What did you find in your long wandering in the snow?
> I love your secret. By God, I will never violate the wings
> of the snow you found rising in the wind.
> Give them. Keep them. Love.

In this constant back and forth between announcing his secret and refraining from telling it, he seems to be saying that if he told you his secret, it would violate his love. Yet he is addressing you there as his beloved, instead of Jenny, who can't "come up" to him, as he implies in the last lines of "To the Muse," "Come up to me / or I'll come down to you."

AW: Yes. He felt he would be too open if he told the secret. I wonder, just a speculation, if he as a small child had exchanged things with his mother, and she made fun of him or teased him or mocked him in some way, so he thought, *I'm not telling my secret thoughts to anybody.*

CD: Do you think his secret, which is unsayable, has more to do with the concept or the secret than the secret itself?

AW: That was it.

CD: I'm also struck in some of these poems, in the later poems especially in *This Journey* and *To a Blossoming Pear Tree* where he often approaches the unsayable before deferring to it—what Robert Bly has called "the interstices between words, the mysterious events that happen when simple words are placed next to one another." In his later poems especially, the more he's on that precipice of the unsayable, the simpler and even more prosaic his writing becomes while somehow remaining poetic. A good example of this occurs at the end of "On the Liberation of Women" where he writes, "What is going to happen when we both die? / I love you best." Such simple yet effective lines.

AW: "So if you're offended by what I'm saying about women, don't forget, I still love you."

CD: And he did.

AW: Yes.

CD: You were born in New York City, correct?

AW: Yes. My parents moved out to Greenwich, Connecticut. And my background was so incredibly different from James's. They belonged to a little group of friends. They had cocktails every night. There were a lot of parties that they went to.

CD: Hardly Martins Ferry.

AW: Hardly Martins Ferry. No, just another world. We had a maid, a live-in maid.

CD: So a difference in class as well.

AW: Totally different class. My grandparents were very different from his parents.

CD: Can you describe your attraction to him?

AW: See, my attraction to him was that he was a poet and that he was so brilliant.

CD: But there are a lot of brilliant, attractive poets.

AW: I hadn't met any! [laughs] In a way we were on the verge of other worlds. I mean, when I married James, my life changed a great deal. I was in the company of such poets as Galway Kinnell, Anthony Hecht, W. S. Merwin, Isabella Gardiner, Jane Cooper, and, of course, Robert Bly. I often went with James when he gave readings, gatherings with his fellow poets in New York, many at the home of Betty Kray, an incredible woman who gave so much to poetry, and some wonderful trips to the Bly farm.

CD: You must have sensed his vulnerability.

AW: Yes.

CD: He needed help, you thought.

AW: Yes. I think it was the second time we went out on a date, I opened the door—I lived in a railroad flat then, it had lights in the hallway, that's where I lived—and he had his hand held out, and there was a button in it. He said, "It just came off my raincoat."

CD: Help!

AW: Yes. Well, immediately, out comes the sewing kit and . . .

CD: I can fix that! Right?

AW: Long after we had married, he confessed that he had wrenched that button off his coat. He knew.

CD: In his poem "Voices between Waking and Sleeping in the Mountains," he writes about his ineffable love for you in the context of his love for trees.

> There used to be a sycamore just
> Outside Martins Ferry
> Where I used to go.
> I had no friends there.
> Maybe the tree was no woman,
> But when I sat there, I gathered
> That branch into my arms.
> It was the first time I ever rose.
>
> If only I knew how to tell you.
> Some day I may know how.

And in the very next poem, "On the Liberation of Woman," he does seem to tell you by repeating the line "I love you best." He's writing about embracing the tree as his beloved here, alluding obviously to the myth of Diana as an objective correlative for his own loneliness, as he also does later in "Entering the Temple of Nimes" and "Leaving the Temple of Nimes" in his posthumous book *This Journey*, though he comments that the tree is no woman.

AW: Also, in his poem "Defense of Late Summer," he writes of "a Japanese girl far from home" as a maple.

CD: He tells and doesn't tell you his secret in "On the Liberation of Women," writing initially, "What you found on that long rise of mountain in the snow / Is your secret, but I can tell you at last," then declaring he can't tell you: "If only I knew how to tell you. / Some day I may know how."

AW: Or perhaps he never wanted me to know how lonely he felt because that would make him more vulnerable.

CD: Loneliness and embrace, solitude and gathering, saying and not saying, in his poems as well as his life, remained in constant tension throughout his career. Both his albatross and his poetic dialectic. Although he never seemed completely willing to give up his "secret," he did in a way; his secret really becomes an open secret when he writes such lines as these:

> In the middle of my age I walked down
> Toward a cold bloom.
> I don't give a damn if you care.
> But it half rhymes with blossom.
> And no body was ever so kind to me
> As one woman, and begins spring
> In the secret of winter, and that is why
> I love you best.

AW: Yes.

CD: Which says to me that he didn't receive some essential love in his childhood.

AW: Yes. The comfort. The nurture.

CD: In his poem "Lying in a Hammock on William Duffy's Farm in Pine Island, Minnesota" the "red-tailed hawk, heading for home" that appears near the end of the poem seems to trigger his survivor's guilt and sudden leap to his startling last line, "I've wasted my life." A confession that perhaps implies how regretful he felt about leaving Martins Ferry.

AW: "How do I dare? When I'm not working, I'm lying in a hammock."

CD: I love the way you speak for him now, throwing your voice into his, admitting things that he probably never would. How does he know that the red-tailed hawk is searching for a home?

AW: I speculate that it was James searching for home.

CD: So the gulf that existed between the actual other—you—and the loneliness he couldn't resolve remained an ironic source of his inspiration, shame-ridden as it was at times.

AW: Yes, because to admit, even to someone who you love and adore, that you feel incredibly lonely ... that's a hard secret to let go of.

CD: Robert Hass makes the point in the same essay I mentioned above that James's loneliness was actually less about loneliness per se than what he called the "solitariness of being, of beings going about their business," like the red-tailed hawk, for instance, "searching for home." But he did admit his loneliness to you in a way, it seems, by writing about the "solitariness of being" he observed in things both animate and inanimate, which I don't think meant he didn't need your company.

AW: In a way, but not coming out and saying it plainly.

CD: "If only I knew how to tell you."

AW: See, he didn't.

CD: What? I'm lonely? What other way is there to say it than "I'm lonely"?

AW: But he couldn't. Somehow he couldn't.

CD: Because the solitude and even alienation he felt so deeply as a kind of state of being was ineffable. Yet, he hopes that "someday [he] may know how." Do you think he ever got to that point?

AW: I think he was working his way toward it, yes.

CD: James's personal life was quite a mess when you met him. His first marriage to Liberty Kardules, his high school sweetheart, had dissolved, and he had been denied tenure at the University of Minnesota in 1964 after spending seven years there.

AW: I was never told very much about that side, but I heard from other people he was doing a lot of heavy drinking. No drugs but drinking.

CD: Allen Tate, one of the eminent fugitive poets and author of "For the Confederate Dead" was chair of the English Department at the University of Minnesota at the time.

AW: Yes.

CD: He denied James's tenure.

AW: Yes, it was a terrible time.

CD: Do you think it was because of the tumult he was going through as much as anything else?

AW: Oh, I think he was certainly unstable, and I don't know what things he was saying to students. He was going out drinking with them, which was not a good idea.

CD: And then he ended up at Minnesota State University Moorhead for a little while.

AW: He went there for a summer. And that was wonderful. But then Macalester College saved him. The University of Minnesota didn't take away his tenure until he got that job at Macalester. He went as a transfer to Macalester, taking a year off from the University of Minnesota to go there. I'll never know how fair or unfair, but for him losing tenure was devastating on top of everything else.

CD: Really, it's amazing he didn't give up.

AW: Or take his own life.

CD: But something kept him going; he had a powerful life force.

AW: Yes. That's a good way of putting it.

CD: Despite the fact that he must have suffered terrible discouragement and even depression at times, along with his bouts of drinking.

AW: He had a terrible breakdown in 1959 and was hospitalized.

CD: That occurred after his breakup with Liberty, correct?

AW: Oh, that breakup was on and off for about three or four years. I'm just learning about it now going through the letters. His most intimate letters were written to Donald Hall. I think he felt Don was more sympathetic to his personal problems than Robert was.

CD: Donald Hall is a great letter writer. He must have been a great help to James.

AW: It was wonderful that he had Donald Hall to write to. They started writing to each other long before he met Robert Bly in 1954.

CD: I forget where they met.

AW: Donald Hall was working for the *Paris Review* and wrote James to ask for poems, and that is how it all began. Their letters, like all of James's correspondence, started out formally: "Dear Mr. Hall," "Dear Mr. Bly." But by their third correspondence, they were on a first name basis.

CD: So you married James about a year after you met him?

AW: A year and a day after I met him.

CD: He had gone through a very rough time for about six years before that.

AW: That's right. Through the whole Minnesota thing. And then for a year after that he was just wandering. He stayed with Elizabeth Esterly in California. He stayed with his parents in Concord, Ohio. He stayed with the Blys on the Bly farm in Minnesota.

CD: So he didn't have a job at all?

AW: He didn't have a job, and he didn't have a home.

CD: What year was that?

AW: His time of wandering, from 1964 to 1966.

CD: And he was probably drinking quite a bit.

AW: Yes.

CD: So this leads up to the obvious question: how did he manage to get such a good job at Hunter College after so much wandering?

AW: I have no way of knowing why he was chosen, but I'm sure those on the hiring committee at Hunter College were impressed by his interview and realized how bright he was. Also he was a popular and well-respected poet.

CD: A huge break. I'm suddenly realizing I haven't asked you how, when, and where you met James.

AW: I met him at a party in April of 1966 when he was in town to interview for the job at Hunter. Before he had actually been hired. The party was given by the Stevensons. David Stevenson was chairman of the English Department at Hunter and his wife Joan, a good friend, taught with me at the Walden School. The poet Josephine Miles gave a reading at the Guggenheim Museum and the party, which was at their home, was in honor of her. Allen Mandelbaum, a colleague of David's, brought Jane Cooper and James to the party.

CD: Did James introduce himself to you at this party?

AW: Actually, we didn't talk to each other at the party. He was sitting across the room from me, and I was sitting on the floor talking to Josephine Miles. James was reciting poetry by heart: some in German, some by Irish poets, as well as many American and English poets. We eyed each other but didn't speak until we met outside on the sidewalk after the party. He said, "I already know your name, but I want your telephone number, to take you home, and to take you out to dinner sometime." Actually we got into a cab with about fifteen other people, and he did ask me out, but not until six months later, in April of 1967.

CD: But he hadn't forgotten.

AW: No, he didn't. He got the job. However, that summer I left New York to do civil rights work in Georgia. Before I left I did get the *Mentor Book of Irish Poets* to take with me because I was very interested in this poet. And I also tried to find a book of his teacher, Theodore Roethke, but I couldn't spell his name and never did get the book. That fall, after I got the book and started teaching again, the Stevensons had another small dinner party, and James was invited but he didn't come. Allen Mandelbaum was there, however, and I thought I had nothing to lose whatsoever, so I went right up to Allen and said, "How is your friend James Wright enjoying teaching at Hunter?" And Allen said, "Oh"—his ears perked right up—"he's giving a poetry reading at the Y. You ought to go, dear." And so I said, "Well, I will, I will. Let me know, but I'll look it up." Allen Mandelbaum called James Wright and said, "That girl was asking about you and you'd better do something." So what he did was he called David Stevenson and said, "I'm giving a poetry reading in November and I'm reserving three tickets, one for you and Joan and one for your friend Miss Crunk." Crunk was my maiden name. It's a Dutch name. And that was how it started. I mean it was all very planned.

CD: So without Allen Mandelbaum's assistance you might never have met James.

AW: Well, I think the Stevensons would have had us over for dinner because they knew I was interested.

CD: Right. So then you went to the reading with great expectation.

AW: Yes, and after the reading to a party at Galen Williams's apartment. She was in charge of the Ninety-Second Street Y readings at that time. When I got there with the Stevensons, James was sitting in a big armchair, and he saw me come in and took my arm and pulled me onto the arm of his chair. And I didn't leave that place for the rest of the evening. And that was it. I always describe it as two incurable romantics meeting each other.

CD: He must have been just as romantic as he was haunted.

AW: Yes.

CD: Even though you were in love with James, you discovered fairly soon just how severe his drinking problem was, which in turn must have caused you to have a few second thoughts about the future of your relationship with him.

AW: Yes. I was worried about his drinking because I had drinking problems with my own family, but once he admitted he knew he had a problem with drinking, I thought, well, that is the first step.

CD: Did you bring up his drinking problem with him?

AW: Yes, I did, and he said, "Yes, I know it's a problem."

CD: And you asked him what he was going to do about it?

AW: I don't think I even said that, I just thought I didn't want to pursue that. To get him to admit it was a big deal. Then I thought, well, we will work on that.

CD: So you started seeing him pretty regularly, and he did do something.

AW: He did.

CD: Pretty soon?

AW: About a year after we were married he decided to go to a therapist, and I thought that was the beginning, and it was. But it was a long time before he joined AA. When he got his honorary degree at

Kenyon, the president of Kenyon said in the little talk before they presented him with the degree that James Wright had fulfilled the promise of his youth. But James said, "No, I haven't because I'm an alcoholic, and that wasn't the promise of my youth." I have an aunt who was in AA, and he called her up not long after his trip to Kenyon, and she took both of us to an open AA meeting. I went to a lot of open meetings with him for the first six or seven months.

CD: I imagine he spoke pretty eloquently at his AA meetings.

AW: As a matter of fact, I never heard him talk. I have it written down somewhere what he wrote in his journal about his first meetings at AA, but after he wanted to start going to meetings without me, and that made sense.

CD: If we could backtrack a bit to 1958, which was such a critical year for James in terms of discovering his own voice and free verse style amid the crowd of his formalist peers.

AW: Okay.

CD: After the success of his first two books, *The Green Wall* and *Saint Judas,* both of which were noteworthy for their formal skill and empathic witnessing to the lost and forgotten of Martins Ferry, James wrote to Robert Bly complaining about the crisis he was having with writing in blank verse. I found this passage in *A Wild Perfection*, the 2005 book of James's letters that you and Sandra Rose Maley so meticulously edited and published with Farrar, Straus and Giroux: "I mentioned having written a 'Farewell to Poetry' even before I saw *The Fifties.* . . . The new imagination is so important, to all living human beings and not just the literati, that I am going to continue to search for it—and if I can find it in myself (though I believe I can), then I will identify and fight for it in others. And this is not mock humility—I see blood in the matter. I really do."

When James started reading Pablo Neruda, Theodor Storm, Georg Trakl, and other modernist European and Southern American poets, he realized, like Bly, that there was really nothing preventing

him from writing outside the formal tradition of English prosody ex-
cept tradition itself and his rather academic critics' expectations. He
felt enormously liberated and proceeded to abandon the iambic line,
a liberation that lasted throughout the rest of his career. I think read-
ers and critics of James's work don't fully appreciate how masterfully
and quickly he shifted from formal to free verse, mastering his own
enjambments and line breaks within a year or two after publishing
Saint Judas. One can only marvel at the inherent skill in his free
verse that instilled his poems with a vital new breath and oneiric in-
spiration. It was as if he had discovered a gift that had been there all
along but felt he couldn't accept until Bly and the modernist "dogs" of
Europe and Central America—Bly's term for the international poets
contemporary American writers and critics were ignoring—con-
vinced him otherwise.

AW: Right. James actually discovered Trakl when he was in Vienna
on his Fulbright scholarship. He wandered into the wrong classroom
and heard his first Trakl poem. He began translating Trakl then.
That love for Trakl was a strong bond between him and Robert. With
regard to Robert Bly's journal *The Fifties*, going to that mailbox and
finding it there was one of the most exciting things that ever hap-
pened to him. It was the turning point of his life, the fulcrum. Those
letters to Robert, their early exchanges in the late fifties were truly
remarkable.

CD: Bly was such an invaluable friend and mentor to him then, as
well as throughout the rest of his career. He continues to comment on
how much he still misses James.

AW: He opened the door; he was his liberator.

CD: What would have happened to James at that point in his career
without Robert Bly's hospitality and mentorship?

AW: I think maybe he really would have stopped writing.

CD: There were several American poets writing exquisite formal verse in the late fifties. In addition to James, I'm thinking of Richard Wilbur, Robert Lowell, Howard Nemerov, Maxine Kumin, James Merrill, Adrienne Rich, Ruth Stone, Sylvia Plath, Anne Sexton, Elizabeth Bishop, John Berryman, W. S. Merwin, and even John Ashbery. Although most of these poets turned to free verse and their own idiosyncratic forms in the mid-sixties and seventies, they started out as skillful formal poets.

AW: Yes.

CD: But also many lesser academic poets who felt compelled to write formally or, as James might have put it, "like slaves to the iambic line."

AW: Well, that was the way one wrote then.

CD: Most poets, except for the beats, were polishing their blank verse in the fifties and early sixties to gain the approval from the academy and its academic critics. James had the nerve as well as the irrepressible need to find a way out of the academic, formal rage that had a choke hold on his colleagues, although he had already written some of the of the most accomplished formal verse of this era and maintained a brilliant ear for the ghost of form. He broke into free verse, concocting variable lines and ingenious enjambments, thumbing his nose, like Bly, at the traditional prosody he felt was antithetical to "the new imagination" and free verse. Bly likes to refer to this poetic rebellion as "letting the dogs in," those European modernists and South American poets—Pablo Neruda, Antonio Machado, Georg Trakl, Federico García Lorca, Theodor Strom, Juan Ramón Jiménez, César Vallejo—who most American poets and readers had never heard of. Also his classical influences from Japan, China, and Italy—Bai Juyi, Tu Fu, Li Po, Catullus, and Horace. I think it's a little known fact that James spent a year on military duty in Japan following the war before heading to college at Kenyon on the GI Bill, where he studied with John Crowe Ransom. At the end of his poem "Ars Poetica, Some Recent Criticism," the first poem in *Two Citizens*, which was published in 1973, he angrily dismisses the champions of received forms by the authority of his own self-abnegation: "Hell, I ain't got nothing. / Ah, you bastards, / How I hate you." As raw as this attack might have been, one gets the feeling he needed to say it.

AW: Yes, exactly.

CD: You were really the first woman then who provided stability in his life.

AW: I helped him organize his life, and I did all the finances because he was quite helpless with that! And then we had all of these wonderful trips to Europe.

CD: So from Martins Ferry.

AW: Quite a leap!

CD: He dedicates his last book *This Journey* to the town of Fano in Italy, then adds, "where we got well, from Annie and me" What did he mean by "where we got well"?

AW: We went to Bari. We went down to Apulia, and it was very scary for him. We had had a very bad experience in Bari. Someone had tried to snatch my purse and pushed me to the ground. We didn't like the city anyhow. We liked some of the things about it, but it was really a scary city. And we were warned: Don't go out. Don't keep your purse on your shoulder. Don't do this. Don't do that. And I heard later that there were gangs there, the drug gangs. And it was a port city. He tended to be very frightened of things like that.

CD: So you started going to Italy in the mid-seventies?

AW: Our first trip was 1970.

CD: That early?

AW: We went to Paris first. James wanted to show me his Vienna because he had studied there. And I wanted to show him my Italy because I had taught there.

CD: Vienna is where he went after receiving his Guggenheim, right?

AW: No, he had a Fulbright during our first trip. He had a Guggenheim during our last trip to Europe. And I wanted to show him my Italy.

CD: You had been to Italy?

AW: I taught there for two years, at the Overseas School of Rome.

CD: I always wondered why he went to Italy instead of France or England or Spain.

AW: Yes. And I loved Italy. And I wanted to go to Italy with him, to a place where I had never been before because I didn't want to be the guide. So we went to Bologna, and it was just a beautiful city. It was the perfect city. He just fell in love with it. And it just became our country. He called it "the country of my heart." After we had that bad experience in Bari, we went back to Fano, where we had a wonderful time in 1972, and it hadn't changed. It was safe. It was calm. And we liked where we stayed.

CD: So there was suddenly this . . .

AW: Resurrection. And there was nothing to be scared of.

CD: What do you think he had been scared of before?

AW: I think—I'm just guessing—in Minneapolis there was that kind of lowlife that put him on guard.

CD: Where he wrote so many superb raw poems, poems like "Hook," which actually appeared in *To a Blossoming Pear Tree* in 1977, many years after he lived in Minneapolis.

AW: "Hook"—such a poem! In doing some research with the papers at the Andersen Library Manuscript Department at the University of Minnesota in October 2012, I looked through many drafts connected with both *Shall We Gather at the River* and *To a Blossoming Pear Tree*.

I will call it Hook.

It was thirty five degrees below zero,
Fahrenheit, for my English friends.
Too cold for the snow to fall
Anymore. I don't.
Have to be told
Any more somebody
Hates usX. As I ran, slowly, I saw
I would miss the bus to Saint Paul.
I missed it.

I was only and y oung man
In those day, on that evening
The cold was so God damned
Bitter there was nothing.
Nothing. I was in trouble
With a woman, and there was
Nothing there but
Me and dead snow.

I stood on that streetcorner perfectlyX awre
Of nothing except the dead fact.
Another bus to Saint Paul would arrive
In another three hours, if I was lucky.
Oh, I am plenty lucky.

At somewhere, a bell
Then beating one, an old man
On the way to Harry's
Paused and stroked my face. Please
Give it to me, he said,
I'll give you anything.

Get away from me, leave me alone, I am standing
      here
Trying to write a book review of the exquisite
Villanelles and pantoums in the dead
Radiance of William F.
Pritchard's
Body?

The old man went away to Harry's,
And then the young Sioux appeared.
Ain't got no bus here a long time.
He said. You got enough to get home on?
What did they do to your hand? I answered.
I had a bad time with a woman, he said, here,
You take this.
Did you ever see a man hold sixty-five cents
In a hook, and lay it on your shoulder?
I took it.

Anne Wright's copy of "Hook," by James Wright

James didn't actually begin work on "Hook" until he began preparations for the manuscript of *To a Blossoming Pear Tree* in 1974, a very tough year for him. His parents died that year, and he had a breakdown after we returned from Europe. I discovered from the drafts that both "Hook" and "To a Blossoming Pear Tree" were originally sections of the same poem he started in 1974. I have a copy of the poem here.

CD: Remarkable. Both poems express such transcendent empathy. I always assumed James had left "Hook" out of *Shall We Gather at the River*, which was published in 1968, and then included it later in *To a Blossoming Pear Tree*. Its style and theme are so consistent with several of the poems he wrote while living in Minneapolis in the mid-sixties, such poems as "The Minneapolis Poem," "A Poem Written under an Archway in a Disconnected Railroad Station, Fargo, North Dakota," "Speak," "The Poor Washed Up in Chicago," and "Rip."

AW: He found life menacing in Minneapolis and even more frightening in Bari.

CD: But you would never know from his poems that he was frightened by the lowlife in Minneapolis. He seems to embrace the downtrodden in the same way his character Judas embraces the mugger's victim in his poem "Saint Judas." He seems to transform his fear of the downtrodden characters he encounters in Minneapolis into compassionate elegies, as in these lines from the conclusion of "Speak":

> I have gone forward with
> Some, a few lonely some.
> They have fallen to death.
> I die with them.
> Lord I have loved Thy cursed,
> The beauty of Thy house:
> Come down. Come down. Why dost
> Thou hide thy face?

And also stony resolve, as in the concluding lines of "Inscription for the Tank":

> I have heard weeping in secret
> And quick nails broken.
> Let the dead pray for their own dead.
> What is their pity to me?

Did you notice this sort of emotional vacillation in him between compassion and resignation? And was Fano a place that healed not only his fear but a lifelong wound of physical and psychological hardship?

AW: I'm not sure why I went on about the lowlife. I think James was always aware of what dark, menacing things go on in all cities and towns. One may not see or experience this kind of life, but we know it's there. Perhaps he felt the only thing he could do about it was write. After his losses in Minneapolis—his marriage, his job, his children who moved to California with their mother, his house on Como Avenue, he lived in dreary places on miniscule funds. He hung out at the bars on Seven Corners, an area now spiffed up, which was a very different life than that of academia. It wasn't skid row, but he may have felt he ended up there. Yes, I agree, he moved between compassion and resignation. I think the return to Fano, a place we had loved back in 1972, made him feel safe. It hadn't changed, and he knew his way around and what to expect.

CD: In his poem "Piccolini" which appears in *To a Blossoming Pear Tree*, James writes, "But those tiny fish which tickle the skin of my ankles are so diminutive that they would have dissolved altogether into droplets of mist at a mere touch of Catullus's fingertip. I reckon that is why he never wrote of them by name, but left them tiny and happy in their lives in the waters where they still have their lives and seem to enjoy ticking the skin of my ankles." Such a different poem than a poem like "Beautiful Ohio" in which he celebrates the polluted waters of his hometown.

AW: Oh, entirely different.

CD: So he moves both psychically and geographically from the polluted Ohio River to the dazzling piccolini at his ankles in a clear Italian river.

AW: Mingled feelings . . . very mingled feelings in "Beautiful Ohio" that he didn't have about Catullus country in Italy. Catullus was the first person he ever translated when he was in high school.

CD: So there is a . . .

AW: Connection.

CD: But it is almost as if he is realizing for the first time that life can be this way—no longer as complicated and conflicted as it had been for him in Martins Ferry and Minneapolis.

AW: He dared to let himself be happy.

CD: In his last few books, *To a Blossoming Pear Tree* and *This Journey*, there is, as Keats would say, such little "irritable reaching" in his poems. It seems as if his newfound happiness—his revelation that he really could be happy—was as important to him as writing poetry itself. Life and poetry seemed one for him. His "new imagination"—the phrase he had read fifteen years earlier in Robert Bly's journal *The Fifties* and latched onto as a liberating term that helped him break out of writing blank verse—seemed more focused on actual events in his life, his love for you, his professional stability at Hunter, his love of such bucolic details and metaphysical topics as the piccolini, "a field outside of Pisa," and the "secret of light," than on fictive or figurative subject matter.

AW: All his late poems, the attention to detail . . . to the insects, the lizards, even the mosquitoes. He also wrote about details in *The Branch Will Not Break* but in a different way I think. He's writing details about the details in *To a Blossoming Pear Tree.*

CD: So he no longer felt the need to witness in such a personal, visceral way to the downtrodden of Martins Ferry and Minneapolis, as he had in his first four books. You must have seen a change in his behavior as well. He wasn't drinking anymore, and he was finding a home for himself outside the Midwest in New York and Italy.

AW: And in Europe he was also away from the pressures of teaching.

CD: As angry and frustrated as James still was at his academic critics by the time he wrote *Two Citizens* in 1973, he was also growing more and more devoted to you. His juxtaposition of philippics with love poems to you in this book is striking. He moves from such public tirades as "Ars Poetica, Some Recent Criticism" and "I Wish I May Never Hear of the United States Again" to deeply private love poems—"Hotel Lenox," "Voices between Waking and Sleeping in the Mountains," "On the Liberation of Woman"—about you. He gives the impression that his marriage to you has become the most important thing in his life. You two are, in fact, the two citizens of *Two Citizens*.

AW: Yes. And a lot of that book is about our trip to Europe. There are some wonderful poems in that book and then some that aren't so great.

CD: He risked pulling out all the stops.

AW: He dared to do it. He really got slapped on the wrist for it too.

CD: What do you think?

AW: I think some people thought the language was too simple. There was one line where he said, "Put that in your pipe and smoke it." The critics were very critical of that.

CD: In response to this criticism he remarked in a *Paris Review* interview with Peter Stitt, "My family background is partly Irish, and this means many things, but linguistically it means that it is too easy to talk sometimes." Did he ever wonder if you had a reaction to his loquaciousness or plain language?

AW: No. No, he didn't.

CD: He just wrote? He didn't talk that much about it?

AW: No.

CD: You went to Europe four of five times?

AW: Twice on big, long trips.

CD: You loved Italy more than Paris.

AW: We loved Paris too, but there was the whole country of Italy. Tuscany and Verona, Venice.

CD: Paradise.

AW: It was.

CD: And of course he had translated Catullus, so he must have felt excited to be in Catullus country.

AW: We went to Sirmione because of Catullus and also James's Latin teacher from Martins Ferry High School, Helen McNeely Sheriff.

CD: She must have been a kind of substitute mother to James, along with Ms. Esterly. Also, his mentors.

AW: Right, they were. I was lucky to spend time with Elizabeth Esterly. Elizabeth and Henry had moved to Cupertino, California. James stayed with them during his time of wandering (1964–66). During the summer of 1968, we visited them together. Both Elizabeth and Ms. Sheriff "discovered" him at Martins Ferry High School and encouraged him to pursue a classical education. Elizabeth invited him to concerts and discussed literature with him. Later, I finally met Ms. Sheriff. She lived in a beautiful old house in Cadiz, Ohio. James and I went there to dinner during one of the summers we visited Ted and Helen Wright in Zanesville, Ohio in 1976 or 1977. She was amazing. Very sharp. She remembered the very place in her class where

James sat. I never saw Martins Ferry until after James's death. We did go to New Concord and Zanesville, the town his parents moved to when they left Martins Ferry.

CD: Did they receive you okay?

AW: Oh, they were wonderful, yes. His mother said, "I thank God for you every day."

CD: So she felt, maybe, you were providing something she couldn't.

AW: I think she thought I was saving his life, but I don't want to take responsibility for that.

CD: Well, you did.

AW: No. No one saves someone else's life unless you pull them out from drowning.

CD: But you almost did.

AW: You can provide a life that helps them. Another woman who helped him was Carol Bly. She was fantastic to him. He said when he went out to the farm, it was the talks with Carol that were so comforting. The work with Robert was very stimulating and exciting, but Carol was down to earth. She was very kind to James, an intellectual companion too. She was very bright and also a writer.

CD: He seemed to love these women who wrote powerful narratives. Carol did and so did Leslie Marmon Silko, who corresponded for years with James and whose letters you also edited in the 2009 book, *The Strength and Delicacy of Lace.*

AW: Right. They had fun. They did jokes. They did pranks, real pranks that were Carol's idea, I think. One year he was there for Easter and she made bunny costumes for them and they got dressed up in their bunny costumes and went into the town of Madison, Minnesota, with a huge basket of hard boiled eggs and gave them to all the shopkeepers. They came to the drug store where Robert had been having a fight with the druggist about who knows what, and James took an egg out and dropped it, and it wasn't hardboiled. James loved that story. He used to tell it over and over again. But Martins Ferry was with him all the time. He carried that baggage with him until the end.

CD: And what was that like for you?

AW: It was fascinating!

CD: Did you ever visit Martins Ferry with James?

AW: I never saw Martins Ferry until I attended the James Wright festivals after James died.

CD: But you visited his parents with him when they were living in another town in Ohio.

AW: They were living in New Concord, Ohio, when we visited them, and then they moved to Zanesville.

CD: What was that like for you, meeting them the first time?

AW: It was another world.

CD: Did he prepare you for the visit?

AW: Well, he was always so negative about Ohio!

CD: But also deeply in love with Ohio.

AW: I know, I know. It was a love-hate relationship. When we first went, all the fields were filled with Queen Anne's lace. It was so beautiful.

CD: As you say, Ohio stayed with him until the end.

AW: Definitely. Absolutely. You see it in poems like "The Flying Eagles of Troop 62," in which he refers to his friends from high school who were trapped there.

CD: As well as in his poem "The Old WPA Swimming Pool of Martins Ferry, Ohio."

AW: He didn't talk about it so much, but it was definitely there. There were times I think he couldn't believe that he was a tenured professor with a PhD, with the admiration of his colleagues and his students.

CD: And a Pulitzer Prize winner to boot.

AW: Yes, and living in a beautiful apartment.

CD: And going to Italy with you.

AW: And going to Italy. It was like, "who is this person?"

CD: So he was just pinching himself the whole time he was at Hunter.

AW: Yes, but I think very gradually learning to accept it. "Maybe I'm worth it after all. Maybe I deserve it."

CD: When he got sick was there anything he said that hinted at how he actually felt about the arc of his life and career from humble childhood in Martins Ferry to nationally renowned poet in his thirties and forties?

AW: You know, when he got cancer, we never talked about it. I couldn't bear . . . we couldn't bear to talk about it. I just thought I'd start crying and that wasn't going to help him.

CD: Right. When you say "it," you mean the illness?

AW: The illness. The fact that it was terminal.

CD: He was so courageous in his letters, announcing his condition so candidly with his close friend Leslie Marmon Silko. In a letter to her dated December 18, 1979, he wrote:

I have learned that I have cancer. It is very serious, but it is not hopeless. My doctor is a good man and a highly skilled specialist, and he has assured me and Annie that the operation—radical surgery in the throat—will save my life. I will emerge from the surgery with a diminished capacity to speak, and this will create a problem, since I make my living by speaking. But there is a good chance that I will be able to continue teaching all right. . . . I have found that I have a number of considerable powers to help me. I have always been happy with my marriage to Annie, for example, but I suddenly have a deeper understanding of how very strong the marriage is.

AW: He was very courageous. He couldn't . . . we couldn't talk about the fact that he was going to die.

CD: Understandably. And yet he maintained his humor to the end.

AW: Oh, when Edgar Doctorow came to see him, he wrote—he couldn't talk—he wrote, "The leaves are falling." And apparently that was some joke they had at Kenyon College. Phil Levine and Mark Strand came together to visit him, and he wrote to them, "I'd rather be in Philadelphia." [laughing] So he didn't miss his sense of humor.

CD: Donald Hall tells the story of James handing him a note that says, "Don, I'm dying." Then writing another note that said, "for a dish of ice cream."

AW: His humor was indestructible.

CD: You both summoned enormous emotional strength in dealing with this sudden bad news.

AW: I don't know how I did it. I call it having emotional novocaine. Like a big shot. I didn't feel anything. I mean that's not quite true.

CD: You were both so young still, relatively.

AW: Fifty-two. Very young.

CD: Galway Kinnell, Philip Levine, and Hayden Carruth helped him prepare *This Journey* for publication?

AW: Yes, and also his good friend, Roger Hecht, who came almost every day to the hospital.

CD: How did James know Hayden Carruth?

AW: We met at Galway's when James and I spent a weekend with the Kinnells in Sheffield, Vermont. Hayden came over for dinner. Then Hayden and James began a correspondence, and they came to know each other well through the exchange of their letters. Hayden sent a postcard to James every single day he was in the hospital.

CD: He and James had a similar trait; they both had such an enormous capacity for feeling so deeply.

AW: Yes. That never ceased.

CD: He seemed to have reached a higher awareness in the last five years of his life that afforded him well-deserved equilibrium and disinterested objectivity. Was that something you realized too?

AW: I realized a change.

CD: Lines like "mercy on me," and "my name no mind," and "I love you best" are just so plain, naked, and powerful.

AW: Yes.

CD: But if somebody isn't reading closely here, failing to understand who James Wright is at this point in his life or what's happening to him, the import and nature of this change might easily elude them.

AW: Those lines about the chickadee.

CD: You mean from "To the Creature of the Creation"?

AW: Yes.

CD: The chickadee appears in the last stanza of that poem, lines that could certainly be an homage to Theodore Roethke, James's teacher. I have it here.

> What have I got to do?
> The sky is shattering,
> The plain sky grows blue.
> Some day I have to die,
> As everyone must do
> Alone, alone, alone,
> Peaceful as peaceful stone.
> You are the earth's body.
> I will die on the wing.
> To me, you are everything
> That matters, chickadee.
> You live so much in me.
> Chickadees sing in the snow.
> I will die on the wing.
> I love you so.

AW: That's the one.

The identity of Jenny has recently been revealed in Jonathan Blunk's new biography, *James Wright: A Life in Poetry*, as Wright's former University of Washington student Sonjia Urseth.

Ed Ochester. Photo by Judith Vollmer

6 / *Ed Ochester*

P oet Ed Ochester grew up in Brooklyn, New York. He earned a
BA from Cornell University, an MA from Harvard University,
and an MFA from the University of Wisconsin–Madison. A
longtime editor of the Pitt Poetry Series (University of Pittsburgh
Press), he is the founding editor of the journal *5AM*. His own collec-
tions of poetry include *We Like It Here* (1967); *Dancing on the Edge
of Knives* (1973), winner of the Devins Award for Poetry; *Miracle
Mile* (1984); *Allegheny* (1995); *Snow White Horses: Selected Poems,
1973–1988* (1988); *The Land of Cockaigne* (2001); and *Unreconstruct-
ed: Poems Selected and New* (2007).

Ochester's work has garnered awards from the National Endow-
ment for the Arts and the Pennsylvania Council on the Arts. For his
contributions to the arts, he received the George Garrett Award from
the Association of Writers and Writing Programs in 2006 and the
Pittsburgh Cultural Trust's Creative Achievement Award in 2001.

Ochester is professor emeritus at the University of Pittsburgh and
is on the faculty of the Bennington College MFA Writing Seminars.

This three-part interview took place at Bennington College on
June 22, 2011.

Chard deNiord (CD): Throughout your career you have often as-
sumed a self-effacing speaker in your poems who has testified to
human folly. Your candor and compassion for the underdog resonate
a rich mixture of erudition, plainspeaking and Martial-like wit for

what you have called "American dumb fuckism." Could you talk about your discovery of this voice? Did you find it in a breakthrough poem or perhaps group of poems that spoke back to you as you?

Ed Ochester (EO): I don't think there is a specific breakthrough poem. What I can tell you, my understanding of it, is that when I was very young—I had just graduated from college—I ran across by happy accident the poems of Ed Field. Ed had just published *Stand Up, Friend, with Me*. I decided then that Ed Field is probably, arguably, the first widely published postmodern poet in America. And what I loved about his work was the colloquial diction, the simple diction, the use of pop-cultural materials, which seemed to me obviously a worthwhile thing, the clear desire not to mystify the material or the composition process. Also, one of the things I really admired about Ed was that he was one of the first widely published poets to talk openly and freely and unashamedly about his gayness, and all of those things combined, it seemed to me, were remarkable. And before that I'd seen the poems of Frank O'Hara, which knocked me out for many of the same reasons, the wittiness, the quickness, the ability to talk out of the present and most of all, what I call "the O'Hara," the ongoing present, in which he starts at one point and works through time in the course of the poem from morning until night, and it's all in the present.

These elements really amazed me, and later in the mid-sixties, a friend of mine introduced me to James Wright's *Shall We Gather at the River* and *The Branch Will Not Break*. The impulses that I had from Field and O'Hara were reinforced by the kind of thing that Wright was doing and the kind of concern about the common man in eastern Ohio who had been screwed by the bosses and worked in the coal mines and factories. And finally, a little bit after that, I met Jerry Stern. He was, before he published *Lucky Life*, among other things the director of Poets in the Schools in Pennsylvania. So we got together on a regular basis in Harrisburg to talk about stuff. He had been publishing for a long time, and he was in his mid-fifties, I think, when *Lucky Life* was published. He had a meteoric rise of fame in as far as a poet can be famous. And what I loved about him—and he was, I think, my oldest continuous friend in poetry and my mentor for that matter too—the omnivorous quality of Stern, being able to write, think about almost anything and more particularly to be able to indicate the thought processes, the way he "leaps," in Bly's word, was just remarkable to me. So all of those, I think, came together, and gave me things, gave me tools to work with. My work, for the most part, doesn't look anything like those writers, but there are elements that are drawn from them all. Gradually, I would like to think my work has been getting a little bit more sure, a little bit more speedy in the application.

CD: I notice that in a lot of your poems, you create catalogues that zip down the page. They are not so Stern-like as your own original litanies, but you do share a similar style of verbal drive and poetic reasoning that builds to memorable fugues.

EO: Stern is interested in doing things that I'm not particularly interested in doing, and he has, as you know, a kind of Talmudic temperament. His mind goes around and around and around the subject until he gets to the essence of it and then *wop!* he makes a statement at the end of the page that often is a leap to something that wasn't there before. And I love that, but on the other hand I've never been inclined to go around and around quite as much. I always have had a sense in my own poems of going in maybe unexpected directions as they start out but of moving in one way and doing it fairly quickly.

CD: In your poem "Packing Lunch," you move from image to image and at one point say, "O love, I'm going on / because the first images are clearer."

EO: And that's one poem that's actually written in one sentence with a semicolon in the middle, and that was the intent of it, to simply get on but not be boring and give a sense of excitement in talking all at once. And I think that in some ways that's Sternian, but it's also not as circular; it's trying to choose individual elements that are pertinent and interesting but it's not going around and around as much.

CD: Not at all. I'm interested in your idea of audience, since by now you've created a kind of myth of self as Ed Ochester in a way that is not dissimilar from Stern's ecstatic, elegiac personas, except in the ways that you've just described. You envision the "poor dumb fuck heads filled with shit muttering to themselves," as you describe the common American, in your poem "Butterfly Affect." Do you think of the "poor dumb fucks" as your primary audience, or other poets?

EO: Well, my immediate audience is a handful of friends and my wife. Past that, I don't know. You know I'm surprised from time to time that someone will come up to me at a reading or I'll meet someone at a college who will say they love my poem x, y, or z, but how they ever got to it or how they ever saw it, I don't know. What I know is that if you stay in one place for a while, and if you're at a place like Bennington where once a year you do a reading, you do tend to get lost inside the exterior of your poems, and I think that people think of me in a way different at this place [Bennington] from the way that I think of myself because they assume that what's there in the poems is me. On the other hand, what I'd like to think is that there is never actual contempt for the poor dumb fucks, since in the poems we all are dumb fucks at least one moment or another, and it is written out of sympathy, out of compassion and—I don't want to say despair—but frustration.

CD: You exercise a delicate balance between compassion and satire in repeating what seems to be a credo in your translation "Beltrolt Brecht: On the Infanticide, Marie Farrar." "So I beg you, don't be angry at her. / Each creature needs the help of the other." And in your poem "My First Brassiere," you conclude

>   that sex has taught me two things:
>
>   don't judge
>   but if you must judge,
>   forgive.

Do you ever feel the line between your compassion for the common folk you call "dumb fucks"—people the speaker of many of your poems seems to identify with—and odious historical characters blurs to the point of invisibility?

EO: I think that it is invisible. I think that one has to speak out against stupidity. I think that's a long-standing tradition for many poets and many poets I admire and so come the comic and the satiric poems. But I think that we also are people living with other people. Human beings are, despite Ayn Rand, social animals, and we need compassion for one another. The Brecht poem is a translation of the early Brecht. He can't deny what is terrible, what is out there, but you can have at least compassion for the subjects of that suffering. That's Whitman after all. "Stand up for the stupid and the crazy," he said. And I think if there is one moral teaching I can remember, I think it was when I was about thirteen or fourteen, I got on my bike and to the horror of my parents rode out to Whitman's birthplace on Long Island, and the nice lady who was in charge gave me some pamphlets on Whitman, and that was the phrase that stuck with me: "Stand up for the stupid and the crazy."

CD: Which is from Whitman's preface to the 1855 edition of *Leaves of Grass.*

EO: Yeah, and I loved it. In school I was the butt of jokes and picked on but not so much that I wasn't able to rescue some people who were much lower in the pecking order than I. That's my idea of religion, I guess.

CD: You certainly don't excuse religion from criticism in your poems.

EO: Organized religion has created so much misery for so many people, so many deaths, so many massacres, so many cruelties, but I think that there is and it's observable in ordinary people and not just in our own age but going back as far as written records, a kind of sympathy for human beings, the wish to help other human beings. It's a kind of natural, inbred Sermon on the Mount, "do unto others." And that's what I see, you know, rather than original sin.

CD: I'm interested in that impulse in you because it seems to be there from the start of your career. You grew up in Brooklyn in the forties.

EO: I was born in Brooklyn but grew up in Queens.

CD: Your father was an insurance man, and did your mother also work?

EO: She worked as a secretary.

CD: Her name was, Viola, right?

EO: Yeah.

CD: And your grandmother worked boiling diapers.

EO: Well, that was one grandmother.

CD: One grandmother.

EO: My grandmother Ochester. The grandmother who lived with us was a person with not quite an elementary school education.

CD: Right.

EO: Her father had owned a delicatessen for a while, and she worked in that, making salads and stuff, and for much of her life, after her husband died at an early age, she lived with her children. We had a house in Queens, which was bought at the beginning of the Depression with the last money that the family had, a family house. My mother's brother lived upstairs with his wife and daughter and we lived downstairs. And my grandmother and her maiden sister also lived in the house, and she spent the rest of her life living in the house, you know, talking to local tradesmen who were friends, meeting with friends from her past life, always in our house, never went anywhere. She was earning her keep, she felt, by doing laundry. She was the cook for great occasions and ordinary days and also had a great influence on me, I think, because she was—what would you say?—a kind of natural Christian. She never cared about going to church.

CD: Like you were just describing a minute ago.

EO: Yeah, but she had a sort of natural kindness, a gift for easing pain for people, friends of hers, the kids in the family, her own children. She was a remarkable human being.

CD: So she must have had a huge influence.

EO: She was the one who raised me really because my mother went to work. She was there every day when I came home from school. For a long time, because I had asthma as a kid—my parents had bought a little place in upstate New York outside of Newburgh—and every summer to improve my health, also to simply improve their lives, my grandmother and I were dropped off in that place, and my parents would come back once a week to bring groceries, but I lived with her for three months at a time, and we had many conversations and we got along amicably. She never disciplined me in any way at all, so I had a great relationship with her.

CD: You were like a son to her.

EO: Very much, yeah.

CD: It sounds like you grew up very close to the street.

EO: The area where I lived was mixed, was basically German, Italian, some Middle Eastern, and German Jews lived in the area, a few Irishmen. It was one of those places in Queens, which like now was just a mixture of striving families. And on Woodhaven Boulevard, which was eight lanes—eight traffic lanes wide at that time—in Queens there were distinct German neighborhoods, Jewish neighborhoods, Italian neighborhoods, various other ethnic neighborhoods, which usually were distinct, but at the same time kids from those communities were all drawn into the high school I went to, Richmond Hill High School, and what that meant is that you met a lot of different sensibilities, and that was very good. One of my very close friends who was Jewish had a mother who loved poetry and was the only mother I ever knew growing up who loved poetry. Another friend of mine, who was Italian, was one of the kids who had a great love for opera, and her father was a metal worker, a craftsman who among other things made the iron gates at the Bloomingdale's store in Manhattan. But to have that diversity of population, that diversity of interests and skills was wonderful because it rubbed off on you.

CD: There must have been a lot of storytelling.

EO: Talking about the old country.

CD: Your background is primarily Polish.

EO: It's Polish and German.

CD: And German. And so this was not a neighborhood where there were a lot of Germans but not a lot of Polish.

EO: No.

CD: Your original family name was not Ochester but . . .

EO: Olshevski.

CD: Which your father or your grandfather changed to Ochester?

EO: My grandfather.

CD: Which sounds Irish, but not really.

EO: Well, this was when my father was very young, as I mention in my poem "Changing the Name to Ochester," but the family had moved to an Irish neighborhood around Chauncey Street in Brooklyn, and apparently, so far as anybody could tell, he changed his name to Ochester because to him it sounded Irish. And of course, no Irishman has ever thought for a second that was an Irish name, since there is no county Chester, at least not in Ireland. It's one of those idiotic things that happen all the time but make a difference in the lives of people.

CD: Do you feel this name change ever affected your identity or sense of yourself as a poet or ancestral image of yourself?

EO: See, I never knew this because my father was so ashamed of his father and what had happened. He was so outraged because his father had left the family, had left my grandmother Ochester. My father, or one of his brothers, would get in touch with their father to tell him about deaths or major changes in the family, but they never spoke about him to the people in my generation. I didn't know any of this until after my father died when I was going through his papers. And when I said to my mother, "why didn't you tell me any of this?" she said, "your father wouldn't let me."

CD: In your poem "Dreaming about My Father," you imagine a post-humous conversation with your father that's heartfelt, archetypal, and painfully remorseful.

> "I'm sorry," he says, as we roll a load of stones
> toward the wall he's building toward the big maple,
> "that I didn't talk to you more—what can I say?
> I was tired and angry—and that I called you
> good for nothing."

But there's a rapprochement in the poem. The poem ends with these lines, "'I know,' he says, 'but it doesn't matter / now that we're here, and we're talking, / now that we don't even have to talk.'" Your speaker—you—appears to feel a clear sense of forgiveness, freedom, and filial catharsis by the end of this imagined conversation.

EO: Yes, all those things. The strange thing about that poem is that I've read it a number of times. I've read it at Bennington several times in the past, and almost every time someone or some people will come up after and say, "that's just like my father." For whatever reason—is it universal? I don't know—but it is certainly common in America for sons to not get along with their fathers or do so at a very elementary level, and so I think that poem is so specific that it talks to everybody.

CD: Yes, and then in your poem "For My Son, Ned," you write,

> I want to say 30 some years after
> the momentous event of your birth, "hello?"
> and "I'm trying to redress the balance"
> and, "welcome to the world."

Maybe things that your father couldn't say to you?

EO: Sure, and I was very conscious at the time of composition that those two poems were going together, that they spoke to one another. I certainly have a much warmer and closer relationship with my son, I think, than I did with my father. But I can tell there's all kinds of strain there.

CD: In a recent interview I conducted with Robert Bly, he quoted his poem "Words a Dreamer Spoke to My Father in Maine," the ending of which captures this paternal-filial wound. "My dead father stood beside me, / But his eyes remained on my chest. / I say to him for the first time, 'Oh look at me when we talk.'" Your poems about your father and son address both the remorse Bly mentions in his poem and the promise of saying what we need to say to our children while we still can.

EO: So much of what we thought about was trivial. So much of our criticism of other people is utterly trivial. A student of mine the other day was using Donald Hall's wonderful line from his poem "One Day," which is a this-is-what-you-shall-do kind of line: "Work, love, build a house, die." And that's a kind of simplicity that covers the major things. And the other stuff isn't necessary, but you don't know it at the time.

CD: Hall informed me that that saying is a Swabian aphorism. It reminds me also of the Zen saying, "Chop wood, carry water." You found a language in poetry that wasn't happening in your family, especially between you and your father, that came obviously a little later than your childhood years. You went to high school, then Cornell, then Harvard, which you liked and disliked, before you finished your graduate education at the University of Wisconsin. Did you begin writing poetry seriously during your PhD studies at Wisconsin?

EO: Well, actually, I would say starting around the time I was in my last couple years at Cornell, undergraduate college, I was writing poems from the time I was in high school but not doing anything close in spirit or in appearance to what I've done for most of my life until the last year or two of college. I think the first poem I really liked was taken when I was a senior in college by the *Beloit Poetry Journal*. And there was one little poem, which was pretty crappy but which had echoes of later stuff, that was published when I was in high school right next to a poem by Bukowski in a magazine called *Epos*. But I didn't have a strong sense of how to put it together, I don't think, until I wound up in Wisconsin, and things came together there for me—friends, my reading, the politics at the time; it all came together, and I started to see some ways out.

CD: Did you receive your MFA there too?

EO: No, I was on the PhD track. I never finished the dissertation, although I finished all the other requirements. At the time you could do that and move on and get a job.

CD: You then got your first teaching job at the University of Florida?

EO: I did, but I didn't like it too much. I then went to the University of Pittsburgh. In the first couple of years, I decided I was *not* going to finish the dissertation, and I went to the then-chair of the department—this was the early seventies—and said, "Well, I'm going to write poems. I'm not going to finish my dissertation." Of course, if you did this now, you'd be out on your ass inside of a week. And his response, Lord bless him, was to say, "Well, there are many ways to the chosen land, just work on . . ." [laughing].

CD: What was your dissertation on?

EO: It was a very long one—the reason it never got done—on James Shirley, the Caroline and Jacobean dramatist who wrote more plays than anyone else from the period except for Shakespeare. And I decided I was going to deal with them all!

CD: Very ambitious.

EO: Well, it was stupidity, I think. I had a polymath as a mentor who didn't tell me that wasn't wise. He just let me go, so it was not to be, but that was one of the great pieces of luck of my life—that I happened to come out of graduate school at a time I didn't have to lock myself in and still managed to get through.

CD: I'd like to return to a question about the arc and conceit of your poetry. You write in your poem "The March of the Penguins" that we are "the first country to pass from barbarism to decadence without an interlude." Do you feel as a poet that you are also an American witness preserving some sanctuary of civilization in this country with your demotic, often ironic voice? I guess this also raises the question of whether Auden was right when he wrote in his elegy for Yeats that "poetry makes nothing happen."

EO: I made a parodic comment on Auden in which I'm at a cabin at the MacDowell Colony in the great cold, and I take a book of poetry down from the shelf to start a fire and say, "At last poetry makes something happen."

CD: That's good.

EO: But the answer to it is that my sense has always been that it's in the arts, and poetry certainly, but also in fiction, nonfiction, and the other arts that things happen in the sense of recognition of what's out there and recognition of possible responses. The terrible thing about popular culture, as much as I love it, is that it increasingly tends to be an instrument of salesmanship, and it's false for many reasons, but it's particularly false for that reason. You know, we're all free, free to buy merchandise. It's in poetry and fiction and maybe some movies, maybe in the spirit of some music, that we get outside of those views or that insistence. And so in that way poetry makes something happen. It allows people to be free in a dimension of their mind. And once upon a time, maybe once again in the future, Brecht and Neruda actually did make things happen in a way, in the sense of encouraging people, awakening people.

———————

CD: You write paradoxically at the end of "Ballerina," "America, close your eyes and you will see me dancing." This line of course sounds like it could be right out of Allen Ginsberg's "America," but you are saying that only when America closes its eyes can it see what it's distracted from seeing.

EO: That's a very early poem, and I wrote that, I think, as more of a joke . . . in a joking way more than anything else. It was meant to be a taunt, I think, rather than anything else. But what the poem is saying is that you can imagine yourself as whatever you want to be, even if there are pressures against you for doing that. And the call at the end is to imagine how that's possible, I guess, or what it might look like.

CD: I'm curious about your inclination to make bold leaps in your poetry, as many poets of your and your preceding generation have also done, conjuring expression that is both humorous and tragic. We see it in Allen Ginsberg, James Wright, John Berryman, Ruth Stone, James Tate, John Ashbery, Thomas Lux, Bill Knott, and many others. I'm wondering why you think, just from a historical or aesthetic standpoint, why this flowering of leaping poetry that was so prevalent in many European and South American modernists took so long in this country.

EO: It's still a minority position in many ways, and I think there are all sorts of reasons why this might be the case, but one is that the poetry that the large majority of people may know, if they know any poetry at all, is poetry that they don't like, which is very serious, which was given to them by teachers in elementary and secondary schools who didn't like poetry either. And consequently, even though you don't read poetry, you know that poetry is a highly serious form of art, and so it's disturbing to see people in the present being satirical, being humorous in poems. The second thing, I think, and there are surely other reasons, but the second thing is the high icons, the major icons of the modernist movement of poetry in English were, although they had their humorous moments, all highly serious people, so . . . capitals on all of these words.

CD: So what happened?

EO: Well, that's what I'm taking as one of the swings, why half of the people didn't write humorous poems before, but in American literature, once you began to get those elements of what I'm calling postmodernism, for want of a better phrase, once you started to get people like Ed Field or Frank O'Hara with some of the poems that were giddy or funny at the same time, those were elements that you saw and wanted to emulate. You wanted to do something of the same. I think it's grown, and I think that in recent years, publication of anthologies like *Stand Up Poetry* has impelled it further. The only thing I would say about this is that a lot of people, including myself, get tired of poetry readings that are basically joke sessions. . . . It's just too monolithic, but that doesn't mean that all the poems or the good poems that have humorous elements, comic or satiric, are joke-telling, you know? They are employing humor in different ways, not just the most reductive of stand-up performances.

CD: I'd like to turn to the theme of loneliness that occurs in a lot of your poems. You write in "Goodbye, Farewell, Auf Wiedersehen Poem," "May we only be lonely / by choice." Has loneliness, as opposed to isolation or privacy, been instrumental in your work as a conceit and a condition?

EO: Well, I mean, not to sound too pretentious . . . it *is* the human condition. Britt and I live by choice in a county not too far from Pittsburgh, but we don't have any neighbors close, and so in a number of the poems that I've written, reflecting where I live, it's very quiet at night. There are not people dancing by in the street. And so there is that. But there's also behind that . . . "you can only be lonely by choice." People need to be by themselves. They can't be and shouldn't be tweeting *all* the time, you know, and holding hands all the time. That's what I mean by "lonely by choice," being alone when you need to be alone and when it's useful to be alone. In the country, you set the terms for that. You can go back to the city if you want. You can be with friends if that's what you wish, but you don't have to be, and you can have a mixture, which to me at least is very pleasant. You know, when I want to bay at the moon, I can be there and I'm happy to be alone, but I'd go nuts if I were in that condition all the time.

CD: Right, right. You've gone to some writers retreats throughout your life like MacDowell.

EO: I've been to MacDowell and Yaddo. I've never done a lot of that because we live in the country and it's so conducive to work. I wanted to go, I think, just to be at Yaddo and see, and to be at MacDowell and see, and I liked both of them. The people I met there were great, but I didn't get arguably more work done there than I do at home when I go to a quiet place. We have two houses on the property. When I go into the old house, down below us, I've got a private room inside and a private porch and I can get a hell of a lot of work done.

CD: We talked about this earlier in regard to "Packing Lunch," the idea of the clear image. Do you feel too much thought or elaboration tends to obscure or ruin poetic expression as opposed to . . .

EO: You mean a revision?

CD: Yes.

EO: One of the things that I do find in revision is that when I'm making a mistake in revision, I'll overcomplicate a poem. I'll start to try to refine the sentiment of the speaker and sometimes, essentially, will just drive it into the sand. I think that often a poem is generated by a conflict of impulses, a conflict of ideas, that hasn't been resolved. And the reason the poem begins is that you've got these warring impulses at work. I try not to investigate those too closely. I like to see what they do once I'm writing, and then maybe once the poem is done, if it is, I have a clear idea where it comes from, and I can generalize and say, "oh, I was doing *that*." But that's, I think, when you murder to dissect. When you're trying to put a poem on the page, you don't want to be too fine in thinking it out.

CD: Right. This leads me to the question about form and your idea of form in your work. Gerald Stern on the back of *Unreconstructed* says in the last sentence of his blurb, "He has turned into one of our very best poets. His poems are gorgeous, brilliant, heartbreaking and formally wise." He uses the phrase "formally wise" there.

EO: Well, that's really very generous of Jerry.

CD: Well, it's true. But in your poem "Unreconstructed" you attack the formalist head-on and say that anyone who uses form should not be trusted. So I'm interested in what form you found for yourself outside the kind of conventional form you attack in "Unreconstructed."

EO: That particular poem was written at a time when there were new formalist anthologies coming out all over the place, and as you know, there may very well be some excellent poems in any individual anthology, but much of it is just cookbook crap. The danger for American writers right now, and at that time, is that for people who aren't too smart, the sense is if you just fulfill the obligations of a particular arbitrary form, that's going to be a poem. That's as idiotic to me as saying if you use end rhyme it's got to be a poem. That's what my poem was written against. I've published a number of people in the Pitt Poetry Series who are very skillful with such forms as the sestina, sonnet, pantoum, villanelle, so on and so on, and I admire that. I use elements of conventional prosody in my own poems, but I'm also one of those people who grew up at a time when organic form made a great deal of sense to me and still does. I do think that, ideally, every content will suggest its own form.

CD: When you say organic form, could you just elaborate a little on that?

EO: Well, basically, this is what Robert Creeley was talking about; this is what Denise Levertov was talking about. The assumption or belief is that in every subject, in every content, there is a kind of germ, as there may be in a seed, that will develop according to the suggestion or the necessity of the subject.

CD: Right, it's very similar to what Bly said in his journals *The Fifties* about the dangers of being governed by the conscious mind.

EO: Yes. Bly, when it comes to talking about poetry, talking about the look of poetry, is a very wise man, and when Creeley, Olson, Levertov, and so on were talking about it way back then, they attempted to define the free verse poem as that verse poem that isn't free but that discovers its own form. And even Frost for that matter said that the poem is "like an ice cube on a hot stove. It finds its way by its own melting." All of these are metaphors for what actually happens in the composition of a poem, and even if you are writing a dandy sonnet you still are going to have some of those things happen. Take Frost's sonnet—"The Silken Tent," which I always say is one of the most perfect poems in American English—it isn't just that the sonnet form is handled so skillfully but that he's found the right way to introduce and to elaborate on the metaphor of the woman as the silken tent, and it's just absolutely gorgeous because the content and its variation fit so beautifully with the demands of conventional form. I will say also that some of the poems of Bukowski, for example, and there are many poems like this, are such that just the really good representation of an interesting spoken voice is enough to carry it. Or the prose poem if you like, may work as a poem because the conversation that's captured, or the voice, is so interesting. It really depends on the forward thrust of speech.

CD: Well, there's a strong, unabashed voice in a lot of your poems. I'm thinking, for instance, of your poem "Snow White," which relies almost fully on a candid, ribald voice, as opposed to some of your narrative poems. In this poem, Dopey says, "Finally got me a blow job from them faggots over in Uncle Remus." "Oh," says Doc, "how wuz it?" "Well, didn't taste too bad." What sort of mode do you shift into when writing a poem with so much voice as this from your more often narrative style?

EO: It's just fun. Another slap at Disney. There are many jokes, as you probably know, based on the seven dwarfs. A friend told me that joke about Dopey's blow job, so I stole it and stuck it in the poem.

CD: It's a poem you probably couldn't send out to a conventional journal.

EO: It will never appear, in all likelihood, in the *Georgia Review.*

CD: Or in the *Kenyan Review.*

EO: Or the *Kenyon Review.*

CD: So you've published a lot of bawdy poems in journals like the *Chiron Review* and *One Trick Pony* and *Nerve Cowboy.*

EO: Yeah.

CD: I was wondering if you could talk about your long history of publishing subversive poems in such journals as *Nerve Cowboy* and *One Trick Pony.*

EO: I've just done it for a long, long time, and it's not a mark of a split personality. I think it's a mark of an integrated personality. But the fact is that some of the better-known, better-established, and larger magazines that publish poetry are not necessarily hostile to a comic poem or a satiric poem, but it can't be too simple a line. There has to be a more highly textured artifact. Whereas magazines like the ones you mentioned, if the poem has a strong motion, a strong reaction on the part of the reader, they're quite willing to do it, at the same time as those magazines don't want to deal with what they would imagine, I guess, to be the fussier poems, the more complicated poems, the more mystifying poems. And that's just the way it is. I have nothing to say about that.

Ideally, magazines will be able to publish a range. But as you know at the present time, it is very difficult for a gay writer to discuss his or her sexuality in a poem in a major university magazine without "texturizing." I don't want to name names, but it just hasn't appeared. And it's very difficult or at least used to be difficult for blacks and minorities to publish in good sound literary magazines. I'm not sure what to say about it except one responds to publishing possibilities. But what I can tell you is that when I'm doing readings, I try to have a mix of the more easily apprehended comic poems and the emotionally complex poems, and I never find in an audience—at least no one who'd talk to me about it—I've never found in an audience rejection of one kind or the other. If it's a successful reading, and people were enthused they'll come up and say, "I loved that one," or I loved 'Snow White' or 'Pocahontas,'" and someone else will come up and say again, "That poem about your father who died, just wonderful." That's the way it ought to be. But it just isn't that way in magazines. And that's not my fault, that's their fault.

CD: That's interesting because you're saying your audiences are responding equally.

EO: In my experience, I'm not just talking about college audiences, but townspeople, local bars, are much more open-minded or omnivorous, whatever is the right word, than many editors.

CD: That's fascinating. You and Judith Vollmer are publishing a lot of poems at *5AM* like "Snow White."

EO: Well, we bring them together. Everybody involved with the magazine in the beginning had the same sense that it would be wonderful to have a magazine that would be—this is borrowing a phrase from Paul Zimmer—"a republic of many voices" and would really reflect the people out there in the United States. So that's what we've tried to do. And it's one of the reasons we've kept it up for so many years—because we think it's important to do.

CD: Isn't it ironic how many American poems that were considered taboo by the mainstream literary journals of their day have not only made it into the mainstream but become classics. "Song of Myself," "Howl," and even "This Be the Verse" come immediately to mind.

EO: Well, there certainly was a lot of resistance to "Howl."

CD: Yes, but just how those poems got into the mainstream of American poetry in the first place is an ironic, telling story.

EO: Well, on the other hand, "This Be the Verse" was written by Philip Larkin, an Englishman, and Englishmen can do a lot of things that American poets can't do in America. I know, it's nutty but that's how it is.

CD: There is a curious and often unpredictable sense of propriety in American publishing.

EO: There is.

CD: Particularly with regard to proprietary boundaries. What con-

stitutes going too far or, conversely, not far enough? Whitman resort-
ed to publishing his own poems in the mid-nineteenth century, and
Thomas Wentworth Higginson passed on both Whitman's and Dick-
inson's poems at *The Atlantic*.

EO: I think that much poetry that really is interesting and really
works but is relatively fresh does not follow old models, has always
tended to come out in the small press, has always tended to come out
in special magazines. You think of Frank O'Hara, who now in many
circles is regarded as a master, and I think he is. He couldn't publish
in most magazines at the time. I think for that matter of Stevens, who
initially could publish, that's true, but at the same time Stevens's first
couple of books did not sell very well. They were not in front of read-
ers all the time. He was too different I think, and that probably is true
not only about poetry but fiction as well. It doesn't mean if I don't like
it, it's got to be good. It doesn't mean that if I don't understand it, it's
got to be good. But it does mean that, I think, people who have been
editing the standard magazines over the years, over the generations,
tend to be narrower in judgment than they should be because they
have an interest in continuing the past and fear introducing elements
that may appear to be in bad taste, which is to say the new. And I don't
know, I think it's necessary if you are an editor, or you are looking at
poems. . . . There is such a thing as bad taste, and I think one needs
to develop a sense of what that means, but bad taste doesn't mean it's
new or has a dirty word in it, blah, blah, blah, blah, blah. You know?
For all of the years that I've been editor of the Pitt Poetry Series I've
tried to be as eclectic as possible, to recognize different kinds of ex-
cellence. I'm not the super reader. I don't want to say I have no faults
in that way, but I certainly have tried to bring people together from
different parts of the poetry universe of the United States, and I think
it's important to do that.

CD: Yes.

EO: And I think particularly in New England . . . this is one of the
things about Bennington College. I love the place, but many of our
New England students only go with the most serious of the New En-

gland poets. And there's nothing wrong with the New England poets necessarily, but there is something the matter with readers who can't branch out or won't branch out or don't know those other things.

CD: How have you been able to sustain your own voice, your own ideas—maybe it's easier than I might imagine—while at the same time spending so much time reading for the Pitt Poetry Series?

EO: There's an easy answer that I have for that, and that is that I've always found teaching with classes I like, with students I like, to really be energizing rather than enervating, and I feel the same thing about editing. And I think that Gertrude Stein and Hemingway—I'm just rereading *A Moveable Feast* now, the new edition—both agreed that they would like to collect Picassos. I can't collect Picassos and neither could Hemingway, at least originally, but at least the notion of collecting poets in the series I edit has always been extremely interesting to me. For all sorts of reasons, just because I like the idea of helping to publish and promulgate work that I think is moving in one of many ways. I like the notion of helping other poets get into print and stay in print. I'm not taking myself too seriously here—but when I look over the list, it's like a bunch of trophies I've won because I got these people in here. I'm proud of that list and of the poems.

One of the new books that's coming out spring 2012, from an author that's new to us, is a book by Martha Collins called *White Papers*, which I think is fantastic. It's basically a history of American racism in poetry. That may sound impossible or bleak, but she brings it off. It's amazingly readable, it's extraordinarily moving, and to be able to have that book in the series makes me very proud. I hope we get it around. And I'm thinking too, one of my friends here at Bennington, Major Jackson, has said in a couple of lectures that white people never write about race relations, and I don't think that it is absolutely, uniformly true, but it's generally true. Martha also knows Major, and I suspect that they've spoken about it, but this in a way is an answer to that neglect in the past, and it's marvelous, and it's powerful.

CD: I think you used the word "electric" once . . . that there has to be an electric quality.

EO: Yeah. I've published books by devout Christians whose religion is the subject of their poems. I've certainly published poems by devout atheists. I've published books by Jews who support Israel. I've published books, and I will be publishing a book, by an Arab American who is on the other side of that fence, and it's not a sense of even-handedness that I want, but a sense of getting powerful statements, powerful collections from different sensibilities, different voices, different minds. And also, I would say, right from the beginning, different identities. I had a conscious notion when we were starting, when I was starting at the poetry series, that the percentage of women poets from university press and trade houses was much smaller than the percentage of women poets writing really good poems that I knew were out there. So one of the things that I wanted to do in the series was to make it evenly balanced between male and female writers. And it has been that for many years, it's the first one to ever be like that, and I suspect if you actually added it up, it might still be the first and only one. I felt the same way about minority writers from different areas, and the list of minority writers in the poetry series has grown, not because I seek out manuscripts and I want to say, "OK, look, we've got minority A, minority B, minority C," but the quality of manuscripts coming across the desk from members of various groups has been both extremely good and larger and larger. It reflects the whole poetry community in the United States, and I'm very pleased with this fact and again that the "republic of many voices" notion is there.

CD: So it's often an embarrassment of riches that you have on your desk, but the burden of having to choose so selectively from them, it must be . . .

EO: The strange thing is that I never had that much of a difficulty. Maybe I'm fooling myself, but there are manuscripts that I hate to turn away because I like the writers, but if I feel that the manuscript isn't ready to go yet or it just isn't working, I try to explain that as carefully and encouragingly as possible. But when it finally comes down to what I want to do, there usually isn't a great struggle. The books declare themselves. And recently, by the way, we moved up to twelve books a year, starting this year.

CD: From?

EO: Seven.

C.: Richard Blanco, the poet President Obama recently chose to read at his inauguration, has published two books with the University of Pittsburgh Press, *City of a Hundred Fires*, which won the Agnes Lynch Starrett Prize in 1998, and *Looking for the Gulf Motel*, which came out in 2012. In a *New York Times* article published on January 8, 2013, Blanco commented in a telephone interview, "Since the beginning of the campaign, I totally related to his life story and the way he speaks of his family, and of course his multicultural background. . . . There has always been a spiritual connection in that sense. I feel in some ways that when I'm writing about my family, I'm writing about him." Could you talk a little about what impressed you so about his work beyond just his ethnic and familial subject matter?

EO: I guess I'll say the obvious. As Galway Kinnell says in "Poetry, Personality, and Death," ideally a poet may get to a point where he speaks not only for his or her own self, but for everybody. I saw that in Richard's poems. Plus, like Frost, he has a sense of humor.

CD: In the same *New York Times* article I referred to earlier, the author of the article, Sheryl Gay Stolberg, observed, "Like Mr. Obama, who chronicled his multicultural upbringing in a best-selling autobiography, 'Dreams from My Father,' Mr. Blanco has been on a quest for personal identity through the written word. He said his affinity for Mr. Obama springs from his own feeling of straddling different worlds; he is Latino and gay (and worked as a civil engineer while pursuing poetry). His poems are laden with longing for the sights and smells of the land his parents left behind." We certainly see this quest in such poems as "America," where Richard redefines the American Thanksgiving experience through his first-generation Cuban eyes. He had this to say about this poem: "My Cuban family never 'got'

Thanksgiving. It was one of those traditions without translation. For Cubans, pork isn't the 'other white meat,' it is the 'ONLY white meat.' This poem originates from one of my earliest memories of the clash between the two cultures that shaped me."

You also came from a family, as you have already elaborated on, that experienced considerable difficulty assimilating into so-called mainstream American culture. Was there something about Richard's American experience as depicted in his poems that resonated with your own American experience, despite the fact that you come from different ethnic backgrounds? Something quintessentially American that ends up as a common cultural experience, despite the different ways you and he might express this experience in your respective poems? I'm thinking, for instance, of your poem "Changing the Name to Ochester."

EO: I grew up in an area of New York City with lots of first- and second-generation Americans—mainly Germans, Polish, Jews, and Italians. Listening to my own and my friends' parents' and grandparents' stories, it always seemed to me they were telling the same story, no matter where they came from—only the incidentals and the accents were different. Not that they all loved one another—every group had its own prejudices and preconceptions about every other—but they were all strangers in a strange land. We still are, I guess. But I knew very early that there was always a diversity of voices in America, and later I was impressed in college to be told that although America had many local dialects of English (not the least strange being my own Brooklynese), no one dialect was superior to another in terms of the ability to communicate, though some dialects were more socially approved (e.g., NPR rather than Gullah). So, yes, when I became editor of the series I wanted to collect that variety of voices, rather than emphasize the same white male, Ivy League–approved poetic voices I learned to appreciate in college. Though I'd emphasize that as a white, male, Ivy League–educated guy, I don't hate those categories either—as Seinfeld's character might say, "nothing the matter with those."

CD: You took over as editor of the Pitt Poetry Series in 1978. Is that correct?

EO: That's right. It was another year until books that I chose came out. The series has grown in terms of sales. It used to be, when I came on board, that if we sold a thousand copies of a book, that was very unusual and absolutely wonderful. And of course, now we sell not huge numbers of copies of all the books we do but we do have books that have gone off the charts, and often will sell quite well, and that support the other books. And that's also the kind of balance I wanted. I mean, I never wanted this to be a collection of books by writers who no one is interested to read, but it seems to me that we have an obligation to support younger writers who aren't likely to sell all that much. For example, Reginald Shepherd, who I think was a genius. I loved the work and I wanted to support him, despite the fact that his books never sold strongly.

CD: You wrote the following in your introduction to the Pitt Poetry Series anthology, *American Poetry Now*, which came out in 2007:

> Some readers have liked poetry in general because they want to read only the great poems. To my mind, that's akin in its intelligence to such thoughts as, 'I only eat great meals,' 'I only play great games of tennis,' 'I only go to great movies,' and 'I only have great sex.' Translated such a sentiment usually means I was forced to take a course about the great poems in the English language and I didn't like it much, but in any event, I've done it and haven't had to read poems again in years. A related question is, Where are the great poets of today? The proper answer is, we don't know yet. Even Shakespeare was not the acknowledged master of the English language in his lifetime.

You go on to emphasize the importance of not purposely looking for "the great poem" in the editorial process. Could you elaborate on this?

EO: Whenever I hear anybody say—and students say this kind of thing because they don't know any better—but whenever I hear anybody talk about projecting a great series of poems, before in fact they've written one, I imagine that they have some sort of garbled notion of writing, as though it's according to a cookbook somehow.

I think anyone who feels that or who thinks that isn't necessarily a fool, but he or she is someone who doesn't really know what they're talking about.

CD: You see all sorts of poetry obviously that comes across your desk, so I'm particularly interested in what you think the state of contemporary narrative poetry is given the incredibly diverse and eclectic nature of the work you consider for publication every year.

EO: It's getting better. For a long time, the narrative poem was for some reason regarded as old hat, as inherently stupid, working against new discoveries of language, et cetera, et cetera. It's all nonsense, you know. Narrative poetry has been one of the basic elements of any nation's poetry for as long as we know. And in recent years, I've seen among students, among manuscripts that I get, many more narrative poems of all kinds than I did, say, ten or fifteen years ago. Somehow the universe has expanded, and I think that the notion of telling stories or having strong narrative elements in poems seems, as it should, normal once again.

CD: For so many years, probably because of the stand-up craze that poetry went through, and to some extent is still going through, there were a lot of glib and weaker narratives.

EO: Yes. Well, that's what I was talking about earlier too, the fact that if you just stand up, and you're just telling jokes and the jokes are kind of narrow and glib, it does wear thin quickly I think. But what isn't narrative? How could you say that narrative is impossible when narrative is Homer and narrative is Chaucer and narrative is just about any poet in the history of the art in the West that you want to name? And for that matter, in many other cultures. The question is: what kind of narrative do you want to develop? What kind of narrative do you want to do?

CD: That's interesting because you associate yourself with a kind of postmodern sensibility, the breaking down of any overarching principles for instance.

EO: Yeah.

CD: But the arc of that postmodern sensibility has culminated in a lot of theory which is not something that you subscribe to. In fact, there are three poems in *Unreconstructed* where you make open fun of Derrida.

EO: Yes. Well the answer to that is, as I was suggesting earlier, no one has ever to my mind defined to the satisfaction of any listener or reader what postmodernism in literature is. And the fact is, when people talk about postmodernism as the theory people have and do in English departments, they're talking not just about a literature but about other cultural developments. So it's a tricky thing to nail down, but some of the excesses, it seemed to me a few years ago, would be otherwise intelligent people talking about the inability of language to seriously communicate. So when you get to that stage you know something's the matter. When we got to that stage in Pittsburgh, back in the early nineties, I couldn't help it. We had a faculty member who was saying these things to his students, and I couldn't resist, because, you know, "denotation was not a function of language anymore," he said. I put a note in his box that said, "Dear Paul, Fuck you. Sincerely, Ed," and he knew exactly what I meant, you know? And I've been telling that story ever since. But we seem to be exploding away from that narrowness.

CD: I think in another one of your poems you say, "Motherfucker, deconstruct that."

EO: Well, that's a serious poem. A nasty person's talking, threatening another, and how do you deal with that, that's evil, and how do you talk that away? You can't.

CD: Right.

EO: So the only thing I would say is that I don't think minds have been settled yet about where we are now, where we've come from—it's probably going to be a number of years before we are—but in poetry you can identify certain elements. Those are things that I was talking about in connection to Ed Field.

CD: You acknowledge in your poem "A Letter to Edward Field" that the book for which he won the Lamont Prize was not received well by critics.

EO: It got a damning review in *Hudson Review*. Again, Ed's book did all of these things that seem strange, offensive, threatening, and so of course it got a bad review. *Hudson Review* now is an eminent but quite conservative journal. And it would be inclined to pan it. But the guy who was doing the review was talking about all of these terrible elements and why it wasn't poetry and quoting some, but they seemed so exciting to me at the time that I had to get a copy of the book.

CD: You say in the poem it saved your life.

EO: Well, this is when I was in the middle of very tedious work, I thought.

CD: What year was this?

EO: It was 1961 to 1962. And I was actually writing or researching a paper for a history of literature class, I forget who the professor was, on the Elizabethan great chain of being. And it's not that I wasn't interested in the great chain of being, and it's not that I'm still not, I am, it's just that it felt tedious then and I just didn't feel like doing it anymore. And when I went out to spend some time, get some water, pick up a magazine off a rack—it just happened to open to that review, and Field was like real life.

CD: You spent so much of your early life in academia before turning to poetry as both your vocation and avocation.

EO: Yeah, I did. I never had and I do not now have any contempt for accurate scholarship. It's always amazed me when I was working in graduate school and later about the positive results that can come from such things. But what I felt at that time was that academic life, if you were going to work as a scholar, was much more constricting than I would wish. People at that time would only succeed if they mined a very small area, and I just didn't want to do that.

CD: But you have scholarly acumen.

EO: But that's different than being in the English department.

CD: That's true, but your formidable knowledge of history permeates your work, particularly European and American history.

EO: I find it very productive material. I'm just interested in history. But what I do find when I'm reading historical narratives and interpretations are interesting mirrors or distorting mirrors of our own time. And the Nero poem for example that I sent you, it's playful and it's meant to be, but it's also talking about things that existed not only in Nero's time but our own. So I don't know, I mean history may not repeat itself, but it offers or repeats certain images and actions that are interesting and are reflections in some ways—*comments* is a better word—on our own times.

CD: In your poem for Judith Vollmer, "Ironies of History," you let history do the work itself. You know it, but it does its own work in the poem as it does at the end of the poem:

> He died of yellow fever in Haiti so that Napoleon
> could marry her off to Prince Camillo Borghese,
> wealthiest man in Italy, one of whose many titles
> was Baron Crapalotri.

How could you beat that?

EO: Talking of history, I brought with me to Bennington the history of Sultan Mehmed II, who conquered Constantinople. I finished it when I was here, but in the back pages of that book the historian mentions that a sultan had been executed by Janissaries about three hundred years after Mehmed, not by beheading, but by compression of the testicles. How could one not use that in a poem? And the historian added that this was a special form of execution reserved for the royal family.

CD: That's fatal? I guess it could be.

EO: Well, I had the same question.

CD: Can you die from that?

EO: Well, I suspect that if they were unremitting, an enormous compression applied, you could.

CD: I'm curious how you have time for your prodigious reading of history in addition to all the hundreds of submitted manuscripts that come across your desk.

EO: One of the things I'm blessed with is that both my wife and myself have very simple tastes. We do not spend a lot of time shopping. We do not spend a lot of time making the home better than it was before. We travel a bit but not a lot. We don't have a lot of things that we do that distract us from our main interests. And our main interests are reading, for both of us. For Britt, bird watching. She just found the 106th species on our property that she's seen and recorded.

CD: Wow.

EO: And gardening. And we both enjoy light and simple cooking. We try to make time to do the things that we care about most, and we're doing it more the older we get. So it's just one of the uses of living in the country that the distractions are fewer.

CD: Yeah. I know you also love classical music.

EO: I try to listen, on days when everything is very well organized, to listen to music at least one hour a day.

CD: Opera as well?

EO: I've never been a great fan of opera. I like classical music, chamber music. I particularly like the Baroque composers. I enjoyed opera when I was a kid. One of my friends took me to the Met when I was in high school, but it hasn't grown on me in later years.

CD: But you also like Neil Young.

EO: I've always liked rock music from the sixties and seventies, and both of those things have been very useful in writing. Years ago, I was able to write and establish mood by having rock music playing very loudly in the background. I can't do that . . . I don't want to do that with any kind of music now. But often if I'm listening to something, it does establish a mood or make a suggestion from the music, what might happen in the poem. So it's useful in that way.

CD: Four years ago at the Association of Writers and Writing Programs conference you had a pretty big scare in New York City. Would you mind talking about this?

EO: I've had two big medical problems in the past years. Back in the nineties, I had a viral infection of the heart.

CD: Pericarditis?

EO: Well, I don't think it was that, technically, but it was some kind of invasion of the heart by a virus, which is very common. I just thought it was the flu, and I let it go, and I finally came down when I could barely breathe. Luckily, my daughter and her boyfriend were visiting us, and they called the local ambulance, which took me to the local hospital, which life-flighted me to Pittsburgh. They stabilized the condition, and then afterward they did the kind of operation where an electric wire is passed up through the groin to the heart, and it let them create new electrical passageways that repaired the damage the virus had done.

CD: Wow. The virus did damage?

EO: Yeah. And what's amazing is that it was just around that time that doctors discovered the heart could repair itself to some degree. So it's been a long time since this happened, but the heart has been getting stronger, and every time I see my cardiologist on the standard visits twice a year, he's been saying, "oh, it looks good, better than it was last time."

CD: Oh, good.

EO: So that has gone well. The other thing was just a burst aorta, you know, that occurred when I was at AWP in New York. I was extremely lucky then in that there was an ambulance waiting in front of the hotel. The guys in the ambulance looked at me, spoke to the person who accompanied me, and they were able to make a pretty good guess what it was, and they took me to a hospital in New York that specialized in that type of repair. And not only that but there were two surgeons. This was a Saturday night...

CD: You're talking about a burst aneurism here.

EO: Yes. And there were two surgeons ready to do some vascular work on someone who was not life threatened, and they were already dressed, so they took me in, and here I am.

CD: You really only had a matter of minutes.

EO: Yes. I was extraordinarily fortunate. So, you know, it's not that I'm thinking that I'm so lucky that I can't be hit by a bus or anything else, but it was amazing.

CD: Yeah. Well, it's interesting, you haven't written about these incidents, but they must, in some way, influence you.

EO: I mention it in a few poems.

CD: Did you?

EO: I did in a poem. I remember in the first one, when I was in the ambulance, thinking to myself, if I ever get out of this, I'm really going to stop fucking around and get to work, and I remember in the second one...

CD: You think you had been fucking around?

EO: Well, I was trying to concentrate my mind. You know, in a different way.

CD: On something else?

EO: No, just more in what I wanted to do. I felt something similar when I was in the ambulance the second time, going away from that hotel in New York. The strange thing about that is I've never viewed myself as the bravest of men, but on both of those occasions, I wasn't frightened. The first thing I felt was, well, if I die, this is really going to make it difficult for Britt and, you know, my friends and the children. But it wasn't fear, it was a concern that others would be unhappy or discomforted. And I don't know if that kind of thing is normal or not. But I think it's interesting that that was my response.

CD: I'd like to read a few lines of yours that read like a credo. "Oh Proktos"—which means "asshole," right?

EO: Correct.

CD: "How many times must I tell you, / whatever blossoms is rooted in the dark." These lines remind me a lot of Theodore Roethke's "The Root Cellar."

EO: I never thought of that. Yes, probably so.

CD: But in so many ways, this phrase, which is from your poem "The Muse," captures so economically both sides of your poetry, the satire and the compassion, the austerity of your youth, and the blossoming of your poetry later on, but your muse . . . you seem to hear the first utterance of your muse in the dark, before it becomes compassionate or funny or historical.

EO: I guess another way of saying it is paying attention to the subconscious, listening to the prompts that you get. Comfrey roots, which grow very deep, seemed to me a very natural image for that. And I guess what I would say is that for most poems that are about interior matters of importance, that's where they come from. Comic poems, satiric poems, they come from the head, from the rational faculties, but the other materials come from somewhere else. That's why I like that cover of *Unreconstructed*, by the way, because it suggest the unconscious.

CD: Yes. It's the brain, but it's also a bush.

EO: It's a bush, but it has that suggestion of underground elements.

CD: Yes. There's another poem in which you talk about the damned who sing.

EO: It's "The Whitehead Metals Stickball Team at Lunch Hour on W. Tenth St." It goes like this:

> There is so much pain, you're a fool
> for not talking about it. But what's amazing
> is how those in pain think it's normal.
> What's wonderful is that it never changes:
> How the damned laugh and sing when they can.
> How the years change everything to gold.

EO: Yeah, I don't know what to say about that. That says it. I don't think I thought of it at the time, but do you remember the original cover of Philip Levine *The Names of the Lost*, where the prisoners are being led along?

CD: Yes.

EO: There's a line, and there's one guy . . . they're not dancing, but there's one guy who's smiling at the cameras as if they're going on vacation, and I assume this is why Levine chose it for the cover of the book *The Names of the Lost*. He doesn't know he's lost yet, or doesn't want to believe it.

CD: Right.

EO: And that, it seemed to me, was very close to what I had in mind at the end of that poem.

CD: The candid admission here, "There's so much pain, you're a fool / for not talking about it," betrays your willingness to mention it despite your knowledge of what it makes you, namely, foolish. But then again, it's balanced with humor and pathos.

EO: Well, a fool in the sense that it's something that anyone with half a brain knows. Why waste time talking about it? There's nothing you can do about it.

CD: Right.

EO: And so we ignore it.

CD: So if you do choose to talk about it, which you do, whether you're talking about your parents, the labor force, a historical event, you do it in a way that emphasizes your inherent rapport with the human condition. You use words like *damned* and *asshole*, instead of more glorious or proper terms, that carry double-edged meanings, both derogatory and familiar, even affectionate.

EO: Well, in a way it's saying "wake up," you know. It's saying "wake up" to the speaker in the poem, I think, very often too. But I think what much poetry in general does, it says "wake up" to what's happening—wake up to your life, wake up to what it's like.

CD: Yeah.

EO: And I do think that is the core of most poetry. People's actual freedom is limited. What seems to be free is you can have a large choice of consumer goods. You know, you can have a large choice of things as long as you don't rock the boat very much, as long as you're not causing difficulty for the people who own it all. I don't have the belief that any individual poem or collection of poems is going to wake up millions of people to that fact. But it is a fact. And I think that the obligation of the writer, insofar as he or she can, is to point to those situations, those moments that are illustrative, and say basically "wake up—this is what it looks like, this is what it is." And I do feel a compulsion to do it. I try not to be preachy, but I go back to my grandmother, the one who raised me, and who would say on many occasions in public and private, "You talk so well you should be a minister." And maybe in that sense I am.

CD: Do you have any favorites among your own poems?

EO: They are usually the most recent ones. When I'm doing a reading I try to do a mix that would appeal to the particular audience. When I'm reading at Bennington, I like to do some outrageous poems that are comic. They always go over well here as a kind of relief from all the excellence around them. And also try to choose some poems that are a little more challenging, which seem to go over well.

CD: You always seem to enjoy reciting "Monroeville, PA" at your readings.

EO: Well, that's the one . . . I mean it's absurd. It's just a couple of lines long. Which is basically a little joke that I think has a point, and people seem to love that. And people who have heard me read two years ago will say, "will you please read or recite 'Monroeville, PA'?"

CD: I'd like to read it to you.

> One day a kid yelled,
> "Hey Asshole!"
> and everybody on the street
> turned around.

EO: And it is actually based on a thing that I heard, and people did turn around. It took me I think ten seconds to write the poem, but the way things go, that's the one that keeps coming up, and so that's why I read it in lots of different situations.

CD: What poets following you whose satirical voices double as voices of witness do you enjoy reading?

EO: People I keep coming back to and reading include Tony Hoagland, who's wonderfully courageous. At times he gets himself into deep water because he does seem to choose the wrong diction for a moment in the poem, out of enthusiasm for the subject. And I think that if I were his editor, which I would love to be by the way, I would suggest a few small changes here and there, but no one in American poetry now is doing more courageous work in confronting the culture than Tony. I think he's absolutely marvelous. Let me mention a couple of poets we have coming up in the series. One book that's coming up is Glenn Shaheen's *Predatory*, which won the Starrett Prize. He's an Arab American poet and former student of Tony's who writes about life in America, life in Palestine. The poems are accurate, cutting, kind of outrageous, and very, very sad, but so true it's like a laser cutting through the crap in the news. The political, which has been taboo for so long in American poetry, is starting to come to life again. And I don't mean propaganda; I mean poems about the public scene.

CD: You think for the first time since the sixties and seventies?

EO: Well, a lot of stuff in the sixties and seventies was not so good; it was a kind of propaganda. And what I'm seeing now are poems that are not preachy interrogations of major aspects of American life. Political poems are starting to appear. There is, of course, never going to be an end to the lyric poem or the poem that is focused inward, but there are other poems in the world that are possible.

CD: Right. Well, now maybe for a last question about the present age. There is such an enormous tent of American poetry now that's both online and in hard copy. As an editor, teacher, and poet who has played such a significant role over the last thirty years in discovering new voices while nurturing the established careers of such poets as Alicia Ostriker, Reginald Shepherd, Peter Everwine, Denise Duhamel, and Lynn Emanuel, to mention only a few, how do you see the current explosion of poetic venues, journals, and events—for example, online magazines, blogs, vanity presses, AWP conferences—affecting the future of poetry as far as either enhancing or compromising the vast array of contemporary poetic voices that only seem to be growing in number?

EO: I think that poetry online and on electronic means is probably going to grow, for one thing because it's more pleasant to read one page on the screen as opposed to a novel or something like that. And that is ideal, you know, for poems. I think what's been the case up to the present is that many online magazines really, with some significant exceptions, have not been juried, have not been edited by people of very good sense or taste, so that I don't go to online magazines very often because what I find is just a mish of a lot of stuff that doesn't look to me very good. I think that once poetry magazines online become as focused as some of the political magazines online, that it will have more of an audience.

CD: That's beginning to happen.

EO: Yes. I think it is. But if you don't know where to find the stuff that you are likely to like or that is good, you don't want to waste your time, and that's what I think a lot of people feel about online magazines right now. And I know for a fact that most publishing poets in the United States, and probably the majority of younger ones, still think that what appears in print is much more prestigious than what appears online. I've had poems online in a number of places, but the only thing that I'll put on there is something that's already appeared in print.

CD: I asked Maxine Kumin that same question, and she responded that it will "all get sorted out in the end." But I think what she was really saying was, "I really don't have to worry about this at this point in my career."

EO: Yeah.

CD: But it must be, for your students here, an intimidating prospect for a lot of them to think about publishing. Do you have any advice for young poets who are trying to get a first book published?

EO: Yeah, lots of advice. First of all, don't be too quick to send out a whole book manuscript if you have some poems that you like. My advice as you know at MFA programs is to write a lot, revise a lot, write a lot, revise a lot, revise a lot, and read your peers and read the greats and read your peers. And not to do it too fast. Patience—Ezra Pound said a hundred years ago "pull down vanity," and one kind of vanity is the notion that you have to send everything out that you write and that it will be published. I like the practice in most MFA programs of not emphasizing publication or not even talking about it until the student is about to go out into the world. The emphasis is on reading and absorbing, writing and revising, and that's what it should be. It's got to be good because among other things the audience is limited compared to other art forms.

CD: And apparently decreasing according to National Endowment for the Arts statistics.

EO: Well, I'm not sure I trust the NEA statistics. At the same time the NEA said that poetry readership was declining, our sales were rising. It's true that every other publisher I hear about—trade and university and small press—has sales that are declining. My business manager told me a week ago (June 2011) that our sales for the last quarter are steady. They haven't grown, but they haven't gone down by a third as they have in other places. It's always been a limited audience, but the audience for poetry is larger now than it was when I was a kid for very good reasons. There are poetry readings everywhere, and when there are poetry readings, there are books available because the authors have them. So there's greater distribution for almost everybody than there was, let's say, for Frank O'Hara when he was starting out and for many others. And again, some people read poems online rather than reading books.

When people talk about the great audience for American poetry in the past, they're talking about the kind of narrative poetry or the kind of lyric poetry that has been replaced by greeting cards, by pop fiction, by romance novels, and so on. Even Longfellow or Whittier and other poets of the nineteenth century may have some absolutely marvelous work but also large stretches of dull shit—it's just television before television. Certainly what happened with the early modernists in terms of readership in the United States—things are better than that now, even though only a few New York houses are still carrying on with poetry publication. But at the same time it's not that there's nobody out there who cares. And it remains to be seen what happens to people in high school now. I'm a little alarmed by the gadgetry that everyone seems to be enslaved to, but at the same time I know ever since I was in high school the general word was that the generation of Americans coming up were total airheads, druggies, fools. You know it's not true, but the word hasn't changed. It's a hatred of the young. Maybe that will be justified with the next generation, but you know, I'll believe it when I see it.

Martín Espada. Photo by David González

7 / *Martín Espada*

P oet, essayist, translator, editor, and attorney: Martín Espada has dedicated much of his career to the pursuit of social justice, including fighting for Latino rights and reclaiming the historical record. Espada's critically acclaimed collections of poetry celebrate—and lament—the immigrant and working-class experience. Whether narrating the struggles of Puerto Ricans and Chicanos as they adjust to life in the United States, or chronicling the battles Central and South American Latinos have waged against their own repressive governments, Espada has put otherness, powerlessness, and poverty into poetry that is at once moving and exquisitely imagistic. "Espada's books have consistently contributed to . . . unglamorous histories of the struggle against injustice and misfortune," noted David Charlton in the *National Catholic Reporter*. In his nine collections of poetry, two books of essays, and multiple translations of Chicano and Latino authors, and as editor of influential anthologies like *El Coro* (1997) and *Poetry Like Bread* (2000), Espada "has provided a good, useful vehicle for disseminating [a] broader cultural awareness" praised *Library Journal* contributor Lawrence Olszewski.

Espada was born in Brooklyn, New York, to a politically engaged Puerto Rican family. He studied history at the University of Wisconsin–Madison and earned his JD from Northeastern University. For many years Espada was a tenant lawyer and legal advocate; his first book of poetry, *The Immigrant Iceboy's Bolero* (1982), included photographs taken by his father, Frank Espada. Espada's subsequent books, including *Trumpets from the Island of Their Eviction* (1987), *Rebel-*

lion Is the Circle of a Lover's Hands (1990), *City of Coughing and Dead Radiators* (1993), and *Imagine the Angels of Bread* (1996), won significant critical attention. Often concerned with socially, economically, and racially marginalized individuals, Espada's early work is full of highly wrought, heart-wrenching narratives. Espada's book *Rebellion Is the Circle of a Lover's Hands* won the 1990 PEN/Revson Award and the Paterson Poetry Prize. Though defiantly and insistently political, Espada's work is also known for its gentle humor. Leslie Ullman concluded in the *Kenyon Review* that Espada's poems "tell their stories and flesh out their characters deftly, without shrillness or rhetoric, and vividly enough to invite the reader into a shared sense of loss."

Espada's other collections of poetry include *A Mayan Astronomer in Hell's Kitchen* (2000), *Alabanza: New and Selected Poems, 1982–2002* (2003), *The Republic of Poetry* (2006), and *The Trouble Ball* (2011). Espada won the Paterson Award for Sustained Literary Achievement with the publication of *Alabanza*; the book was also named an American Library Association Notable Book of the Year. *The Republic of Poetry*, which deals with the political power and efficacy of poetry, was a finalist for the Pulitzer Prize. Taking cues from documentary poetics as well as formal argumentation and Espada's ongoing fascination with Chilean poet Pablo Neruda, the volume interrogates the role of poetry in the public and private spheres: poems range from odes to poets like Yusef Komunyakaa and Robert Creeley to treatments of the Chilean revolution to antiwar polemics to ironically sage instruction poems for young poets.

Espada has edited two important anthologies of Latino and Chicano poetry: *El Coro: A Chorus of Latino and Latina Poetry* (1997) and *Poetry Like Bread: Poets of the Political Imagination* (2000). The poets across these two anthologies hail from across North and South America, bringing an important yet underrepresented group of poets into English translation. In addition to his work as a translator and editor, Espada has also published two volumes of essays and criticism, *Zapata's Disciple* (1998) and *The Lover of a Subversive Is Also a Subversive* (2010). In the *Progressive*, poet Rafael Campo commended Espada's courage in *Zapata's Disciple*, maintaining that he is one of only a few poets who "take[s] on the life-and-death issues of American society at large." *The Lover of a Subversive Is Also a Subversive* considers the role of poetry in political movements. According to poet Barbara Jane Reyes, "To be a poet, Espada asserts throughout this series of essays, is to be an advocate, to advocate for those who have been silenced, and for places that are unspoken. . . . Our work as poets can empower the silenced to speak." Espada himself has never wavered in his commitment to poetry as a source of political and personal power. In an interview with Bill Moyers, Espada spoke to the impact of poetry on the lives of second-generation immigrants who discover the power of their own experiences through the form: "Poetry will help them to the extent that poetry helps them maintain their dignity, helps them maintain their sense of self respect. They will be better suited to defend themselves in the world. And so I think . . . poetry makes a practical contribution."

This interview took place on March 23, 2014, at Martín Espada's home in Amherst, Massachusetts.

———————

Chard deNiord (CD): A lot of people know who you are from your poetry, but would you mind starting by talking about your early formative years in Brooklyn, specifically what it was like growing up there in the late fifties and sixties? You didn't start out as a poet, but your childhood experience in East New York informs a lot of your work.

Martín Espada (ME): I was born and raised in the East New York section of Brooklyn in 1957 and grew up in the Linden projects. My father was from Puerto Rico. My mother was born Jewish in Brooklyn. When I was young, she became a Jehovah's Witness. My father's Puerto Rican family and community embraced us. That was the culture around me. My earliest memories of East New York have to do with my father's activism. When I was seven, I had a rudimentary political awakening due to the fact that my father disappeared. He was allied with Brooklyn CORE, the Congress of Racial Equality. CORE targeted businesses and industries with boycotts if they did not hire African Americans and Puerto Ricans. One such business was Schaefer Beer. Community organizers had a unique platform in 1964 because that was the year the World's Fair took place in the city. Schaefer had a pavilion there, and protesters targeted that pavilion, among others. There were hundreds of arrests, my father included.

CD: Why?

ME: When a city puts on a big show, a World's Fair or an Olympics, it tries to contain the undesirables, especially the political undesirables. In 1964 there was a roundup of dissenters who descended upon the World's Fair. They were not permitted the usual niceties, like a hearing or a phone call. My father was arrested and disappeared into the jail on Hart's Island in the East River, which also serves as the potter's field for the city of New York. My mother didn't know his whereabouts. Being only seven, I concluded that my father was dead. I would sit holding a photograph of my father and cry. He was gone approximately five days. Then one day he walked through the door. I said: "I thought you were dead." I started crying and he laughed; I recall seeing his gold teeth. Later, he tried to explain himself. He understood that he might want to involve me in some of his political activity, so from time to time he would. My father was a community organizer, with a storefront operation called East New York Action. He would bring me there, and I would occupy myself while he worked. I used to draw. I remember seeing picket lines and drawing them. I remember hearing stories about rent strikes, protests against landlords, and drawing. There were drawings I discovered years later on the backs of leaflets announcing demonstrations. I was immersed in an ethos of protest. For example, I remember my father playing a Phil Ochs song called "The Iron Lady" for a friend of his. The iron lady was the electric chair. It was a song against capital punishment. I stood there and soaked it in, not saying a word. Of course, my father was a photographer. He photographed the community and the civil rights movement as it unfolded around him. Those photographs hung on the walls, and those images impressed themselves on my psyche. I was not a red diaper baby per se; my father was too independent to ally himself with any political party. He was one of the first Puerto Rican leaders in New York to build coalitions with the African American community. At the end of 1964, he spoke at a rally for school decentralization. One of the other speakers was Malcolm X. My father's most famous photograph was one he snapped of Malcolm that day. I thought this was how everybody grew up.

CD: You must have demonstrated a genuine interest in your father's activism.

ME: I did. On the other hand, he was my father. I was his son and wanted his attention. Whatever he was doing, I wanted to be part of it. Wherever he was, that's where I wanted to be. I wanted to know what all the yelling was about.

CD: What kind of role did your father play in his community?

ME: My father loved his community and loved justice. By the time I was nine or ten, the political climate closed in—and I literally mean *climate* because the city was burning. There were riots in East New York. I recall skies filled with smoke, as if the city were under siege. My father was out on the street, acting not as agitator but as peacemaker, trying to get everyone to negotiate.

CD: Were you bilingual as a child?

ME: I had the same rickety command of Spanish many Puerto Ricans born and raised here would have. I worked hard to assure that I was fluent. And I made a discovery: when you are the most bilingual person in the room, nobody cares whether you have total command over the irregular subjunctive. It was a matter of turning this combination in my head until I reached the right numbers. Then it all came tumbling out.

CD: You've written several poems about your father, but two that stand out in your books are "My Father Is a Guitar" and "The Trouble Ball."

ME: My father died a little over a month ago in February, at age eighty-three, of a heart problem, which makes the poem you mention, "My Father Is a Guitar," disturbingly prophetic, since it was written years ago. The other poem, "The Trouble Ball," was a poem that I wrote in collaboration with him. Late in life, my father wanted to tell stories from his early days. He knew that I was a conduit. He sent me an email detailing the first time he went to a major league baseball game. This never came up before. And suddenly it did. Some background: The great Satchel Paige pitched for the Brujos (Sorcerers) of Guayama in the Puerto Rican winter league. My father worshiped Paige and the other Negro leaguers. Those players were prohibited from playing in the major leagues and would be until 1947, when Jackie Robinson famously broke the color line with the Brooklyn Dodgers. We tend to associate the Dodgers and Ebbets Field with all things progressive. But in 1941, six years before Robinson, Ebbets Field was just as segregated as any other ballpark and the Dodgers as segregated as any other team. No one told my father. He went with my grandfather in 1941 to see the Dodgers play the Cardinals and waited for Satchel Paige to show up. Around the third inning my father, who was eleven, asked his father, "where are the Black players?" He asked, "¿dónde están los negros?" His father whispered, "no los dejan," or "they don't let them play here." His heroes would not appear on field that day. Moreover, he himself could never go out there with a glove or a bat. He also saw that everybody else in the stands was white. This was more than a single act of racism. This was the discovery of a systematic, institutionalized racism accepted by everyone around him. And baseball was his religion. He eventually ended up living on West 108th Street in an Irish neighborhood and played for a team called the Crusaders.

CD: There is a wonderful picture of him winding up on the mound like Satchel Paige on the cover of your book "The Trouble Ball." The last stanza of the poem captures beautifully your father's first childhood shock and outrage over racial injustice—an outrage that lasted his entire life. Here it is:

> There was a sign below the scoreboard at Ebbets Field: *Abe Stark*,
> Brooklyn's Leading Clothier. Hit Sign, Win Suit. Some people see that sign in dreams.

They speak of ballparks as cathedrals, frame the pennants from
    the game
where it began, Dodger blue and Cardinal red, and gaze upon the
    wall.
My father, who remembers everything, remembers nothing of
    that dazzling day
but this: *¿Dónde están los negros? No los dejan.* His hair is white,
    and still
the words are there, like the ghostly imprint of stitches on the
    forehead
from a pitch that got away. It is forever 1941. It was The Trouble
    Ball.

ME: Yes. My father participated in the underground economy. He
played semipro ball. The money came from gambling. One of the great
pieties of baseball is this attitude toward gambling that comes from
the Black Sox scandal of 1919, when the White Sox threw the World
Series. Flash forward to the mid-1940s: a whole culture of baseball
predicated on gambling and involving teenagers. There was a Dem-
ocratic Party ward boss on the Upper West Side who organized the
Crusaders, bought the team bus, uniforms, bats, balls, gloves. He also
put up the stakes, the money to gamble on the games. Teams played
for a few hundred dollars, winner take all. The organizing principle
for playing semiprofessional baseball in the city was gambling, the
stakes came from the Democratic Party ward boss, and the cops
looked the other way. You can see my father as a pitcher on the cover
of *The Trouble Ball.* He's seventeen years old in that photograph, em-
ulating the high leg kick of Satchel Paige. He was a towering figure in
my life; I imagined he threw a hundred miles an hour. He didn't, but
he mastered every crafty pitch in the book. He threw the curve ball,
spins, shoots, the knuckleball. All those pitches came out of this tan-
gle of arms and legs, which is how he pitched a no-hitter one day. The
kids trying to hit him had never seen breaking pitches.

CD: I assume "the trouble ball" in the poem is the knuckleball?

ME: The "trouble ball" refers to a pitch in Satchel Paige's repertoire. It was Paige's changeup. He threw a variety of pitches and gave them some rather poetic names.

CD: The line, "It is forever 1941. It was the Trouble Ball," resonates both plainly and metaphorically as a poignant utterance of witness toward America's entrenched legacy of prejudice toward people of color.

ME: The past is prologue, as the Bard said. The pitch that gets away is the pitch that hits you in the head. It is forever 1941. Whatever your personal disasters are, they're always going to be there. Of course, he was marked not only by that incident, but by the color of his skin. My father was a dark-skinned Puerto Rican, a brown-skinned man. He was denied education and employment, harassed and arrested by the police. Most notably, something happened in December of 1949 while he was in the air force. He took a bus from San Antonio, Texas, to New York City to see his parents on Christmas furlough. The bus stopped in Biloxi, Mississippi, where my father was arrested and thrown into jail for not going to the back of the bus. He spent a week in jail. My father said it was the best week of his life because he figured out what to do with the rest of it. He left the air force and got involved in his community, in the social movements of his time.

CD: At the end of your poem "My Father Is a Guitar," you write,

> Sometimes I dream
> my father is a guitar,
> with a hole in his chest
> where the music throbs
> between my fingers.

There is a clear sense of transmission there; as if he is passing his mantle, which is his heart, onto you.

ME: It's more a sense of helplessness. There's a hole in his heart, and I'm trying to put my hand over it. There's music, but I can't cover that hole. At some point we learn that the people who brought us into the world will someday leave it. I didn't lose anyone close to me for some time. Then it started happening, and it hasn't stopped.

CD: It won't stop.

ME: Ultimately, I look at it and think: how could I have possibly known?

CD: You had an innate sense of his mortality.

ME: He had been advised by his doctor to stop working. He worked until the very end. It wasn't until a few months before the end that he was able to take a deep breath because he got a big disability payment from the Veteran's Administration. He was a mechanic in the air force. In order to work on the planes, they had to turn the engines on full blast, and so his hearing was permanently damaged to the point where he went deaf. So the VA gave him some money.

CD: It seems that you were hurt into poetry, as Auden said of Yeats in his elegy for him, by the injustices that you witnessed around you from a very early age. But that hurt was also your father's hurt, as if you had not only inherited it, but experienced it in a way that led you to write about it.

ME: I took on that pain and, more importantly, the resistance to it. That resistance defined him because it wasn't simply about being hurt. He chose to resist. Me too.

CD: To fight it.

ME: I began collecting my own injuries. Some of those injuries came when my father moved us out of Brooklyn. Many people saw Long Island as the promised land. They left the city in an exodus called white flight. In fact, they were trying to get away from the likes of us. We didn't get the memo. We went to Valley Stream, Long Island, a working-class enclave composed of Irish, Italian, and Jewish communities. I think there were two other Latino families in Valley Stream.

CD: Your dad was working by that time as a photographer, right?

ME: When I was born he was working for an electrical contracting company and doing photography as a sideline. Because of his skill at community organizing, by the mid-sixties people started paying him to do that. He ended up working for the community development agency under Mayor John Lindsay and later worked for the New York Urban Coalition. He was involved in advocacy on behalf of Puerto Rican drug abuse programs and Puerto Rican addicts trying to rehabilitate themselves. It wasn't until 1979 that he got a grant from the National Endowment for the Humanities to create the Puerto Rican Diaspora Documentary Project, a photo documentary and oral history of the Puerto Rican migration. That resulted in more than forty solo exhibitions and a book called *The Puerto Rican Diaspora: Themes in the Survival of a People*. But that was a long time coming. He was almost fifty years old when he finally got the opportunity to practice his art full time. Meanwhile, there were attempts to improve our station in life, which is why we left Brooklyn and ended up in Long Island. I wrote a poem called "Beloved Spic," which chronicles the experience of Valley Stream. I heard that word more often than I heard my own name.

CD: You've also written a poem titled "Revolutionary Spanish Lesson" that begins, "Whenever my name is mispronounced."

ME: In Valley Stream I would have been glad to hear my name mispronounced. Instead I was called "spic" or on a good day "greaser." Of course, there was physical violence too.

CD: Such constant brutal hurt.

ME: There was constant fighting, harassment, and isolation. For all the times I can remember either punching or being punched, there were other experiences that were even more lacerating. I remember being quite taken with a girl in one of my classes. She seemed to be taken with me. We would sit in the corner and talk. One day we were sitting, talking, giggling, when her friend approached and whispered something in her ear. Then this girl, who had been so affectionate with me up until that moment, looked at me with big round eyes and her mouth wide open and said, "Are you a spic?" Often I would respond to that word with fury, but on that occasion all I could summon was sadness. I said, simply: "Yes, I am." Sometimes you accept how other people define you, even if their definition of you is utterly cruel. Those moments are indelible.

CD: Powerful stuff.

ME: I wonder whatever happened to her.

CD: I can only hope she's reading your poetry. Turning to your college years, you attended the University of Wisconsin, correct?

ME: I went to the University of Maryland first, and I dropped out after a year. When I dropped out I began collecting various bizarre forms of employment. When I was still in high school, I was a bindery worker at a printing plant.

CD: Is that where your poem "Who Burns for the Perfection of Paper" comes from?

ME: Yes, that's right.

CD: That's a great poem; it reminds me of Seamus Heaney's poem "Digging," in which he turns from digging potatoes with a shovel to digging for poems with his pen. Like Heaney's poem, the end of "Who Burns for Perfection of Paper" captures your metaphorical shift from physical labor of making legal pads to writing.

ME: I went to Northeastern University Law School and was surrounded by people using legal pads who had no idea how they were made. We don't know how things get made. We take those things for granted and the people who make them for granted. I wrote the poem "Who Burns for the Perfection of Paper" with that in mind. In the years prior to law school, I made my way out to Wisconsin. I thought Wisconsin was where Oregon is. I went there for the ocean. What I found was the coldest weather of my life.

CD: But you stayed there.

ME: I stayed there. The weather was terrible, but the education was good.

CD: And you wrote that fascinating poem about the woman you married there titled "Isabel's Corrido."

ME: Isabel. I married her to keep her in the country. It didn't work out.

CD: Did you write much poetry in high school and college?

ME: I wrote my first poem at fifteen, thanks to a teacher in Valley Stream. Every day someone was using my head for a conga drum, and yet I wrote my first poem there. I had a teacher in the tenth grade by the name of Mr. Velleca. He approached some of us sitting in the back, trying not to be seen, young thugs that we were.

CD: Did you consider yourself a thug?

ME: I was more thugged against than thugging.

CD: Were you a pretty big kid by then?

ME: I was still at the bottom of the food chain. What you realize is that you cannot project that appearance or everybody will abuse you. It's a prison yard mentality. I did my best to avoid looking like a victim. That day I was sitting at the back with the other young thugs. Mr. Velleca came up to us said, "Young thugs, I have an assignment for you. I would like you to reproduce your own version of *The New Yorker* magazine." He held up the magazine. We had never seen *The New Yorker* magazine. We were all New Yorkers, but that was a very different New York. He handed it to us, and we passed it from hand to hand down the hierarchy of thuggery. So it was passed down until it came at last to me, and the only thing left unclaimed at the back of the magazine was a poem. I said something like, "Oh man, a poem?" I had actually failed English two years earlier, in the eighth grade. I did not want to fail English again. Anyway, I sat down next to the window. It was raining that day, so I wrote a poem about rain. I don't have the poem anymore. I had no idea it would be historically significant. I only remember one line, "tiny silver hammers pounding the earth," to describe rain. I had just created my first metaphor. I did not know what a metaphor was. Someone explained it to me a few weeks later, and I went strutting down the hallway. But I discovered at that time that I loved words. I loved banging words into each other and watching then spin around the room and maybe jump out the window with the rain. I wrote in high school on and off, didn't have anywhere to go with it, and eventually stopped. I started again during my first year at the University of Maryland. I would write these poems about growing up in Brooklyn, but this made little sense at the University of Maryland in College Park. I'm sure everybody thought I was making it all up, the professor included. I was discouraged from pursuing that tack and took that criticism to heart. At the same time, I took an English course, an introduction to modern poetry. There was Eliot, Pound, and Stevens, nothing to which I could relate. Nobody thought to introduce me to Whitman, Sandburg, Hughes, or anyone in that tradition, which I would discover on my own and embrace. I became alienated and dropped out. It took me a long time to get educated.

CD: That's because you had lost something you found, you know, your first experience with poetry, something meaningful, and then it not leading anywhere that was viable because of this curriculum.

ME: I drew the not-unreasonable conclusion that whatever I must be doing, it isn't poetry. That other thing is poetry, since it's in the *Norton Anthology*. Little did I realize that I would end up being published by Norton. But I was getting Ezra Pounded. I thought, "I must not be doing it right." So I stopped.

CD: So when did you start again?

ME: I had dropped out and was working at a variety of jobs. A friend of my father's, Luis Garden Acosta, came to visit and brought with him an anthology called *Latin American Revolutionary Poetry* from Monthly Review Press. The editor was Roberto Márquez, who taught at Mount Holyoke College and would become a good friend. Roberto's anthology included Pedro Pietri, a New York Puerto Rican poet. Next to Pietri there was Nicolás Guillén, the Cuban equivalent of Langston

Hughes. In fact, he and Hughes were close. They met in Spain during the Spanish Civil War. There was a book published in the late 1940s called *Cuba Libre* featuring poems by Guillén and translations by Hughes. Not only was Guillén in this anthology; so was Ernesto Cardenal of Nicaragua, years before Nicaragua would be in the public eye during the Sandinista Revolution.

CD: FDR made a famous remark about the Somoza dictatorship in Nicaragua that reflected the realpolitik of U.S. foreign policy toward Central America.

ME: In a conversation with Sumner Welles, the ambassador to Nicaragua, FDR said, "Somoza may be a son of a bitch, but he's our son of a bitch." That incident turns up in a poem called "Zero Hour" by Cardenal, which appears in that same anthology. All this was a revelation to me.

CD: And Neruda must have been in there.

ME: Neruda is not in that anthology, but I discovered him too. Here was a tradition to which I belonged. I started writing again and never looked back.

CD: Your first book, *The Immigrant Iceboy's Bolero*, was published in 1982.

ME: Yes. I was twenty-four years old and living in Madison, where I got involved with a vibrant community of poets. I completed my education at the University of Wisconsin–Madison. I got a BA in history in 1981. I had two important mentors: Herbert Hill, the former national labor secretary of the NAACP, who taught me the history of the civil rights movement, and Steve Stern, a professor of Latin American studies, a specialist on Chile.

CD: You were on your way as a writer, but you decided to go to law school.

ME: Well, the only drawback to my first book was that nobody read it.

CD: Welcome to the club.

ME: No one read my second book either. Why not go to law school? I had never heard of an MFA. This was alien to me, and I'm not sure it would have been the best thing for me anyway. I went to Northeastern University Law School in Boston, got my law degree, and practiced as a tenant lawyer in the Latino community of Greater Boston. I published my second book after I got out of law school, *Trumpets from the Islands of their Eviction.* Then my third book changed everything. I published *Rebellion Is the Circle of a Lover's Hands* with Curbstone Press. Curbstone was a dynamo, and the dynamo behind the dynamo was a guy named Sandy Taylor.

CD: You wrote a poem for him.

ME: Two poems. Bob Hershon at Hanging Loose talks about "lifers." He's referring to people who commit themselves to poetry for life, who do everything they can for other poets and poetry. Sandy Taylor was a lifer. With his wife Judy Doyle, he cofounded Curbstone Press in the mid-seventies. They began to publish Central American poets at a time when most people in the country thought Central America meant Ohio. Then they published *Rebellion Is the Circle of a Lover's Hands* in 1990. They were so industrious. Sandy didn't go anywhere without a handcart full of books. I once saw him sell a book of poetry to some guy he met in a bar.

CD: He believed in you.

ME: Absolutely. He believed in me, in poetry, in politically committed poetry.

CD: But he must have known that you were an important find.

ME: I had many fathers, and he was one of them. He was more than a mentor. Sandy sent Curbstone poets into the community. That's how I ended up doing a reading at a boxing gym for a team of young amateurs. That's how I ended up doing readings in prisons, halfway houses, community centers, and bilingual education programs, with the understanding that the nontraditional audience is, in many ways, the most traditional of all.

CD: But your poetry must have suddenly connected with a wider readership.

ME: We published a bilingual edition. I collaborated on the translations with Camilo Pérez-Bustillo because it's damned difficult to translate yourself.

CD: And you were still working as a tenant lawyer?

ME: Yes. I was a poet-lawyer. The media discovered me and reacted as if they had stumbled across a bizarre creature, like something out of Greek mythology, with the body of a lawyer and the head of a poet running out of the woods.

CD: Sounds like Yeats reference to the Sphinx in his poem "The Second Coming."

ME: I was slouching toward Bethlehem. So the media seized upon this persona.

CD: When you say media you mean ... ?

ME: Television, radio, newspapers. Sandy Taylor knew what to do with those opportunities. The book won a couple of awards. I got an award called the PEN/Revson Fellowship. I also won the Paterson Poetry Prize from the Poetry Center at Passaic County Community College. Maria Mazziotti Gillan is still one of my biggest supporters.

CD: So you must have also been reading voraciously. You didn't go to an MFA program or a PhD program in English, so came to poetry on your own with a strong background in primarily history. Auden recommended in his curriculum for poets that they specialize in another field besides poetry, as well as speak a foreign language. You have done both these things.

ME: I got a JD, which in the halls of an English department is considered the equivalent of a GED.

CD: But you were reading Whitman by this point and also Neruda.

ME: I came to Whitman by first reading the poets influenced by Whitman. I did it backward. It was by reading Neruda that I discovered Whitman, by reading Ginsberg that I discovered Whitman, by reading Sandburg that I discovered Whitman, by reading Masters that I discovered Whitman. All roads lead to Whitman. I became obsessed with Whitman. I would carry *Leaves of Grass* under my arm, underlining it and reading it aloud to anyone who would listen and even to people who wouldn't listen. I became fascinated with translations of Whitman into Spanish, which sound like Neruda. In fact, when I visited Chile, I read Whitman in Spanish at Neruda's tomb.

CD: You seem to have been influenced by both Whitman's ecstatic voice and his use of the transpersonal self in his speaker. Such a speaker manifests in much of your poetry where you either cross over from yourself as the poet to your subject or you assume as a persona the identity of your subject. I'm thinking of the speakers in your poems "Jorge the Church Janitor Finally Quits," "Portrait of a Real Hijo de Puta," "La Tormenta," "Jim's Blind Blues," "The Legal Aid Lawyer Has an Epiphany." These poems contain characters with whom you either become or empathize with what Keats called *negative capability*—that ability to exist in "uncertainty, mystery, doubt without any irritable reaching after fact or reason."

ME: I am not always the "subject" of the poem when I make an appearance in the poem. Often I will appear on the edge of a poem to essentially contextualize the narrative and let people know: yes, I was there, I saw this, I heard this, I can say this.

CD: Like your poem "The Hole in the Ceiling."

ME: That's me. That's my hole in my ceiling. Yes, there is a speaker who represents more than one self.

CD: But there's also a lot of narrative, telling stories about people who would otherwise be completely lost and forgotten. You write with a compassionate obsession that seems utterly natural, in which you witness to a myriad of anonymous figures who have suffered persecution, torture, and alienation. You're tireless in doing this, betraying a political and social energy that emanates from your early exposure to injustice through your father's community work in East New York—a sense of moral outrage that has carried over into your adult life that perpetuates the personal and social hurt that inspires your poetry. But you also write about the converse of suffering and injustice, such poems as "The Republic of Poetry" in which you describe a utopia where poetry is not just an anodyne but a way of life, a kind of beatific government of poetry where every citizen is consumed and informed by poetry. It reflects your visionary muse. Instead of witnessing to and lamenting torture victims in Chile, you extol the real possibility of civic bliss through poetry. The last four lines of "The Republic of Poetry" capture the radical poetic law of the Chile you experienced during your visit:

> In the republic of Poetry,
> the guard at the airport
> will not allow you to leave the country
> until you declaim a poem for her
> and she says, *Ah! Beautiful.*

ME: The preoccupation with justice is as natural as breathing. Having said that, I'm not sure "tireless" would be the way I would describe it because I'm tired.

CD: I know you must get tired.

ME: I'm exhausted, actually.

CD: What I'm talking about is the spirit in you that's tireless.

ME: I have something to say. One of the most useful things any teacher ever said to me came from Hugh Seidman in Madison. He said: "you have a subject, something to say, and that can't be taught." He made me realize how important it was that I had something to talk about. As far as my obsession with justice . . .

CD: It's a fire.

ME: It's a fire. It's an acknowledgment that we have not solved the problem.

CD: And we're not going to.

ME: No human society has ever solved the problem of justice. No legal system has ever solved the problem of justice. No philosophy has ever solved the problem of justice. This remains a great, unsolved problem. I don't understand people who wonder whether poetry can address the question of justice. This is not a matter of stating the obvious, not a matter of taking the side of the angels and being done with it. This is about addressing one of the great, confounding problems of human existence, as Whitman did and as the poets in Whitman's tradition have done ever since. I experiment with the utopian imagination precisely because the definition of utopia keeps shifting depending on what we accomplish. We have never solved the problem of justice, but we have eliminated certain injustices, have reduced certain forms of injustice. There are injustices that move in cycles. They subside and then rise again. Yet we must never give in to cynicism, which is fashionable. We must never give in to hopelessness, which is trendy, and which the hopeless cannot afford. Neither can I.

Take that poem "The Republic of Poetry." Every image in that poem comes from something I witnessed or heard about in Chile during the celebration of the Pablo Neruda centenary in 2004. To see a society at that moment so immersed in poetry was a mind-bender. Poets in this country spend so much time collaborating in their own marginalization. We accept it, laugh about it, mock it, but only rarely do we attempt to change it.

CD: Even from within.

ME: Look at the way we talk about ourselves.

CD: In light of what you just said about cynicism and hopelessness and cleverness, which is rampant in a lot of poetry today, how do you feel as a poet teaching at the University of Massachusetts, trying to make sense, continuing to be a witness to injustice around the world, specifically in this country and Latin America?

ME: When I left the practice of law, there were people who asked me what I would write about. That was twenty years ago. I have found something to write about. I always will. There's so much more to say. Last year I got an email from a musician in Newtown, Connecticut, by the name of Jim Allyn. Jim was organizing an event for National Children's Day in June, a response to the massacre at Sandy Hook Elementary School in Newtown the previous year, where a gunman killed twenty children and six educators. He invited me to be part of this event with music and poetry, where two of the parents of the murdered children would speak. I wrote a poem for the occasion called "Heal the Cracks in the Bell of the World," which I read at this gathering. There's a poem that has nothing to do with my being Puerto Rican and everything to do with my being human.

CD: Well, you have a wonderful poem called "Cordillera" which ends with these lines:

> and wild sow
> in green plátano thicket,
> searching, like those
> beggars' hands,
> for bread and sight
> and salvation.

You write about the metaphorical sustenance of poetry here in both physical and spiritual terms, as both bread and light. Poetry appears to supplant religion for you as a human activity that can lead someone to salvation.

ME: I have seen too much of religion to think of poetry as a religion. People sometimes say to me, "Poetry saved my life." Often these individuals are referring to being incarcerated or struggling with a history of violence or drug and alcohol abuse. Poetry offers them an opportunity to recognize the humanity in themselves and the humanity in others, to see that the impossible is possible. It goes back to the notion of utopia at which we customarily sneer. When my grandfather was born in 1890, much of what we take for granted today was considered impossible. The abolition of lynching was considered impossible; the eradication of polio was considered impossible.

CD: Would you say poetry saved your life?

ME: I often speak about or on behalf of others, so I don't think of poetry in terms of poetry saving me, but I don't know where I'd be without it.

CD: You probably would have been fine if you'd stayed a tenant lawyer instead of becoming a poet, fine in the sense that you would have made a decent living while also helping people.

ME: If I had been a tenant lawyer, and only a tenant lawyer, I would have made a contribution. It was extremely intense work, and, suffice it to say, you don't always win.

CD: Well, if poetry didn't save your life, then can you say that it brought you to another level of awareness that you didn't realize you were capable of, an awareness that has made all the difference in your life?

ME: Poetry took me to places I never would have gone but for poetry, enabled me to meet remarkable people I never would have met but for poetry, enabled me to tell stories I never would have told but for poetry.

CD: In going to Chile and meeting poets there and getting to know Clemente Soto Vélez and so many other poets as well, not just poets but all the people you write about, many of whom you've elegized, you must feel enriched to a point you couldn't have imagined before you became a poet.

ME: Clemente Soto Vélez was a mentor, a poet, a political prisoner incarcerated for his leadership role in the independence movement back in the 1930s. He was the first of many fathers I would lose.

CD: Would you mind naming some of your other fathers in poetry?

ME: Clemente Soto Vélez was tremendously important to me. So, too, was Andrew Salkey, a poet from Jamaica who taught at Hampshire College. So, too was Robert Creeley, an extraordinarily generous man. There was a British poet by the name of Adrian Mitchell, a wonderful writer and activist. There was a writer by the name of Piri Thomas, who wrote a book about the Puerto Rican experience called *Down These Main Streets.* Then there was my dear mentor and friend, the historian Howard Zinn.

CD: Right, you were in his documentary *The People Speak.*

ME: Howard was another extraordinarily generous man, a true visionary who enabled us to see how the world might be if we set our hands to the task. He was able to do that because he would take some "utopian" notion and demonstrate where, historically, this had occurred before and remind us of how far we'd come. He would talk about the labor movement and make clear that, yes, at one time the eight-hour day was utopian, the minimum wage was utopian, unemployment compensation and workers compensation were utopian. We take all these workplace rights for granted, and we spit on labor unions today. I recently wrote a poem about the Paterson silk strike of 1913. Why don't we talk about this history?

CD: What do you think it is about politics in this country that heralds progressive literature one minute and then demonizes it the next?

ME: We need to look more closely at the history of this country and how that history contextualizes the way we read poetry. Cary Nelson has published important studies of left poetry from the 1930s and 1940s. What happened to that poetry? McCarthyism was a cultural as well as a political phenomenon. The Cold War was a cultural as well as a political phenomenon. Think about Tom McGrath, a blacklisted communist. Think about Ed Rolfe, the poet laureate of the Abraham Lincoln Brigade, the American volunteers who went to fight against Franco and fascism in the Spanish Civil War of the 1930s. Nelson makes it clear that the academy capitulated to McCarthyism. All those loyalty oaths, all those firings, all those people whose literature disappeared from the anthologies and the syllabi. The fact remains that we internalized a certain value system that too many of us apply to this day when we talk about political poetry.

CD: What have you been working on recently?

ME: I am now focusing on my father's mortality. I consider mortality every day, and that changes my focus. My writing in the last few years has come in fits and starts as I necessarily dealt with whatever crisis happened to be brewing. I try to write my way out.

CD: You've been amazingly prolific over the past thirty years, not to mention ambitious in both the historic scope and magnitude of your subject matter.

ME: I know my rate of production, and I'm slowing down.

CD: That's not necessarily a bad thing.

ME: I need to find a rhythm. When I'm under pressure, on deadline, I do my best.

CD: How would you say your experience of witnessing to the uncovered and forgotten cases of life-numbing suffering and injustice in such places as Chile, East New York, Nicaragua, and the ghettoes of Boston has redounded on your own sense of the poetry business in this country? You are now a well-known poet who holds a lucrative job at a prestigious university. Do you find that your acts of witnessing and elegizing otherwise forgotten heroes of their communities, those whom James Agee called "famous men and women" in his book *Let Us Now Praise Famous Men*, has provided a clear perspective for you, as far as what's just and socially important vis-à-vis poetic fame?

ME: I am well aware that it is not a meritocracy out there. The injustice in the poetry world that most troubles me is the injustice against the older generation of poets who never get their due. I am thinking of Latino poets now.

CD: You mentioned several poets a few minutes ago from the thirties and forties who were wiped off the face of the literary map.

ME: Clemente Soto Vélez died in 1993 and was buried in an unmarked grave. It's one thing to talk about the neglect of a poet, quite another to visit his grave in the mountains of Puerto Rico and find it unmarked.

CD: Still is?

ME: There is a marker now because I bought one.

CD: But no family?

ME: Unmarked. As I put it in a poem for him, this is how the bodies of dissenters disappear. There are many unmarked graves in the world, and many of the people buried in them were on the losing side. I think of Clemente Soto Vélez when we talk about poets who never got their due. With Camilo Pérez-Bustillo, I translated Soto Vélez into English, but he died shortly after the book was published. Then there was Jack Agüeros, a Puerto Rican poet who did not publish his first book until the age of fifty-seven. He had a period of great productivity for about a decade and then fell victim to Alzheimer's disease. He died in May 2014. I wrote the foreword to Jack's first book, called *Correspondence between the Stonehaulers* and published by Hanging Loose Press. He published several collections of poetry with them. He also published a collection of short stories with Curbstone called *Dominos*. He translated a poet by the name of Julia de Burgos, a beloved poet from Puerto Rico who died young in 1953 from complications of alcoholism and poverty and was buried in an unmarked grave. The unmarked graves are everywhere. That to me is the great tragedy. It's not simply that a poet does not get his or her due but that there are real consequences for not getting your due, up to and including an unmarked grave.

CD: And the poetry not being published or read.

ME: Think about where the publication of poetry may lead. Think about the way it flows, about the opportunities that arise if your poems are published and read, if you are able to work, whether you're teaching or lecturing or giving readings. The awards, the fellowships, the money that we've been told isn't there in fact is there. Poetry reflects the hierarchy in the society as a whole. Poetry is not immune to the social forces that surround it. It has to do with the distribution of wealth.

CD: Do you feel fortunate as a poet who has written about a lot of the same subject matter your Puerto Rican colleagues, fellow poets, have written about and not been that recognized for?

ME: I feel fortunate to have heard the stories and passed the stories on. I feel fortunate to bear witness and then report on what I have witnessed. I feel fortunate to have been inspired by certain individuals and entire communities. I feel fortunate to have a means by which I can express my joy and my grief. I feel fortunate to have a relationship with a certain audience, a certain community that speaks back to me.

CD: And each time you hear that audience speaking back to you, you must think, "well, if Clemente or somebody had had a different stroke of luck here or there, maybe that would have happened with him or with somebody else." But you seem very cognizant of the larger voice of poetry.

ME: I'm cognizant of that voice. I'm also cognizant of what I consider to be a debt that I owe to the generations that came before me. Some of that is grounded in a traditional Puerto Rican sense of what elders mean, what ancestors mean. I bring that understanding to poetry when I write poems about Soto Vélez or Salkey or Creeley or Mitchell or Zinn. In the elegies I am doing more than mourning a loss. Now that my father has died I am writing those poems about him.

CD: Your style of writing is often Whitman-like, with anaphora, the drum beat, the celebration, the praise. One of your books is called *Alabanza*, which means *praise* in Spanish.

ME: Whitman's influence runs north and south. Whitman influenced poets who influenced me, like Neruda. When I write in that voice that seems to be in Whitman's idiom, it's also Neruda's idiom; it's the idiom of all the other poets who are part of the Whitman tradition, in English or Spanish. Sometimes their experience is close to mine, sometimes not, as is the case with Edgar Lee Masters and *Spoon River Anthology.*

CD: But an American kid of thirteen or fourteen could pick up any of your poems and understand them—read them and be moved by them immediately.

ME: I hope so.

CD: They are not difficult in a way that is off-putting.

ME: I don't believe in difficulty for its own sake. The cultural, political, and historical information I want to convey is difficult enough without muddying the waters.

CD: I interviewed Robert Bly several years ago and I asked him what the one thing was he did in the late fifties and sixties he felt was most significant as far as changing American poetry with his journals *The Fifties* and *The Sixties,* and he said publishing Neruda. I said, "Well, what did Neruda do?" He said, "He let the dogs in." He then commented that the so-called academic poets of the fifties had banished the dogs. Have you ever had a conversation with him about this?

ME: I've had the opportunity to encounter Robert Bly on two occasions. Many years ago we did a panel on Neruda together at a poetry festival in New York. More recently, in 2013 Bly received the Frost Medal from the Poetry Society of America, and I received the Shelley Memorial Award. I had the opportunity to read at the awards ceremony with Bly. I introduced myself and said, "Remember me?" I gave him my book, and he saw my name and said, "Oh yes!" We owe Bly a debt for what he did to bring Neruda to the attention of English speakers. Bly was not only translating Neruda but translating particular poems that, as Bly said, let the dogs in. The dogs had been thrown out of the house when McCarthyism, the Cold War, and the New Criticism came in. What Bly did when he reintroduced the dogs, when he brought Neruda into the conversation, was to reinvigorate American poetry in a way that was the polar opposite of the suppression American poetry had suffered. I appreciate Bly for doing what he did when he did it.

CD: I really see you carrying on in the tradition of Neruda, Clemente, and Whitman. I had the fortunate experience of meeting Kjell Espmark, the former chair of the Nobel literature committee, a few years ago during one of his reading tours in New England. I asked him why more American writers aren't being considered more seriously for the Nobel Prize. He was tactful, but it was clear from his answer that the Nobel committee hasn't felt for some time that American writers in general are international enough, which I felt was a nice way of saying they're not political enough, though the Nobel committee would never admit that. Do you get a sense now that that's changing, that there is more appreciation for poetry outside the country? You've spent your writing career trying to wake American readers of poetry to different voices.

ME: So is America waking up?

CD: I guess that's a good way to put it.

ME: I think America wakes up and then nods off again. Every time I think things are moving in the right direction, they move in the wrong direction. Whether we're talking about politics, history, or poetry, things move in cycles. Change is not linear. Change does not move in a straight line. We lose ground, and then we gain ground back again.

CD: Czesław Miłosz wrote in his poem "Dedication," "What is poetry which does not save / Nations or people?"

ME: On the one hand, we now live in a culture that is less literate than it has been in years. On the other hand, this is a culture that craves meaning, and poetry often presents people who crave meaning with the meaning they crave. Not for nothing do we find poets invited to speak at ceremonies of great importance, from weddings to memorial services. There is a hunger for what we have, and I think we have to honor that hunger by trying to feed it.

Stephen Kuusisto. Photo by Connie Kuusisto

8 / *Stephen Kuusisto*

S tephen Kuusisto graduated from Hobart and William Smith Colleges and the Iowa Writers' Workshop and is also a Fulbright Scholar. He became a dual faculty member at the University of Iowa, where he teaches creative nonfiction in the English department and also acts as a public humanities scholar at the university's Carver Institute of Macular Degeneration. For years, he has acted as a speaker on education, diversity, public policy and disability. Kuusisto learned to read Braille at the age of thirty-nine and continues to produce professional works of poetry and literature.

Kuusisto wrote a memoir entitled *Planet of the Blind* (1998), which jumpstarted his career, landing his poems and essays in such magazines as *Harper's*, *The New York Times Magazine*, and *Partisan Review*, and various anthologies. He also made appearances on *The Oprah Winfrey Show*, *Dateline NBC*, and *BBC*. *Planet of the Blind* catalogs the lifelong struggle of societal acceptance as well as personal acceptance of his blindness.

His other works include *Only Bread, Only Light* (2000), a collection of poems that portray the strangely beautiful world of visual imagery and extraordinary yet delicate language. *Letters to Borges*, his most recent collection of poems, was published by Copper Canyon Press in 2013. Currently, he is in the process of writing a collection of prose poems for Copper Canyon Press entitled *Mornings with Borges*. He is also working on a set of political poems that address disability. Kuusisto founded with his wife, Connie, Kaleidoscope Connections

LLC, a foundation that helps to raise awareness of disability. He presently serves as the dean of the honors program at Syracuse University.

This interview took place on March 23, 2014, at Providence College.

Chard deNiord (CD): Stephen, not everyone "who is hurt by mad Ireland," to quote W. H. Auden's phrase from his elegy for Yeats, or by mad America or fate or anything else, turns to poetry. Would you say you were hurt into poetry, and, if so, when exactly?

Stephen Kuusisto (SK): That is a great question, Chard. When I was a child, it was very clear, growing up in the 1950s and early 1960s, that being a person with a disability made me an outlier—to borrow that term made popular now by Malcolm Gladwell. Teachers didn't want me in public school, and my mother *did* want me in public school because she felt that I would have a limited experience of life if I went to the Perkins School for the Blind in Watertown, Massachusetts. She felt strongly that I should live in the world, but the world was very conditional, and teachers didn't want me in mainstream classrooms. This was long before the Americans with Disabilities Act and long before acceptance of children or adults with disabilities in the village square. So early in my life I felt a sense of ostracism and loneliness. Able-bodied kids didn't want me to play with them, and there were no sporting programs for kids with disabilities, so my world became the world familiar to all artists who discover the arts early in life—it became an isolated and rather beautiful, but very private, kind of experience. I spent time in the attic of my New Hampshire grandmother's Victorian house playing with her old wind-up gramophone, looking through old steamer trunks full of curios from ocean trips long past, looking at the parts of old clocks, and playing, really, alone for long periods of time. So even by the age of seven or eight, I had a *very*, very intense kind of inner life, and that inner life is a thing that many artists will tell you—whether they're dancers or painters or poets, what have you—that they early on had that sense of the wonder and strangeness of being alive.

One of my favorite movies is Ingmar Bergman's *Fanny and Alexander*, which, I think, in many respects details that kind of childhood sense of provincial culture and wonder set against the backdrop of the strange adult world. So you don't have to be a disabled kid to experience this, but I think disability in my case created the dynamics where it is possible to just drift into solitude. I spent a lot of time in the New Hampshire woods by myself, listening to birds. By the time I discovered poetry—in the sense that one has an experience of it with a good high school teacher, and then you go to college and discover that there are living poets among the faculty at the school you go to—a kind of wonderful connection happened between that early foregrounding of the inner life and the discovery that, what Auden called "the cave of making," poetry was really a portal to the intricacies and beauties of the inner life. So in that way, when poetry arrived for me, I'm not sure that it assuaged a sadness so much as it gave me a *corridor* to very powerful places that were already constructed—a kind of rich and unaffiliated place in my head. I think that's a different way of thinking about poetry than a kind of standard view of confessionalism, where you're simply narrating what hurt you. For me, poetry was more than that—it was an opening to all kinds of richness that I had stored up.

CD: This really must've had something to do with your discovery of language in concert with these very interior, private moments that you're talking about.

SK: In my early childhood I lived in Helsinki with my parents—my father was a Finn—so I spoke some Finnish, and Finnish is, of course, a rather glorious language with its vowels, funny consonants, and wonderfully outspread sounds. So from the age of four, I loved the glorious sounds of language. Then, to go back to the disability theme, if you're mainstreamed into public school, and a lot of kids don't like you there, you become a really rich talker. Of course this is a story familiar to the Irish. I still tell the story about being on a playground around the age of five or six, and a bully came up to me and he said he was going to make me eat a handful of dirt, and I said to him, "That looks like really terrific dirt! I like that dirt, and I'm going to eat it, but before I do, I want you to sample these acorns!" I had shelled some acorns, and the bully had no idea that acorns are bitter and will make your mouth swell up, so he ate them, and that was the last of him—he went away and left me alone. You learn quickly that language is your friend, and inventiveness is your friend—a story also familiar to many other kinds of children, right? Some grow up to be comedians, others grow up to be lawyers, but you learn quickly that language is your friend.

CD: That actually segues right into my next question. You suffered merciless bullying growing up, and yet somehow you've retained a kind nature. In fact, you write in your memoir, *Planet of the Blind*, that "the blind are static creatures, capable of joyous mercy to the self and to others." Could you just elaborate on how both your blindness and poetry imbued you with such a joyous nature, despite the privations you've suffered with the blindness?

SK: You know, the only bad review *Planet of the Blind* ever got was from a blind woman in London who said that I was just "too cheerful"—that my vision of blindness was just "too beautiful." I knew what she meant—the reality of disability in these United States and around the world remains a very difficult one. It's steep, it's stark—people with disabilities are 80 percent unemployed, and their support mechanisms—the services available to them—are increasingly being reduced. It's a very steep road, to say the least. So I wouldn't want to answer this question without first saying that there are some very hard realities having to do with disability, and my blog, *Planet of the Blind*, is often a place where I will write about these sorts of problems from a social-cultural perspective, and I teach about these problems in courses on disability and public policy, and disability and history.

On the other hand, what makes you an artist? It's an affection for the minutiae of experience and for the mystery of experience, and for the improbable nature of experience. You become by necessity, I think, as an artist a meditative soul. I know of no artist who doesn't have a heightened quality of apprehension and awareness about time, about the moment, about imaginative possibilities. So I think, in a way, that art is about hope. It's to say life is not static—it's moving. It's moving all the time. Somebody asked Lead Belly, the great blues guitarist, "How do you play the twelve-string guitar?" He said, "Well, you gotta keep something moving all the time." Donald Hall, an incomparably good American poet, talks about "reasons for moving" and that "you keep moving all the time, whether you're walking or writing, that the flow of your imagination is what matters." Well, that's the flow of the spirit. So you can have a very dark moment one moment, but then you can turn the corner and be in a rather remarkable and beautiful situation. To stay open to that—to that changeable possibility both of life itself with its improbable glories, and also the flow of the mind, and the way in which both the subconscious and the natural world will move and change—is a kind of spiritualism. That's why Jung liked looking at poetry so much. So, in that way, I think the poem offers us an ongoing hopeful range of possibilities.

You mentioned Auden—you know, in that poem where he eulogizes William Butler Yeats, he says a hopeful thing: "The poet has died, but he will become his admirers." Examined at its core, that's an incredibly hopeful thing—the poetry goes on in strangers. It goes on in the extended culture of the living. This is a very hopeful thing all the time. So to get back to blindness, I think if you live well with a disability, and you've learned a kind of, as Daniel Goldman would call it, emotional intelligence—how to step back from a situation, even if it's unsettling, and look at it and bring your imagination to bear on it, then, in point of fact, you do become mindful that there are some joys in even what appears to be a kind of deprivation. That's a very familiar thing for poetry.

CD: You're making me think of twenty things at once here, as far as the connection between blindness and kindness and its relationship to poetry—that heightened awareness that you're talking about, a kind of spiritualism, as you referred to it—because certainly there are many artists throughout history, as well as poets, who have hardly been kind, and you would think that poets *would* be kind, given what you said about the relationship between art and hope. So I'm thinking there must be something in the nature of an artist who's also kind. You must have thought about that, especially in light of the difficulty and privation you've experienced from learning to negotiate the world, suffering bullying as you did, and not being soured by it.

SK: I think being alert is part of the equation. Nowadays, in higher education, many people are starting to talk about "contemplation study," studying the way in which contemplative mindfulness—certainly a notion known to Buddhists and known to spiritual people generally—can be harnessed to think about the surface of critical thinking. You can slow down, you can breathe, you can open up your curiosity and your thought processes and be more attentive and apprehensive to what's going on around you. When you can achieve that, your world becomes larger. In my first book of poems, which was called *Only Bread, Only Light*, the title poem takes place in the Bronx in New York City, where I'm walking around, and . . . you know, blind people see a little bit, most of them do—99 percent of them do—so some see colors and shapes, as I do, and if they get up close to something, they can actually make it out, and some see nothing at all, but most see something, so what does that mean? What is the experience of seeing something bright, and in what way is it suggestive of art?

Everyone knows that you can go look at a Jackson Pollock painting and see kaleidoscopic and beautiful shapes and colors and that in fact in a good Pollock painting there are layers of paint, and that even suggests depth psychology, that there are layers of this thing, so we know that in abstract art that the world isn't figurative, but it can be beautiful. Well, it turns out that blind people see the world the way Pollock did—many of them do. So in this poem, I describe walking around in the Bronx and the beauty of that. I say, "At times the blind see light, and that moment is the Sistine ceiling. Grace among buildings. No one asks for it—no one asks." That's the beginning of the poem, but the sense of this is that beauty can strike you in rather improbable and surprising ways, even when you weren't thinking about it. Emily Dickinson's famous line, "There's a certain slant of light" . . .

CD: "On winter afternoons" . . .

SK: Right, that this was, for me, a "certain slant of light" that struck me as amazingly beautiful, right? Then I say, "After all, this is solitude. No one asks for it, it just happens. This solitude—daylight's finger, Blake's angel parting willow leaves." Blake, who looked out the window as a child and saw angels in the branches of a tree, right? Then I admonish myself: "I should know better." I'm getting too sentimental. "Get with the business of walking in the lovely, satisfied, indifferent weather. Bread baking on Arthur Avenue—the first warm day of June. I stand on the corner for priceless seconds, now everything to me falls shadow." So this beauty comes and goes very quickly, but it's an astonishing thing when it's there. It has an angelic quality to it—an unasked-for, beautiful giftedness to it.

CD: Wonderful. It sounds to me, though, that you've done as much work spiritually as you have poetically, and that you've wed the two.

SK: When I was a teenager, I began starving myself. I was very depressed about being blind, about not fitting in, and I had a lot of emotional turmoil. I actually starved my way down to ninety-six pounds. Nowadays, we know that that's anorexia, and we know that boys can have anorexia. Back in the early seventies, this was a mystery to every physician that my parents took me to, and I was placed in a mental hospital where I spent about ten days, and they couldn't get to the bottom of it, so I went home. It was right about that time that, for reasons that are very obscure to me, I decided one Sunday morning to get up and go down the street to the local Episcopal church, and I took part in communion. That ancient ceremony of the blood of Christ and the body of Christ—the wafer and the wine—was really a powerful moment for me. I felt a keen sense of uplift, of possibility, of astonishment, of love, and even, dare I say it, a sense that I had a reason to live. That's a hard thing to talk about—those moments of intense spiritual awakening are difficult to talk about, in part because so many charlatans and bad-talkers have taken that space in the public sphere. But for me that was a ritual and spiritual breakthrough. I don't forget it. As Huck Finn would say, "I dasn't forget it."

I'm also interested in lots of spiritual traditions, so I've read widely in Buddhism—I even thought at one point in college that I would major in religious studies and focus on Buddhism. As you know, and we mentioned Gary Snyder last night in our dinner discussion, our generation of poets has been richly influenced by people who have studied Buddhism ardently. I'm a great admirer of Auden, I'm an admirer of Kenneth Rexroth, I'm an admirer of Gary Snyder, I'm an admirer of Red Pine, I'm an admirer of Sam Hamill—poets who have explored the intersections between creativity and mindfulness and peace and divinity. These things have sustained me greatly, as they have many poets.

CD: You've written brilliantly about what you call "the abstractions" in which you think. In fact, in your memoir, *Planet of the Blind*, you write, "The tapestries of Paradise woven without me, the vague sepulchral room I am going toward—a rooming house of separation. I listen to old opera records—Caruso, Gigli, Schipa—"Deserto in terra solo"—the barbarian blood of loneliness whooshing through the capillaries behind my ears." Could you talk a little about this?

SK: Did I write that?

CD: You did!

SK: That's pretty good.

CD: I hope I pronounced those names correctly. Could you talk a little about just how you see doubly, that is, in your abstractions and the physical world that you perceive? Your last book of poems, *Letters to Borges*, is filled with poems that address and expound upon this question.

SK: I remember a college course circa 1975 where a wonderful poet named Jim Crenner, who founded the magazine *Seneca Review*, was talking about what, back in those days, people were calling "the deep image." There was a whole school of poets that came of age in the sixties in America who were taking some of the techniques of surrealism from the sixties and bringing it to American English. We remember W. S. Merwin who in the mid-sixties began writing images that were powered by surrealist association, where things were put together that don't necessarily belong to create a sense of surprise and wonder. Robert Bly, James Wright, and others were all doing this, and critics began calling this return to surrealism the "deep image school."

One of the things that Jim was talking about in this class on that particular day—and this was a revelation to me—was that it's possible in poetry to write something in an image that can't be seen. Now think about that—if you're 99.9 percent blind, and someone tells you it's possible to write imagery in poetry that can't be seen in the visual world, that's a fantastic thing to hear! My little ears perked right up! Jim gave us some examples; he read a line from one of Robert Bly's poems in which Bly says, "The poor and the dazed are with us. They live in the casket of the Sun." I think those lines are in a book called *The Teeth Mother Naked at Last*, but I'm not sure. In any event, Jim said, "How would you draw the 'casket of the Sun'? Any attempt to draw it would be wrong. You simply feel it. It makes an associative leap possible in your mind—it creates a sense of feeling." Later, in a poem that I put in my first book, *Only Bread, Only Light*, I borrow an idea from Lorca, who was also a great imagist: "The little boy went looking for his voice. The king of the crickets had it." The idea that the boy's voice is now inside the cricket—well, that's an image you can't draw, and you can't very well paint it, you couldn't photograph it. It creates an interior sense of emotional fraction and comprehension. So that's part 1 to your answer, right? I discovered that you could do things with images that just simply didn't rely on being a sort of journalistic narrator of the visual world. Discovering that was beautiful.

Then there's another thing—any time you use a noun, you're creating an image. So if I say "lighthouse," "wheat field," "alarm clock," and "battle ship," you will see these things. The ancients thought this was wonderful; they thought that poets were almost mystical because they could call up these images in the minds of others. That's the power of oral tradition poetry—that the poet as reciter and narrator could create visual tapestries in the minds of others. That's powerful too, but as a blind person who doesn't necessarily know what a herd of buffalo looks like, I can still put it in a poem. So people are confused by this. They say, "You write so clearly about the world that you can't see! How can you do that?" I say, "Of course! It's just nouns!" Nouns *and* an understanding of how surrealist imagery can work to produce complex emotional states. So those two things are at work in my work. At work in my work? Or employed in my work?

CD: Following up on that, you also write in *Planet of the Blind*, "But my life lacks the greater integration that comes with wandering the galleries of self, pausing to read the hard words about failure, incompleteness, and self-forgiveness. I have no self-forgiveness—I've learned how not to starve myself, learned how to savor the words, but I cannot accept who I am." That's a tough admission.

SK: That's a tough admission. *Planet of the Blind* tells a story about being a person without affirming language for disability, and about finding that language. Finding that language had, in my life, a good deal to do with finding how to move. For many years, owing to the way I was brought up—my mother wanted me to be in the public sphere and yet simultaneously withheld any of the emotional or technical support I would need to be a successful blind person—I lived a kind of charade of being in the world, hoping to be seen as a visual person, but really insufficiently capable of living an adventurous or outgoing life. That's, by the way, not an unusual story. Years later, I discovered that many people who have low vision or are going blind in midlife often experience this—they go through a long period of denial and don't get the help that they need in order to be in the public sphere in a safe, outgoing way. The other thing is that in the fifties and sixties, being disabled meant having a ruined identity. There's a famous book by Irving Goffman, the apologist, called *Stigma*, and it's about disability and what he called "the politics of spoiled identity"— that the general public views disability as a pejorative, a second-rate condition. So you really belong in an asylum or in a special school or someplace behind an iron fence—you don't belong in the village square. That was a very pervasive idea when I was young.

We forget now in 2014 how much the Americans with Disabilities Act has done over the last twenty-five years, a quarter of a century now, to open up that space. The idea that people are in public going to the theater, going to the stadium, going to the play, going to university, what have you—that was absent in the sixties. Absolutely absent! So I grew up with this terrible wound, and the wound said, "You don't

belong, and you shouldn't be seen as one of those 'spoiled identities.'"
Disability was absolutely a reduced and sad condition. So how do
you claim it? How do you say, "I refuse any longer to be in the closet
about my gayness," or "in the closet" about my sense of disability? You
simply decide at one point, "My life is too narrow, it's too closed—it's
suffocating me." In a new book I'm writing for Simon and Schuster on
getting a guide dog for the first time—the story is somewhat in *Planet
of the Blind*, but this book is almost entirely about dogs—I actually
describe how I would rehearse public space so I could walk around in
it and pretend that I could see; that I chose to go to college where my
father was on the staff, and I knew how to memorize all the footsteps;
that when I went to graduate school at the University of Iowa I went
to Iowa City three months early, and I memorized the goddamn city.
There's a whole section about me going all over Iowa City and memo-
rizing it so I could wander around it. Well, you can do that—it's possi-
ble to do that—but then what happens when you want to go someplace
you've never been before? You don't do it. In fact, you go nowhere—you
stay in a very small circle.

CD: You did that in Helsinki.

SK: I went to Helsinki because it was a city I knew. I could actually
kind of wander around a small district of it and get away with it. But
what happens if you want to go to New York for the weekend, or you
want to go to Atlanta, or you want to go hear the Metropolitan Opera,
or go to Boston and see the Red Sox, or anything? You cannot do it
unless you know how to navigate in the world and do it safely. There
came a moment when I realized I'm absolutely unable to satisfy my
thirst for knowledge and my curiosity about the planet with my sad,
closeted blind identity.

CD: This gets back to the hurt that we were talking about. You're
describing it and fleshing it out here in a way that's really vivid. You
called it a "wound" a minute ago.

SK: I think it is a hurt, and it is a wound, but all hurts and wounds
also, of course, are opportunities. If you're able to step back and look

at your circumstances almost as though you're a character in the audience seeing the play that is your life, you see that there are broader things in play. So for me there came a moment when I realized I would not be able to live in the world unless I knew how to walk in the world. So, first I signed up for orientation in mobility training, which is the training that blind people receive to walk places with a white cane. The white cane allows you to sweep it in front of you and walk down the street, and it also tells the public, "Here comes someone who can't see." That was the one thing I never wanted to do! I didn't want people to know I couldn't see because I feared that I would be absolutely rejected. That, of course, is a fiction! It's an enormous, destructive fiction passed down to me by my crazy mother. Probably the same fiction that people who are in the closet with their sexual identity experience—that if you come out, people will reject you. Well, of course, it turns out that's not true. In fact, once you burst through the door of that fictional closeting, you discover that the world is much more interesting than you had supposed.

People say to me all the time, "How can you go so many places when you can't see"? I say, "Because nine out of ten people are beautiful!" There are a lot of bad people in the world, but they're way outnumbered by the good people. You're treated well! People are good! So I learned how to walk with a white cane, and then I realized, "You know, if I get a guide dog, the dog will engage in this thing called 'intelligent disobedience.'" The dog will not let you walk into traffic and make a mistake. So if you really love cities, as I do, then bingo! a guide dog is really a great thing. Once I got the guide dog, obviously, as you know having had dogs, the whole world responds to dogs. I can't go out in the world with a guide dog on any single day and not have affirming, positive, human interactions. It's a thing of beauty. So what formerly seemed like such a deficit becomes just another part of the human, complex, joyous carnival. You're in the world, safely traveling and going to where you want to go, meeting interesting people, having rather fabulous conversations with strangers—isn't this what we all want?

CD: Yeah. In your poem, "At the Winter Solstice in Iowa City," you write to Borges, "If only they'd given you a dog, you'd have known blindness stands for nothing." So you're saying that your relationship with your two most recent guide dogs, Corky and Nira, compensates for and even transcends your blindness?

SK: You're not a metaphor, right? You're not a metaphor. You're not imprinted upon by cultural assumptions. No one is the conductor of metaphor in the public sphere, so I don't have a baton, and I can't direct how people in a throng will perceive me, per se, so I can't say that there aren't people who see me move through the Chicago O'Hare airport or walking in downtown Providence, Rhode Island, and say, "Oh, look, there's a blind person with a dog. He must be sad. His life must be reduced." I can't change a thousand years of cultural baggage, but I can tell you this: for the most part, as I am sailing down the street with a very fast, smart guide dog or moving quickly through the airport making a connecting flight with an incredibly smart, assured dog, and we're just moving along with greater control and capacity than a lot of people who are stumbling along in the airport, people look at me and go, "Wow, that's a kind of superhero—man and dog sailing through the unknown together!" They're really excited about it! It's also a thing of beauty to be in the company of an animal, and people respond to it. I was moving through the airport the other day, making a connecting flight on my way here, and I was riding through the Newark Airport on an electric cart with my dog sitting on the seat, and dozens of people were pointing and smiling, and they were joyous at the sight of a big Labrador Retriever riding through the airport like the queen of Sheba on a palanquin. It's a great sight!

CD: That's right. You've always had, it seems to me, a joyous nature, but your comment earlier about not being able to forgive yourself really struck me because I think of both the emotional and physical pain you suffered as a young person at the hand of bullies and society in general. Those wounds don't seem to be oppressive or painful to you anymore. Am I wrong about that?

SK: I think every artist knows something about the severe critic who lives inside. I won't say I don't have anxieties—I am a harsh critic of my own work, and I have a Type A personality, as many people who don't give up on writing do. Many people who are intellectuals and artists know that there's a severe critic on the inside, that you're working very hard all the time. People who tend to write beyond their twenties tend to be people who write every day, they're hardworking.

So the knives are out on the inside with a lot of intellectual and artistic struggle, but as we grow older, we find names for the things that oppress us, and we give them new names, and we build a different kind of dramatic relationship with those things, which is, of course, what Jung was always talking about in archetypal psychology—that you could rename your monsters and give them new stage directions. That was really the core of wave 1 psychoanalysis—to find new narratives for your suffering. As we do that, we become more inventive, more ironic with the things that oppress us, so we become more flexible, more malleable, certainly. We can even take some amusement from the things that bother us; we can say, "Oh, I know that voice. That's an old voice of approbation and misery. Be gone—you have no power here today! I've heard you a zillion times and I'm done with you." I think we grow those capacities as we continue to mature and think critically about the nature of our own suffering. I also think that as we grow and mingle in the world we find so many occasions for goodness. What sustains the Dalai Lama? What sustains Bishop Tutu? It's not a dusty book—it's about moving in the world among beautiful people and feeling the shared power of goodness and of good intentions. That's the thing, right? We want poetry to be part of culture, we want our art to be part of a communitarian hopefulness, we want the things that harm us and the outworn cultural semiotics of our differences to be washed away, we want to be equal to our hope.

CD: Those are two different things going on there: of course, there's that interior self-critic in every strong writer who is often merciless and omnipresent, but there's also another voice that's more spiritual and religious that can also be quite judgmental. You say it was hard for you to forgive yourself. You were under the weight of a lot of rejection and bullying when you were growing up. Just how were you able to talk back to that self-incriminating voice through your poetry, as well as through your conversations and interactions with others, to a point where you no longer felt either socially alienated or overly self-critical?

SK: In the new book I'm writing—the memoir about guide dogs—I describe day one of going to the guide dog school. You don't get your dog right away—you have lectures because they're going to give you this superbly trained animal, but before you even get the animal, you have to sit down and hear about what the animal has been through and learn what its experience of being trained has been like and to have a little sense of what a guide dog's world has been about. One of the things that they said on day one—the trainers, the people who have trained the dogs are now going to work with you to bond with an animal—one of the things they said was, "Your dog has been trained with praise, and guide dogs are told at every moment of their day, 'You're a good dog. You are a good dog. That's a good dog.' When they stop for a curb, when they're watching the traffic, when they stop for stairs, when they avoid somebody on roller skates, when they go around a low-hanging tree branch, they're going to do a hundred things a day that are good and necessary to keep you safe, but each time that that happens, your job is to say, 'Good dog!'" To even ham it up a little bit—you're like the Swedish chef on *Sesame Street*, "Good dog!"

I remember when the trainers said that to me I thought, "Can I do that all day"? Then I thought, "Well I've heard of the talking blues." We've all heard of the talking blues—that you just go on all day kind of singing the blues. *Everything's pretty bad out there, and I'm just gonna tell that bluesy story.* We've got a culture for the talking blues. I think most Americans, by the way, are addicted to the talking blues. They spend their days walking around seeing everything that afflicts them, and they've got to make sure that they're going to let you know, right? So I thought, "Wow! The guide dog school's telling me that I have to learn how to walk around all day and say what's good!" That becomes spiritual practice because a guide dog will, as they say, at least fifty times a day do something that requires you to say "Good dog!" I defy you to not feel good when you praise a dog and its tail just goes back and forth so that there are these unambiguous and continued moments of small happiness all day long.

CD: Well, it seems to have affected you profoundly!

SK: You're not the same person after you do that! If you were to just go around all day saying, "Good thing! That's a good thing," they might lock you up! At least when people look at the dog they know you're praising the dog, but it's really a way of saying "Good thing! That's a good thing!" That's a form of practice.

CD: It's had a contagious effect, it seems.

SK: You're not the same person anymore. Dendrites change.

CD: So would you say you're a different person since you wrote that passage?

SK: Absolutely!

CD: So you're not as vulnerable anymore to brown studies, or to the . . . ?

SK: I do suffer from depression, and I take medication for it. By the way, people who have disabilities often have what they call polytrauma, where you've got more than one thing going on.

CD: Your mother suffered from depression.

SK: Yes. So I take an antidepressant, and I exercise, and I'm very mindful of the circumstances. Can I fall into a three- or four-day funk, where I feel old and ugly and immaterial in some kind of cosmic way? Absolutely. But then again, what are the ways out of that? You keep moving, you keep saying "good dog," you hope to bring what you know about suffering and empathy and compassion to others, and you stay in the world. Those are, by the way, the solutions for depression. What does a good therapist tell you? If you're too alone with your depression, the first thing they say is, "You need to volunteer somewhere. You need to get out of your apartment. You need to be in the world."

CD: This poem here is, I think, very pertinent to what you just said. From *Letters to Borges*, "Why Poetry Surpasses Your Friends":

> This is a poem with a gut ache and a broken lamp.
> It used to be a hole; it used to be a burst tire.

Just so, you're the only one in the world.
You catch insects of thought—

All the white-legged annihilations.
The poem knows. Says: *I am gall, I am heartburn. God's most
    deep decree.*
Bitter would have me taste: my taste was me.

Friends?
A bitter mystery?

It is good some days to keep quiet.
Our friends are disheveled wandering stars.

SK: We're all in it together, aren't we?

CD: Yeah. But it sounds like you're saying something very important for you, here, about the role of poetry with regard to its ability to surpass your friends.

SK: Well, I'm also saying something a little tough-minded there, aren't I? I'm saying, "Suffering ye will always have with ye."

CD: And it is you?

SK: And it is me, it is consciousness itself, it is the mortal condition, and yet the more we know it and the more we understand it . . . the word is *architectonic*—multiple layers of assignment and perception are available to us. Suffering isn't just suffering—there are a hundred types of suffering. That poem was dedicated to my stepson, who was having difficulty in his teenage years, and that's my way of saying, "Don't worry—there will be other sufferings, and they'll be more interesting!" There's something almost a little—and I mean this in the best sense— Jewish in that poem. *You're suffering now? Wait 'til you try this!*

CD: If we could get back, just for a moment, to the way you see. Again in *Planet of the Blind* you write:

Reading is hazardous, and to me the words of poetry are onions, garlic, fennel, basil, the book itself an earthenware vessel. Reading alone with a magnifying glass—nothing on Earth makes more sense to me than Wallace Stevens' poem "The Pleasures of Merely Circulating": "The angel flew round in the garden, the garden flew round with the clouds, and the clouds flew around, and the clouds flew around, and the clouds flew around with the clouds." My spastic eye takes in every word like a red star seen on a winter night. Every syllable is acquired with pain. But poetry furnishes me with a lyric anger, and suddenly poems are wholly necessary. Robert Bly's book *The Light Around the Body*, for example, expresses it as an almost mystical combination of wonder and rage about the Great Society. He depicts a world gone so awry that the very pine stump starts speaking of Goethe and Jesus. The insects dance. There are murmured kings in the light bulbs outside movie theaters. All of it is glorious like my boyhood discovery of Caruso in the attic, Bly's voice, among others, Breton, Nerval, Lorca follow me in the dark.

SK: That's right. By the way, that's true for all of us who discover poetry. As Bly says, "These poets become secret friends who are with us always." He says that about his own relationship to Lorca. Isn't that glorious?

CD: I want to get back to Bly. There are two things that really stand out in that passage for me: what you call "lyric anger" and also that poem by Wallace Stevens, in which he keeps repeating, "the clouds flew around and the clouds flew around." There are two different things there, but I just thought those were fascinating observations.

SK: Well the lyric, of course, is fragment, isn't it? When we talk about lyric poetry, we're talking about poetry in which the writer does not know where he or she is going. The poem arrives on the page with a kind of wonderful jazzy improvisation, and then you get to step back and say, "Wow! Look where I went! I started with a vague feeling and a couple of syllables, and lo and behold, this poem has unfolded on the page and it surprised me—it's taken me somewhere I didn't suspect I was going to go." This is the joy of reading a good lyric poem—you're as surprised by its little journey as the poet who wrote it. Lyric poetry is surprise poetry. In narrative poetry, the poet knows where he's going. There may be glorious things happening in a narrative poem, but in general terms the poet has a pretty good sense of knowing where it's going to end up. We can talk about *Paradise Lost* as a great example of a narrative poem—Milton knows where he's going to go. So the jazzy, unexpected surprise of the lyric poem is incredibly attractive.

If your world has been—as mine was from childhood onward—a conditional one in which you don't know where you're going and you can't see effectively ahead, in point of fact you also become a kind of lyric intelligence—you learn to make from the sudden and the surprising things that make sense. There's a wonderful book by Gregory Orr called *Poetry as Survival*. It's from the University of Georgia Press, and it's a book I recommend to just about everybody because it's so terrific on the subject of how poets bring out of chaos sense through the lyric. I wish I could quote off the top of my head what Gregory Orr says in his terrific introduction to that book, but one of the things he says is that death in the family, divorce, the loss of a job, sudden illness—all of these things create horrific crises in the mind, and how to go forward is not apparent, and the lyric poet seizes that moment and makes out of fragmentary thinking a whole new garment.

CD: Well, it's the uncertainty that Keats talks about in his definition of *negative capability*—mystery, doubt, uncertainty.

SK: That's exactly right. Gregory Orr even mentions Keats. In the opening of *Letters to Borges*, I have a poem called "Emily Dickinson and the Ophthalmoscope," and why don't you read the opening of it?

CD: "Emily Dickinson and the Ophthalmoscope":

> A bird, dun-colored and nearly bald, flits above the retina and
>   vanishes
>   Like a Calvinist toy—a straw doll lost in the snow.
> "I'm a girl going blind," she thinks. "Soon I will be dark as a hat
> Or something we might lace."

Of talk there is no use—
The tongue itself is banked.
One might speak to sleeves
Or the buttons of Father's shirt.
   Still, the bird returns
And walks across the eye
Like Milton's Eve, dream-walking.
        "To think what I may tell it," she thinks. "That's the
        trick—
A small, blind wisdom as winter ends."
        She sees the bird already knows;
It bathes itself,
then tucks to clean its wings.
    My cocoon tightens, colors tease,
    I'm feeling for the air;
    A dim capacity for wings.

SK: Emily Dickinson was the first person in the state of Massachusetts to be examined with the newfangled medical device known as the ophthalmoscope. This was in 1855, just before the Civil War. She became aware that her vision was failing, and she went to see a Harvard eye doctor who had this newfangled device that had come over from the Netherlands. If you've had an eye exam, you know what an ophthalmoscope is—it's still in use; it's still necessary today. It's a flashlight with a mirror, and it allows the eye doctor to look into the back of your eye and see your retina. So it's a way of seeing into, at least in a preliminary way, the interior structures of the eye. The eye doctor who examined Emily Dickinson concluded that her retina looked okay and was therefore able to conclude that she wasn't going blind. That was Emily Dickinson's big concern—that she was going blind. What the eye doctor could not discern with an ophthalmoscope is what's behind the retina. As you may know, if you know a little bit about the structure of the eye, behind the retina there are things called rods and cones. The rods and cones have to do with the absorption of and the distribution of light to the optic nerve. Emily Dickinson, it seems pretty clear, actually had a genetic condition that affects the rods and cones. It's a kind of rod-cone dystrophy. What that means is that daylight was exceptionally painful for her, which, by the way, explains why she lived inside, seldom went out, and even greeted people, if they came to meet her in the middle of the day, behind a partly closed door. She'd sit on one side of the door and they would sit on the other.

CD: I also think in her thirties at some point, which would've been around the same time she went to Boston, she woke up one morning unable to see. She said, "I had a sudden terror this September." I think she was referring to that time when she suddenly realized she was blind.

SK: A contemporary eye doctor would say this was rod-cone dystrophy. In other words, in strong sunlight she wouldn't be able to see, which is, by the way, pretty terrifying. So you can go to a library, and on the fifth floor, where all of the Emily Dickinson books are located, you'll read every kind of analysis about why Emily Dickinson became a recluse: she was a lesbian, she hated her father, she was depressed, just simply too shattered by life to be in the world. But it's very clear that she actually was day blind, for which there would've been no solution in her time. Well, that's interesting in a number of ways. It speaks to why she's such a great poet of twilight . . .

CD: "A certain slant of light."

SK: "A certain slant of light." Winter afternoons . . .

CD: They blinded her.

SK: Well, no, she would have been able to see that. At the end of the day while light is vanishing would have been an incredibly great moment for her.

CD: I would've thought it might have been too bright for her.

SK: No, no. As the sunlight is going she would have great clarity of vision. It also explains why she kept her desk away from the window, facing north in a room. So I found that very interesting, obviously, since I think a lot about the nature of vision loss and creativity and the lyric occasion of making things out of the imprecise.

CD: What about a "lyric anger"?

SK: What is a lyric anger? Literary anger differs, by the way, from being hotheaded on the bus. Literary anger is a kind of vituperation—it's where you're willing to state what it is that afflicts you, what it is that ails you, and give it a new name. Literary naming is to give something a new name—to put down on paper the possibility of a new name. Narrative anger is just simply calling the umpire a foul name or getting into a fight with somebody who has cut you off in traffic or something like that. That's not interesting. But lyric anger is a kind of polysemous opportunity to rename things. So if the world is difficult for you, you have the opportunity to be renaming it at every turn.

CD: Because you're angry at the world?

SK: Because the world is oppositional to you. I remember hearing a scratchy—I'm going back to Lead Belly again—a scratchy Library of Congress recording of Lead Belly made by John and Allen Lomax. They're interviewing him, probably in the 1940s, and somebody asks him about the blues. I forget the question precisely, but Lead Belly says, "There never was no white man who had the blues." The way that he said it, I understood—upon hearing it the first time, probably as a kid in junior high who was listening to records—that in Lead Belly's world, the blues are all around him every minute. If you listen deeply to his songs, this proves to be true; he wakes up in the morning and "the blues are walkin' all around his bed," he says. He opens the door and "Lordy, lordy," here comes his own coffin, "comin' right in the back door." At every turn, there's something happening that's telling him, "You don't belong," and *man* it feels bad. On the subject of whether white people can have the blues, well, of course they can. There's an amazing poem by Adrienne Rich in her book *An Atlas of the Difficult World* that's addressed to a single mom who's suffering, and it's done in a kind of litany, line after line: "This is for you. This is for you. This is for you. And if you don't think that's a blues, that's a blues, baby." So of course anyone can have the blues. But in order to have the blues, you have to know something about being conditionally accepted. So I do think that there are a lot of privileged white people walking around who don't necessarily know this conditional feeling—it only happens when they feel a little injustice at the Department of Motor Vehicles. But if you have a disability, there are a lot of doors slammed in your face all the time. Something's not right. I travel with my friend Bill, who uses a wheelchair, and it's amazing how day by day, almost hourly, there's something that afflicts him that is a problem. So lyric anger is an acknowledgment that the world's full of these obstacles. And then what are you gonna do about it?

CD: There's such an evocative dichotomy in your work between that inspirational anger that you've just described and what you write in "Letter to Borges from Grazer Schlossberg": "I'm trying to learn patience through tenderness." There are these complementary feelings that exist in you almost at the same time and perhaps one more at one time than another. I think you've also said in another interview, I think with Kenneth Warner, that tenderness and impatience are becoming more and more important to you.

SK: That's a way of describing the growth of your psyche, isn't it? The Beatles, on *Sergeant Pepper's Lonely Hearts Club Band*, when Paul McCartney sings, "I used to be mad at my school, the teachers who taught me weren't cool," he's changing his scene—"man, I was mean, but I'm changin' my scene." This is what it is to grow up, right? To put some distance between the early sense of the woundedness, the vulgarity and the hypocrisy of the world, and that you don't necessarily accept it—that the world is vulgar and hypocritical—but you learn how to be a trickster, you learn how to sustain yourself in the midst of it, you learn how to take from the rough the ingredients you need to make something tender, to use that word. That's what it is.

CD: But without anger, and without a kind of fierceness that you feel sometimes toward injustice or toward trespass or toward an oversight, you don't have the necessary energy to write the poem or to express a pertinent thought about something that's insulted you or insulted the community.

SK: Well, also as you grow older and you find this tenderness that we're talking about—the sense and ability to slow down and be curious and engaged and thoughtful with what you're thinking—what goes with that is the capacity to be ironic about what you're feeling, so that you're angry at your country because it's bombing children in Iraq. I wrote a poem, it's in *Letters to Borges*, called "The War Production Canzone," which is about the military industrial complex and the cruelty of American foreign policy. It's a chant about my dishwasher, which is made by the same company that's dropping bombs on Iraqi children, that my dishwasher can be used to bring back the dead. Well, what am I doing there? The poem is an authentic crying out against American imperial cruelty and the way in which our consumer industrial culture feeds injustice. It is all of those things, but it's also very, very darkly funny, even though it gives no quarter. It says that these rascals who make these devices are drenching the world in blood. At the same time, they're selling you a dishwasher. That's lyric anger.

CD: Absolutely. You also write in this wonderful new book a poem called "Letters to Borges from Madrid":

> I wanted to call my father, long dead,
> Tell him the mind is a fit tribute to the world.
> The whores knew as much, fingered their matches, and found
>   objects:
> Combs, fingers, rings, spectacles, reminder notes from strangers.
> Even where there isn't much light we live eye to eye.
> It's a shame, really. There's no one to call.

I love the line "the mind is a fit tribute to the world." That's something you seem to want to tell your father . . .

SK: It's the opposite of "the mind is a terrible thing to waste."

CD: ... but didn't have the chance to. But to get this down in the poem, is the regret at the end of the poem an indication of that?

SK: Well, we can make tributes even with sad things. I remember going to a temple—a monastery in Greece—and seeing by the altar little tin plates made by the villagers, each one of them showing a part of the Body that was broken. They were leaving them there for the Virgin. The broken things are tributes, aren't they? I don't know, how old was I? Maybe twenty when I saw that. But implicitly grasped it, that the broken things are tributes.

CD: Was this something that your father didn't grasp?

SK: My father had a very profound, Scandinavian, mind-over-matter pragmatism. He was very Finnish and very Lutheran, and he had no emotional vocabulary. So if he was in suffering, he would bottle it up, and say, "You've got to put your best foot forward." That made him a singularly unfit parent for someone with a disability. It made him unfit for navigating a rather complicated relationship with his wife, my mother, who was depressed and had substance abuse issues. So he had no vocabulary for the mystery of living in a world of human pain and of sad facts.

CD: So when you say that "the mind is a fit tribute to the world" ...

SK: Well, you know, what do I mean by that? The Elizabethan said, "The poem holds a mirror up to nature." "The mind is a fit tribute to the world"—that if you're clear enough about the strange, peculiar, what-is-ness of the world, then at certain moments your poetry can just reflect it back. You don't have to know the answer to how to make people happy, you don't have to know how to resolve the suffering in a Madrid café, you don't have to be a journalist and report it—you just simply display it, and in that display you are like those Greek peasants leaving a little broken dish on the altar. Sometimes that's enough. That's a delicate thought, and that's a lyric thought. The lyric is also delicate. The lyric doesn't end like the *1812 Overture* with big guns. They won't make a cereal commercial with the big guns going off from a lyric poem.

CD: At the end of that poem, you say, "it's a shame there was no one to call." Of course, you're calling everyone who's reading this, except for your father. So your father stands for maybe all those folks who aren't getting that.

SK: He does.

CD: What can you do about that?

SK: That's right, and for that there is no solution. There's again, going back to Robert Bly, a poem in one of his books about driving. He's going to drive down to Minneapolis to get his daughter, and he says, "The wing of the 747 lifts without volition, and for that there is no solution." He's got this long list of things for which there is no solution. That's one of the ingredients in the lyric poem—that there are these conditions in life, we observe them, and we keep moving.

CD: Maybe we could conclude with this, your ars poetica: "Instant poems are like blue eggs—the blind kid could always find them, alone in the woods. Let others play baseball with a fat rule book."

SK: Is that from the blog?

CD: That's from you!

SK: I'm sure I said that, but I'm wondering if I wrote that on my blog....

CD: It could've been. I just have it down here in my notes as your ars poetica. I'm not sure where I read it, but I remember copying it down from either a book or a website.

SK: Well, yeah, that's right. You find things by chance, and they're rather glorious. Rule books don't let you have any chance. Baseball's interesting because it always seems to be a duel between chance and the silly manmade rules. They've got a rule for everything in baseball except chance.

CD: But the fact that the blind kid always finds them . . .

SK: Well, if you get down close to the ground, you find stuff! Nobody else sees it.

CD: That's really good. Without the rules. I guess I do have one more question for you. Would you say that your partial sight has instilled in your poetic sensibility a heightened appreciation for the significance of imagery as well as symbolic representation? I'm thinking of a line in your poem "Borges: They're Knocking the Wind Out of Me in Iowa City": "In a dream an old man was wearing a red shirt, the first I ever saw." This red shirt takes on the kind of significance William Carlos Williams's red wheelbarrow does. It's stunning how many vivid images you employ in your poetry, for someone with partial sight.

SK: I remember as a child going into the woods and getting down on my hands and knees and seeing the orchid that you find in the New Hampshire woods—they call it the Lady Slipper. It's very beautiful. Getting as close as I could to that Lady Slipper, there, down among the pine needles, that's how I see the world. So the image for me is both, as it is for all poets, an opportunity to display beauty and to bring something shimmering into the field of the poem and thereby share it with readers. There is a sharing of beauty that is at the core of all the arts, but at the same time, it is also an improbable discovery. The "it" meaning the Lady Slipper—that I would find it at all.

CD: Or the blue egg.

SK: Right. And I'm so amazed always at that finding, both literally with ruined eyes, but also in terms of poetry. You know, as a poet, that you write something down that feels right, and you're astonished. So there's a duality there—I'm astonished to see things at all in the world, and then I'm astonished to be able to capture some essence in the poem. That's a sort of dual, twofold quality of wonder. There's a poem in *Letters to Borges* where I walk around the Finnish city of Turku, and I try to call a famous poet who has left Finland and now lives in Sweden, and he dies shortly thereafter. I call him up—his name was Saarikoski—and I say, "Saarikoski got on the line. 'Maybe we will meet one day in this mad world,' he said. Today I traced a clean circle with my feet, though I didn't see the city in which I walked. I thought of the candles in Turku's church—candles, cold as glass, even in summer." That's to say, "Sometimes we don't get the connections we want. Sometimes we don't see the things we want. But *man*, isn't the world mysterious and interesting, even when we don't know it is." It's those little things. I think you mentioned William Carlos Williams and that famous poem of his where he's going to the hospital for people with tuberculosis and he just sees broken glass by the side of the road.

CD: "On the Road to the Contagious Hospital"?

SK: Yeah. Those are the little lyric moments where those side things become remarkable.

CD: And what you're seeing, you're looking for and finding.

SK: I find things in spite of my failure to find things. I think that's right.

CD: The blue eggs.

SK: You know, I wanted to see this poet very much, and he didn't want to see me because he was an introvert. Why should that be any different than not seeing anything else? Yet there's this small, delicate, wonderful, unforeseen kind of beauty. I just wander into an empty church, and there's something rather lovely.

CD: Well, you're clearly blessed with the capacity for wonder.

SK: Without that, what do we have?

CD: That's innate in you and something that I don't think you take for granted at all, but it does not exist necessarily in others.

SK: I think it might be a genetic twist. Probably I have a great-great-great-great-grandfather who was a Finnish warlock.

CD: Your parents, in the way you described them, sound like they had no idea how to think about you.

SK: No, they had no idea how to think about my blindness. They did understand that I was very, very imaginative and had all kinds of talents. In fact, when I told my father I was thinking about going to graduate school to study poetry and writing, and I was split between this idea and going to law school, he said, "Oh, don't go to law school. The world has too many lawyers. Go be a poet."

CD: Well, good for him!

SK: Yeah, I thought that was a wonderful thing for him to say! He liked poetry; he read it, and he particularly liked Galway Kinnell. But he liked Bly and went to poetry readings. He bought a little dinghy—he had a little summer house up in New Hampshire where he kept his boat on a mooring—to get out to his boat, and he named it *Dragon Smoke*, after Robert Bly's essay on "leaping poetry" and the ancient Chinese idea that if you wrote a poem, you would disappear in the sky and leave behind a little dragon smoke.

CD: He sounds like he had a poetic sensibility.

SK: He did. Everybody does.

Peter Everwine. Photo by Micah Langer

9 / *Peter Everwine*

P eter Everwine was born in Detroit and raised in western Pennsylvania. He has published seven collections of poetry, including *Listening Long and Late* (2013), *Figures Made Visible in the Sadness of Time* (2003), and *Collecting the Animals* (1973), which won the Lamont Poetry Prize in 1972. In a review of the collection *Keeping the Night*, the editor of the *Olives of Oblivion* blog noted Everwine's "uncanny ability to combine the abstract with the real" through his juxtaposition of "sparse style" and "dense images."

He is the recipient of multiple awards and honors, including a Pushcart Prize, fellowships from the National Endowment for the Arts, and a Guggenheim Fellowship, among others. His poetry has been featured in the *Paris Review,* the *American Poetry Review,* and others. He also translates poetry from the Hebrew and Aztec languages.

He has taught at the California State University–Fresno, and Reed College. He lives in Fresno, California.

This interview took place in Grafton, Vermont, on July 20, 2010.

———

Chard deNiord (CD): Good morning, and thank you for agreeing to talk to me. I'm curious to begin with about the influence translating Aztec poetry has had on your own work. Could you talk a little about that influence, the influence of the Nahuatl poetic tradition on your own poetry?

Peter Everwine (PE): I came to Aztec poetry at a fortunate time. I hadn't been writing, had no idea of what it meant to be a poet beyond a vague idea of general ambition. The poems—I read them in Spanish—let me work toward a language other than what Phil Levine once called "the language of princes." At that time I had no real knowledge of the Aztecs or their poetry, but I liked what seemed to be their way of rooting themselves into a world of simple things like birds, flowers, precious stones.

CD: I'm reminded of this in your own lines from your poem "On Modern Travel." "Thus to the ruins of the universal / is added the desolation of the particular."

PE: They had a vertical way of thinking. So you have a bird, but the bird is at the same time a mythic bird. And then it's also the soul of a warrior or a king. And they could collapse all of this into one image. I found it beautiful because it wasn't primarily visual, unlike the particulars so often found in William Carlos Williams.

CD: As in these stanzas from "Song of the Red Macaw" from your book *Working the Song Fields: Poems of the Aztecs*:

> Who am I? Flying, I live,
> and sometimes I make songs:
> flower songs, butterflies of songs—
> such as reveal my sentiments,
> such as express my heart.
> I arrive at the side of others. I descend
> and alight on earth, the red macaw of spring.
> I stretch my wings beside the flower drums,
> my song lifts and spreads over the earth.

PE: Yes, and there's one that asks the song-maker to dress himself in plumes that are as red as morning light. You can read that as a lovely lyrical touch. But then you remember that the Aztec national god was a solar god—the bird in dawn's light carries a degree of the sacred. That was a shared knowledge.

CD: I think you're referring to "Bellbird Song":

> The Golden bellbird! It's your song,
> the beautiful one, rising
> from the blossoms overhead.
> perhaps you are the god's bird,
> or a king in his stead—
> first to see the dawn's fire
> and now singing.

PE: Yes.

CD: So the image is actually more than just the thing itself?

PE: Yeah, though it is a bird. I don't think the Aztecs saw their world as abstract.

CD: The image according to Pound is "an intellectual and emotional complex in an instant of time," but it also carries with it a kind of implicit narrative or story in the Aztec poetic tradition.

PE: I think Aztec poetry deals with connecting worlds in a shared code—I suppose a kind of allusive metaphor–driven poetry.

CD: The Aztec image arcs from the thing itself to some transformative resolution or idea or other image. So one thing was always more than just one thing.

PE: Exactly.

CD: The multiplicity of the single thing. Can you think of another example of this?

PE: Well, in another poem, Montezuma, presumably the maker of the poem, calls the jade stones in his necklace his companions, then says he looks into their faces and sees nothing but eagles and jaguars. It all seems very odd. But jade is part of his wealth, and eagles and jaguars are also elite classes of warriors. A lot of things are getting hooked together in a few words.

CD: And what kind of leap, either forward or backward, do you see in Williams's notion of the image or thing?

PE: It seems to me that what you really get in Williams, and what, I think, is easy to miss sometimes, is the energy in the movement of his images.

CD: In what he called the variable foot.

PE: So there was always a way in Williams where the poems were kinetic. It wasn't just a matter of seeing for him; it was a matter of hearing that American voice. That quick, nervous voice.

CD: Good point. And he was writing *Desert Music* around this time you were in Mexico in the mid-fifties.

PE: I lived in Mexico in 1968, though I'd traveled there earlier.

CD: In your poem "Collecting the Animals," you conclude with these shaman-like lines:

> What were the animals but ourselves
> flashing with the wind, stripped down,
> simple at last—the lives
> that go on evading us
> yet move
> in shadows at the field's edge, in trees
> flowing away like water on the far hills.
> And what is there to grieve?
> Here are the tracks they made
> in this place.

And in your poem "We Meet in the Lives of Animals," you vivify a slaughtered cow with shamanistic reverence and human deference:

> "Here," she says, cradling
> a cow's bloody head from which she scrapes
> its stringy flesh. "Here,

hold open its eyes.
It will see our hunger."

PE: Well, that was something I felt. The cow incident was true. I don't know how much I can claim to be shamanistic.

CD: Silence is as important to you as the voices of the animals. You write in your poem "Distance": "Once more I find myself / standing on a dark pier, holding / an enormous rope of silence."

PE: Yeah.

CD: There's a tension between the voices in your poetry and the silence you listen to just as closely. I see this in many of your poems. Any close reader of yours hears the silence as much as the language in your poetry.

PE: It's a companion. I also don't work from a very large vocabulary. I think I have a very simple vocabulary. Very spare. And I don't know if that's deliberate; it's just the words that I react to. And I think at the same time what lies behind a word—its associations and its resonance, its shadow—has been important to me. That may be a religious sense of the world, but if so it's also much of the Aztec poetry I know—often a very melancholy view of the world.

CD: I see.

PE: I don't want to make too much of it.

CD: I don't know if you can.

PE: I don't want to make it into a Zen-like thing.

CD: That's why I don't want to say shamanistic sensibility only either.

PE: Yeah.

CD: But it's something that's very natural and distinct in your work.

PE: It's the way I hear poetry. I don't know what the experience of writing poetry is like for you or for other people, but it seems to me that my aspect of trying to write is really about trying to listen.

CD: And receive.

PE: Yeah, and the silence is a large part of that for me. And if it gets into the form, it's because of the way I'm hearing it.

CD: Yes. You let it sink in . . . the silence.

PE: In the poem and the language that comes out of the silence. This may sound like nonsense, but silence helps me to slow down a poem, to adjust a phrase or line or inner movement to its emotional weight.

CD: Right. So the Nahuatl language of the Aztecs electrified you, helping you find your own voice that incorporates the religious quality of ancient Aztec poetry, much of which you've translated throughout your career, as well as your own hierophantic quality.

PE: Yeah.

CD: You must have returned to Fresno with a new mission following your sabbatical in 1968.

PE: Yeah, it did feel different.

CD: You were talking to your lifelong friend and colleague Phil Levine a lot about your work then, as you probably still do?

PE: We don't talk a lot about our own work. We talk about wine.

CD: You were born in the same city.

PE: Yeah. I once introduced Phil at a reading, and I gave this facetious introduction in which I said my mother had a dream that she had to go to Detroit because she saw the initials P.L. I had to be born under these initials (laughing).

CD: I'm sure that got a laugh. So you came back from Mexico and started writing again.

PE: Yes.

CD: For the first time in years.

PE: Right.

CD: And what came out?

PE: Well, the first book that came out was a book of Aztec translations, *In the House of Light.*

CD: So you wisely stuck with that.

PE: I did.

CD: Rather than saying, "Okay, I'm ready to write on my own now."

PE: I was doing both.

CD: You were doing both, but you pursued the translations first.

PE: It seemed to me the most available material. I really didn't have a book otherwise. And then came *Collecting the Animals* in 1973.

CD: Right. Then came *Keeping the Night* in 1978.

PE: Yeah.

CD: So the translating was really an apprenticeship for you.

PE: That's a great term for it.

CD: Rather than doing your apprenticeship in Iowa, you did it in Mexico on your own separate journey.

PE: [laughing] To the sorcerers ...

CD: With the Aztecs.

PE: I did another book of Aztec translations in 2005 with Sutton Hoo Press, a limited edition. I then found a publisher at Eastern Washington University who was willing to do a selection of my Aztec translations. Chris Howell was instrumental in this.

CD: And that is the recently published book titled *Working the Song Fields.*

PE: Yes.

CD: Congratulations. You mentioned earlier that a lot of Aztec poetry is melancholy, as is yours also. Is your work melancholy because of this influence or simply because you're melancholy by nature?

PE: Probably a case of the two meeting on common ground. The Aztecs ask a lot of universal questions about what life amounts to, and I think there's enough simplicity in their work that you're not ever afraid of imitating them. There's no sense of individual virtuosity in the Aztec poets, partly because it's an oral folk process, partly because they understood the whole system of symbols that was behind every word. I've never been very crazy about highly ornamental poetry.

CD: And when you just used the word *virtuosity*, did you mean it in that sense?

PE: Yes, also that need to be original and unique.

CD: Do you feel that ornamental quality in a lot of, say, Western poetry, say, a lot of poetry in the fifties? I'm thinking particularly of Lowell, not that he was merely decorative or ornamental but lapidary and dense in such books as *Lord Weary's Castle* and *Life Studies.* Does this avoid a truth-telling or lack of pretension that Aztec poetry emanates?

PE: I don't think I want to make that kind of judgment. There are all sorts of people who love that.

CD: That music?

PE: That music. And you can't say that that doesn't belong in the world of poetry. It's just one I don't react to very much. I suppose if you go back historically—I like reading Donne, but I prefer Ben Jonson. These two poets seem totally different to me, and I think of someone like Zbigniew Herbert, that marvelous poem where he says there are poets who close their eyes and a garden of images come streaming down. I don't think I've ever been in that position. And the thing is, I'm not sure I ever want to be in that position. I get plainer and plainer, and sometimes I worry about that, but there's not that much I can do about it.

CD: Because?

PE: Because I think it tends to push me toward a more garrulous statement, diffused narratives, bumbling around in the furniture of narrative, and I don't know if I'm very good at that.

CD: But I was wondering; you said you were worried about becoming more and more spare.

PE: Oh, I'm not worried about that. I'm worried about being more and more confused and garrulous. More talky. And I also want to avoid poetic bullshit.

CD: Do you feel like you're becoming too talky at times?

PE: Yeah.

CD: Why?

PE: Well, because there are ways in which, when I think back to certain poems, how spare they were and how an image worked in that sparseness, and I don't find that same sense of a single image that explores the content of the poem. I've come less and less to that.

CD: Do you know why that's happened?

PE: I think it's part of the way we age, or part of the way I age.

CD: For instance in the poem you wrote recently about a buzzard, do you find yourself writing more garrulously than what you might call essentially?

PE: Not so much in that poem, but there are poems I've written lately that do seem much more given over to the narrative. And what happens, or at least part of what I think happens, is when you start using particulars, in that way of narrating the poem, the particulars tend to stay there as things, and I like particulars that sort of suggest everything behind them. It's a way of understating rather than simply stating.

CD: So it sounds like you're talking more about the lyrical impulse than the narrative.

PE: Exactly. And I love the lyrical impulse. Where I'm trying to find it now is more and more in the old Eastern poets and the Aztecs.

CD: Oh, still in the Aztecs.

PE: Well, I'm pretty much finished doing the Aztecs though—I mean I've done enough of that; I want to get out of that.

CD: Just because you feel like you've finished.

PE: I think so, yes. I think I've done enough and I think I've explored what was interesting for me to explore in those books.

CD: So when you discovered Aztec poetry, just as Bly and Wright were discovering Trakl, Rilke, Strom, and Neruda, among other European modernists in the sixties, you were pursuing Aztec poetry that led you also in a foreign direction that redefined your muse. You translated yourself as well as the Aztecs, discovering a spare, indigenous, archetypal, anonymous voice that became your own in English.

PE: If you read those Aztec poems, it's really hard to tell who wrote them.

CD: They follow an anonymous folklore tradition, as you say.

PE: Exactly. And maybe that's also what I mean by our intense interest in virtuosity and voice and it doesn't exist there. I mean, it exists in the sense that sometimes in the Aztec poems you get an announcement of who the writer is or who the poet is, but this seems more formulaic than individual.

CD: As in they might refer to "the old woman" but not "so-and-so," specifically.

PE: No, it's not "so-and-so." And I don't even think you can trust it when he says "I'm King So-and-So." I think it's maybe somebody who is making that voice up. So there is something attractive about that; I can't say it's faceless. It's deeply human.

CD: Were you influenced by any other poets or traditions of poetry at the time you were translating Aztec poetry?

PE: I must have been. But they are really hard to name. Yvor Winters, of course, some of those poems are wonderful. J. V. Cunningham, early on. Certainly a number of European poets. It's hard to tell exactly who I chose, consciously or unconsciously.

CD: Right. Were you reading other poets at the time, like Galway Kinnell or James Wright or Robert Bly or Phil Levine?

PE: I certainly read all those poets, sure. And you know there were people who said that I belonged to the deep image school, people who said I was a symbolist, people who said I imitated Mark Strand's surrealism. I mean, after a while if you listen to everybody, you don't know who the hell you are. You know, I had all those marvelous classmates. The people you mentioned—many were classmates of mine at Iowa.

CD: So they—Phil Levine, Jane Cooper, Donald Justice, Robert Dana, Henri Coulette—must have influenced you in some ways, either consciously or unconsciously.

PE: Had to. And that whole generation out of Iowa was a very significant one.

CD: They really changed the direction of American poetry.

PE: It was a simpler world then.

CD: So it was a simpler time but also a momentous time.

PE: There were a lot of crosscurrents, and I don't know how many crosscurrents there are anymore because I don't keep up as much with what is happening.

CD: Right. Well, contemporary American poetry has become such an enormous tent in the last twenty years.

PE: There are little groups all over the place.

CD: And so many different rings inside this enormous tent. But I would rather talk about your specific lineage and experience as an Italian American poet. Did you ever feel that your German last name concealed your ethnic identity?

PE: I've never felt it was concealed. I certainly never concealed it. I love the background I came from. It was rather funny when I talked about my childhood during my visit with Ruth Stone the other day, telling her I came from uncles who started out in the mine and so forth. She assumed I had a tragic childhood because of the word "mine." But I think I had a very good childhood, despite the very hard times of the thirties.

CD: Your father died when you were very young, correct?

PE: He died in a car accident before I was born. For the first years of my life my mother and I lived in my grandmother's house in Leechburg, Pennsylvania, and my grandmother mostly took care of me because my mother worked. I'm not sure how it affected me. Sometimes you don't really know what in childhood gets to you. My grandmother didn't know English. All the family that came to the house, my uncles for example, spoke the dialect. So as long as my grandmother was around, that was the language. A very loud language. And the language I was born into at that point was an Italian dialect. So in some ways, I know, that had to affect the way I listen to the music I hear in words. I can remember being in situations later on with my stepfather where I couldn't think of the English word and I would use the Italian. That was part of my growing into that family.

CD: How long did that last?

PE: It lasted until I left home at fourteen. When I started school I got less and less accustomed to it. The curious thing is when I went back to Italy some years ago and went to the Canavese area, I could understand much of what they were saying.

CD: What dialect was this?

PE: It's called Piedmontese.

CD: You said it's partly from Occitan?

PE: Well, it's part of that, so in some ways, it's almost as much Provençal as it is Italian.

CD: And how many people still speak it?

PE: Oh, fewer and fewer.

CD: Must be a very small little group.

PE: The old, so to speak. The young go to school and learn proper Italian. And so I think it's being phased out. There is a body of work in the dialect.

CD: That goes back to the Troubadour tradition in the eleventh and twelfth centuries?

PE: Yes, but also up to modern times when writers were trying to keep the language intact.

CD: And that must be increasingly difficult.

PE: Absolutely. The curious thing is my grandmother had come to America, and as the years went along, she probably spoke a purer dialect then those who were living in the dialect region. There wasn't that element of change going on.

CD: You experienced much loss early in life, your father, your family's dialect and Italian way of life. Do you think that these losses were formative influences in shaping your personality and poetry? What you call your melancholy strain?

PE: I think it is part of my temperament. Part of it comes out of family certainly, and it's very curious. Although it doesn't much get into my poetry, I'm often very happy.

CD: I see that also.

PE: I'm always a little stunned by my own sobriety.

CD: Well, it's not so much sobriety, I think, as a deep sadness and bittersweetness.

PE: It's true. The book of prose poems that Bill Kelly and I just did called *Traces* carries that sense of losing, and if and when I get a new book, that will be a section.

CD: What's clear in your last book of poems, *From The Meadow*, particularly in such poems as "Elegiac," "Fragments," and "Lullaby," is the quality of two worlds, this world and the other. These two worlds are especially poignant in the conclusion of "Lullaby." Your speaker hears a mosquito which makes him

> stop and think
> how driven we are—even the least—to hear
> world's incessant undersong
> even if it was never meant for us,
> or never anything but clamor we wanted to be song
> and how much we love it, and with what sadness,
> knowing we have to turn away
> and enter the dark.

PE: And that's a poem I'm grateful for. If I could write a bunch of those poems I would be happy. I might lose all melancholy.

CD: That's a really beautiful poem with a finely crafted symmetry. It starts with the lines "Last night in the dark, something / came near and frightened me," and ends with the lines, "knowing we have to turn away / and enter the dark."

PE: It seems to me that one of the pleasures I get from that kind of poem is discovering a form in which you can return to previous elements of the poem and yet discover an inevitable weight has been added. And what you talk about, that symmetry, is really a form. Expectation and surprise, perhaps.

CD: Yes.

PE: I think of these poems as sometimes establishing a rather formal relationship to the experience. And at the same time an intimate relationship, if you can combine them.

CD: There's great intimacy there. Your poems are consistently elegiac, and by that I don't just mean sad or mournful. There is a joyous quality in them as well. Do you think you conveyed this elegiac quality to your student Larry Levis, who was such a powerfully elegiac poet?

PE: I don't think so.

CD: You don't?

PE: That would be giving me high praise indeed.

CD: Well, I think you deserve it.

PE: But I mean Larry had so much talent. I knew Larry when he was just beginning to write.

CD: He was your student at Fresno State during a very formative time in his early development as a poet.

PE: I did have him in several classes. But I think Larry just had that melancholy gift. I don't think that can be taught. I think you can only come to it from experience.

CD: But he might have learned some of the forms for it from you.

PE: That would be nice to think so. By the time he died, he had invented so many of his own complex forms. He had found a whole closet full of forms he could use.

CD: Was he an elegiac poet as a student?

PE: He was always a little dark, but he was also very funny.

CD: In your poem "From the Meadow," you mention a tiny figure at the end of the poem calling to someone who may be you. Do you recall this figure?

PE: I do remember—

> though from the meadow where you stand looking
> over your shoulder, that tiny figure you see
> seems to be calling
> someone,
> you perhaps."

CD: Do you see this figure as the past, the poet or perhaps the divine?

PE: I don't think it's divine.

CD: Perhaps death then?

PE: No, I don't even think it's death. I think it's the child you leave, his innocence, and yet bear him with you lifelong.

CD: So the stanza preceding this one:

> But now you know right what lies ahead
> is nothing to the view behind?
> How breathtaking these nostalgias rising
> like hazy constellations overhead!
> little to go by, surely

That makes wonderful sense from the speaker's perspective as an adult directing himself, as well as the reader, to recall the "breathtaking ... nostalgias" of childhood as it also looks toward the future.

PE: That's the most immediate sense, as well as a figure way in the distance. And summoning you or calling to you as if to say, "Are you there?"

CD: Can you remember? Is it saying that? What it's like to be a child, to have that sensibility?

PE: To be that sensibility, to be what you were, to be what in many ways you still are. Because I don't think we just leave it; I don't think we just separate ourselves from that. It's part of our history.

CD: But something is gone. Otherwise it wouldn't be summoning you, right? And what would you say is gone?

PE: I wanted the figure to remain rather ambiguous. Summoning you is one thing. But what if it's calling you to wait for him?

CD: Could you elaborate on that?

PE: You know, I have the sense that, I can name it—I can say "the child"—but even by naming it, I've already put a limit on it. I think that what I like in the poem is that it didn't quite have a limit; there remains something a little mysterious about that little figure. And I feel that about the continuum of our lives. We have a background. We can say, "Well, I was a child," but it lives in us. It calls us back. It's funny; I was talking to Ruth Stone about children, and she said we never grow up. There's a truth in that. So I didn't know what it was calling. Because I think that ambiguity . . . well, the poem does end with the word *perhaps*. And the poem does deal with the failure of the innocent vision.

CD: When you say "how breathtaking these nostalgias," you're not afraid to call it nostalgia, to name it nostalgia.

PE: I'm not afraid at all.

CD: Which is, you know, often viewed as an almost willful despair, an overly romantic quality one might have about the past, a kind of emotional stasis.

PE: We sentimentalize it, and if we use that kind of word we say well, that's the kind of poetry that looks at the past and says, "Oh, it's wonderful and sentimental." I have nothing of that; well, I don't think I do.

CD: No, but if an intensity of feeling in a poem is combined effectively, transcendently, with memory—with remembering—it can be enormously evocative, as is the case, I think, of many of James Wright's poems, such poems as "A Blessing" and "Beautiful Ohio," for example.

PE: I don't think you can live without some nostalgia. How can you do it? How can you not remember with nostalgia your first great love? How can you forget your first long trip on a train? I don't know.

CD: You make this point in your poem "The Heart":

> I imagine I hear it singing still
> so that the woods return, and the boy,
> and the spring evenings—
> O love, O mercy,
> O passing years!

That child again, the boy. There is really more of the past in a lot of your work than the future or thinking about the future.

PE: That's true—that's exactly right. And I suppose that goes with that sense of loss.

CD: Your poetry has become a memorable record of losing and living, which are often the same thing, and the joys of course as well that occur between the losses.

PE: And I hope also it becomes kind of record not of what has been lost but how you live with loss. I don't mean that in any pedagogical way, but that is what one does. You learn how to live with it.

CD: But how to do that in a way that is, as far as the poetry is concerned, newly evocative in the context of your own life.

PE: Exactly, in my own life. I don't pretend to instruct people.

CD: Right, but when you say for instance in "The Heart," "In a small white room I saw my heart after it broke." It's not just you who saw your heart after it broke; it's in a small white room.

PE: That's what I love about the possibility of poetry. And I'm not talking just about my poetry but really about poetry, that you can be truthful, accurate. It was a small white room.

CD: There actually was a small white room; you aren't just being poetic here?

PE: There was. That's right. But at the same time that accident has a whole resonance behind it, and I love it when that can happen.

CD: What do you mean by *accident* exactly?

PE: The philosophical sense of *accident*. It could have taken place in a red room; you could lie and make it a red room. I don't know. I love it when you can be truthful to a situation in life. And at the same time catch that resonance that pushes you.

CD: In his poem "Capri" Czesław Miłosz refers to these real places, these "accidents" as you call them, as "immense particulars."

PE: That's a wonderful phrase.

CD: You mentioned you didn't have a large vocabulary . . .

PE: I don't.

CD: But you certainly possess your own verbal music, are sophisticated and well read. You choose not to use language in an ornamental way, in a decorative way, as you said before. Of course there are great poets such as Shakespeare and Keats who break the spare language rule, but their elaborate eloquence is not your model.

PE: Well, you know, if you bring up a poet like Keats, I mean how can you not love some of those odes? They're so beautiful, they're so breathtaking, they're so heart-wrenching, but you know when it comes right down to the truth of it, I prefer Coleridge's conversational poems. I would rather read Coleridge's "The Nightingale," frankly, than Keats's "Ode to a Nightingale." I'm sure people would say I'm foolish.

CD: You like something more about Coleridge's colloquial speech. You prefer Coleridge's poems in *Lyrical Ballads* to Keats's odes?

PE: I don't know how to explain it exactly. Coleridge is more intimate with his experience. Less aesthetic but more rooted. He's more colloquial, and he puts himself into the narrative. In "The Nightingale," where he holds his child up to the moon and the nightingales are singing all`around him, what an incredible intimate moment that creates between a father and son and the world. And Keats is off listening to this gorgeous music lulling him to death and it's beautiful; he's so young, but it's so far away, and there's so much language being generated. Coleridge has that deep gravity of his experience in his poem. And I think the last passages of that poem have a music that is the equal of Keats. You hear it again in Wallace Stevens at the close of "Sunday Morning."

CD: Right, or in Coleridge's poem "Frost at Midnight."

PE: Yeah, "Frost at Midnight," a little fire, thinking back.

CD: And his son is in that poem too.

PE: Or "The Lime-Tree Bower My Prison," where his friends go on a hike and he travels with them in his mind. And he's got their rhythm in his lines.

CD: There's a spoken quality to a lot of your poems as well.

PE: I think so. I hope so.

CD: Yeah, but at the same time the lyric is so resonant in your work. If I just pick randomly from *From the Meadow*, as I'm doing now, one see this immediately:

> There is in me, always,
> you and the absence of you.

> There is in me, always,
> that road that leads to a field
> of flowers we once knew

> in that place where you were young,
> there, where Memory keeps a life
> of its own in the dark,

like a plant that waits patiently
year after year, asleep and folded inward
until the appointed night arrives

when it stirs and wakes
and opens out—Oh dream flowering
Darkness flowering into darkness!—

forms, figures made visible
in the sadness of Time.

You combine lyrical expression with speech here in a memorable way.

PE: Well, I would like that to be true, Chard.

CD: Those lines are from your poem "Elegiac Fragments." Your voice is quiet and often private. Do you feel your voice remains in that zone in most of your poems?

PE: I do, because I think my sense of speaking in the poem doesn't create a very large public space, and I try even in public readings to create that private intimate space. I think there are poets who work wonderfully in public spaces, Whitman you mentioned. I heard, when I was young, Dylan Thomas read, and he just practically knocked me from my chair. I had never heard a voice like that. Or language like that, and although he was speaking about rather private experiences, the voice and the language were extremely public, I thought. I try not to. I don't think my speaking voice in my poems is public. I can do nothing about that.

CD: Well, that's just the nature of your work and your sensibility. And yet at the same time, this private self that you're talking about that is so closely focused on your own particular subject matter, whether it's a cow or a field or a white room, or any of these things, crosses over from your deeply private self to your reader.

PE: I hope so. That would be something I certainly desire.

CD: I mean it's the great paradox of the lyric, isn't it—the private self, writing about deeply personal things and connecting with others, mostly strangers, through the magic of his or her language?

PE: Exactly. That's what we all want.

CD: And create poetry in the process.

PE: Isn't that what you want in your work?

CD: Absolutely. But how do you do it? Create a transpersonal self that crosses over from personal particulars with meanings, music, and imagery that move the reader?

PE: Who do you speak to when you write?

CD: To myself.

PE: Talking to yourself? Me too.

CD: I think I start there, and then when I realize sometimes when I read the poem out loud to myself, I need to hear with a third ear or see with a third eye that I have become too self-absorbed here, too runic there.

PE: We sit around punishing ourselves.

CD: This is one of the things about Ruth Stone that I'm always impressed with. Just when she's about to descend into darkest sadness, she somehow finds her way out, usually with humor, saving her poems from despair or facile brown study.

PE: Absolutely.

CD: Right? You noticed that about her work.

PE: You quoted her poem "Curtains" to me the other day, a poem addressed to her dead husband, Walter, which she saves at the end with the angry but comic retort, "See what you missed by being dead?" I mean that's an incredible ending.

CD: She's really hearing with her third ear, right? She realizes if she had gone on talking about Mr. Tempesta in the apartment it would have just gone nowhere.

PE: It's a wonderful shift. I love those moments where poems shift like that.

CD: And you know sometimes, not in her case, but it can be too funny or too light, running away too far in the other direction, but by the time you say in your poem "The Heart," "O, mercy" at the end, it's not funny but still evocative for the integrity of the sentiment expressed there.

PE: Well, that's a nice phrase. Though it's very hard to tell sometimes. Maybe, maybe not. Maybe it's not so hard to tell if there's integrity. Maybe we can spot fake rhetoric.

CD: Yeah. I mean do you ever show your poems to Phil Levine or anyone else?

PE: I sometimes show them to Phil, sometimes my friend Connie, or Chuck Hanzlicek, sometimes to Bob Mezey.

CD: And they tweak it or tell you where to revise? Do you almost have a new book ready for publication?

PE: Well, pretty close, I hope.

CD: Pretty close, but are you actually fighting this narrative impulse? You talked about worrying about becoming too narrative, and you can hardly find a narrative poem in your selected poems here.

PE: Partly what worries me, you know, coming back to vocabulary: I do have a simple vocabulary, that's the truth.

CD: But that's for a reason.

PE: It's for a reason. And also I'm not very good at description. You may have noticed that I don't describe things much. I have details, I have objects, but I don't spend a lot of time describing them. I'm concerned that if I'm writing more narratively now, maybe I need more description.

CD: But you're just finding that your new poems are turning in more narrative direction.

PE: In a couple of cases.

CD: Is that because you feel like you have some stories to tell that you haven't told? That don't work in the lyric?

PE: Yes, I have some stories.

CD: I know you do. Because those prose poems are perfect examples. Like your uncle?

PE: Yes.

CD: Well, that's just one, but all of those.

PE: Yeah, they're stories or anecdotes.

CD: And because they're stories, there has to a little description here and there, right?

PE: They move in time differently.

CD: But again, we talked about your lyric poetry being poetry as witness to these losses in an enormously evocative way lyrically throughout your life, but now you've moved to a point where you feel the lyric can't do all that work. It's a little like when Pasternak decided that he couldn't write poetry anymore because it wasn't large enough to contain the kind of witnessing he felt he needed to . So he wrote *Doctor Zhivago*. You're feeling that they're stories that you need to tell about your life, your past.

PE: Can't do it.

CD: Can't, it's the wrong form. It's the wrong form, wrong genre.

PE: But I'm always afraid someone's going to look at it and say, "Jesus! That's a dumb story."

CD: But they're not saying that!

PE: I'm saying that!

CD: I mean, these prose poems, why did they come out as prose poems? Why didn't they come out as verse poems?

PE: Total accident. Chris Buckley wrote me and so I said okay, I'll sit down and try to do some. But I didn't feel like I could do it piecemeal; I wanted some thread.

CD: Yeah, but there was something you found about that form that you liked, that you could work in. as opposed to lines. And here you are thinking about lines your whole life, obsessively, right? Short line here, long line here, free verse. And now suddenly you're not thinking about the line any more. Is that liberating?

PE: It's liberating to a degree.

CD: You feel liberated?

PE: In those poems I certainly did.

CD: Do you want to write more of them?

PE: I don't know, maybe. It's an attractive form. And you can do it with a great deal of precision, though the form easily lends itself to indulgence and silliness.

CD: You're obviously not feeling like, "all right, I'm done."

PE: No, not yet. Not yet. It may come, but not yet, I hope.

CD: That's lucky. You feel lucky?

PE: I do indeed.

CD: Because you're still writing?

PE: I'm writing. My life is full. I have friends. I'm just full.

Stephen Sandy. Photo by Star Black

10 / *Stephen Sandy*

S tephen Sandy was born and raised in Minneapolis, Minnesota, and earned his BA from Yale University and his MA and PhD from Harvard University, where he studied poetry with Robert Lowell and Archibald MacLeish. He was the author of eleven collections of poetry, including *Man in the Open Air: Poems* (1988), *Thanksgiving over the Water* (1992), *The Thread: New and Selected Poems* (1998), *Black Box* (1999), *Surface Impressions* (2002), *Weathers Permitting* (2005), and *Overlook* (2010).

Sandy's meditative and observant poems scrutinize the natural and human world. Of *Weathers Permitting* (2005), John Hollander commented that "throughout this book rural matters are considered with a profound, rather than a light, urbanity—an urbanity of intellect and diction and authoritative rhythmic control." In his eight-part *Surface Impressions: A Poem* (2002), Sandy addresses the family, American history, faith, ecology, and technological change. In a review, poet and critic Peter Campion observed that "with concision and vivacity he portrays how emotions and thoughts collide with the sheer material of the world. . . . Sandy has a unique gift for getting one image to segue into another with a fluid sharpness that any cinematographer would envy."

Sandy traveled to Japan on a Fulbright Visiting Lectureship and was honored with fellowships from the National Endowment for the Arts, the Vermont Council on the Arts, and the Ingram Merrill Foundation. He translated ancient Greek poets, taught at Harvard University, Brown University, and for many years at Bennington College, and was the poet featured in the documentary *The Biologist, the*

Poet, and the Funeral Director (2007, directed by Harvey Edwards). He died in 2016.

This interview took place at the home of Stephen Sandy in Bennington, Vermont, on October 10, 2012, and April 16, 2014.

Chard deNiord (CD): I'm curious to know when you first started to write poetry.

Stephen Sandy (SS): Childhood. I was seven or eight, I guess. Seven would be good. Soon I started to save poems. My grandmother Caddie was influential because she had a typewriter (unlike my mother or father). She typed up my early efforts on her pokey little Underwood portable. I had begun to write; some of her typescripts still survive.

CD: That must've been second, third grade!

SS: Yes. Hitler's invasion of Poland remains a key because I was moved by that, through Caddie's reactions, the Blitz and such mighty events. I recall standing in bright afternoon sun with Caddie at the front door of our house, she waiting for the evening paper; when the paperboy brought it to her, she unrolled it to the headline—and gasped. I asked what it was; she said, "Hitler has invaded Poland. He has started the war." As well, about this time, I found Powers Department Store. (Of course this was thanks to Caddie; did she know she was child-minding?) They had a book department with a little alcove of "fine" editions as well as a shelf (behind glass) of rare books. One or two of these I coveted, a Tennyson, for example (it was housed in a box), his *Poems of Two Brothers*. His first book—the brothers wrote it when teenagers. I asked Caddie for that for my birthday, and she obliged. I treasured it for years—and sold it only to help pay graduate school bills.

CD: Had you read his poems somewhere?

SS: No. Of course, growing up in a quasi-Victorian household, I'd heard the Bard's name and seen it on a book spine or two. But it was years before I read that collection. Since it did not discriminate between one brother and the other's work, eventually I looked in a volume of his poems alone. Another was the vastly popular suite of poems by Alice Duer Miller called *The White Cliffs*, rhyming narrative propaganda on behalf of the British, who in 1940 expected invasion. I saw that it was published during the Blitz, and it was poetry. I don't remember it, but I wrote a poem called "There Will Always Be an England," which rhymed and was perhaps two or three quatrains. Later came "The Fairy Dewdrop Maiden," inspired by Tennyson, an effort of scant merit indeed.

CD: That's intriguing. . . . I'm curious why you even responded to poetry and to Tennyson in particular and to *The White Cliffs*. I mean, what happened? Was it the music? Was it the content?

SS: The music and the content I suppose. Mind you, I didn't sit down and plot out exactly what I would write. I just did it. I did realize very early that poetry was deeply important to me. It was mine. Or perhaps because lyrics were brief and I didn't have to read those long narratives. Just right, maybe, for a kid too young for Shakespeare?

CD: You learned to read when you were six or so. And there was something about poetry as opposed to other children's books or stories that appealed to you. But right away?

SS: Yes. In a childish way I liked the idea of reincarnation. I came to dream or imagine that I had been a poet in another life. Thus a matter of retrieval. By the time I got to puberty, I knew that poetry was a path for me. And maybe, thanks to Arthur Waley, that I had been Chinese. Yet just as I don't read Waley translations anymore, I slowly outgrew those fantasies of another world.

CD: If you felt that you had been a Chinese or Japanese poet, because of your interest in . . .

SS: Never Japan. Always China. And I know my folks—they just couldn't figure me out, and they didn't like that. And they said, "What is this China stuff?" My parents used to go to New York on business; they drove because my father loved to drive. Thus they could bring stuff back like Yankee warm-up jackets. I asked for a book called *Chinese Art*, an English publication, an introduction for the Burlington House Exhibition of 1936–1937, put on in London to raise money for the regime of Chiang Kai-shek. They brought me the book, and it made some difference in helping me along. The Minneapolis Art Institute had a good Chinese section, and I used to like to look at those things but not at the time when I was first interested in China.

CD: When did you actually start reading Chinese poetry? Did the sense of having been a Chinese poet come even before you started reading Chinese poetry?

SS: You're being very detailed. I did not read poetry in Chinese for years—until I studied with Phebe Chao at Bennington.

CD: It's fascinating that your interest in Chinese poetry and also your love for books, especially beautiful books, has continued throughout your life. It wasn't something you discovered in college or graduate school or later on, but this goes way back. Your parents must have thought you were precocious.

SS: I think they were pretty annoyed by it.

CD: Different?

SS: Of course. I don't know what they really felt, but I read a lot, and I was, yes, perhaps a bit precocious. I was reading Proust in the big two-volume edition . . . that would've been when I was thirteen or fourteen.

CD: *Swann's Way*?

SS: First I read *Combray*. My parents called me to a conference.

CD: Like you'd been a bad boy?

SS: Yes. They actually did not want me to read Proust because they had heard things about him. They were sitting on a sofa in the living room. I still remember sun coming through the windows, shades drawn on either side of them, so there was light through the translucent shades. I was standing, they were sitting. And one or the other said, "We realize that you are an unusual young man, and we've decided that you are an intellectual."

CD: They said the word "intellectual"?

SS: Yes. I didn't know what that meant, though I'd heard the term before.

CD: Said in a derogatory way?

SS: Yes. And they went on, "Now it's alright to be an intellectual, but we don't want you to spend too much of your time on it and hang around reading books, and so on."

CD: You were around thirteen then?

SS: Yes. I had done something wrong. All they said was they didn't want me reading Proust. So I didn't read anymore Proust for a long time. And still I have never finished it [chuckles].

CD: Was Proust really considered that controversial a figure?

SS: I think Proust was back then because the word on the street or the golf course would have been that he at the very least had led a suspicious life. Needless to say, they didn't bring that up, and I would have had no idea what that meant. But there was something untoward about Proust, and that was just one of many forbidden things. . . . During the Second World War we had what were called "Bible girls," who helped out at the house and lived there, because my mother was working for the Red Cross, and my father went every day to his business. The Northwestern Bible School was run by Billy Graham and was where he got his start as a public figure. There was a German refugee who came to live with us; her name was Edith. Very nice. Tall and thin. She taught us to count to ten in German: "eins zwei drei vier fünf sechs sieben acht neun zehn." When my mother found out that this had gone on, Edith was fired on the spot.

CD: Because those were war years?

SS: Yes. There wasn't much reasoning behind their responses. Mother's father had died very early; he was a physician in a rural setting, and he rode off one night never to return. It was hard to find what happened, but probably he had had a heart attack or a stroke. So mother was brought up by her mother, Clara, whom we called Caddie. I think there was a lot of protectiveness in Evelyn's mother for her daughter. She had a narrow view of what could be accepted. They were from Iowa, where it was illegal to teach German from the First World War until 1950 or so because of the two wars. Yet there were so many settlers with German roots; the largest ethnic minority in Minnesota was German, not Scandinavian.

CD: So here you are reading Proust and identifying with Chinese poetry and poets, which was, understandably, upsetting to your parents. But rather than conforming to their wishes and playing football you continued reading literary novels, maybe secretly, and writing also, throughout high school.

SS: Yes. Soon however they took me out of public grade school, with my brother, and sent us to Blake School, a country day school, hoping to give us a good education. Mother at one point was in charge of the parent-teacher group at Robert Fulton—our public grade school—and didn't think too much of it. It was a strange place. For example, my kindergarten teacher, Miss Easthagen, loved by all, nevertheless hanged herself one weekend—at the school. Happily, I had gone on to first grade.

CD: You received a rigorous classical education?

SS: Well, in a way, yes. It was a good education. The school required Latin, a modern language, and the usual English and math and so on.

CD: And you were writing also at that age?

SS: Scribbling, yes.

CD: And thinking of yourself as a budding poet?

SS: No, I didn't. There were other aspects—musical. My mother played the piano. My father danced. My brother took up the clarinet; I took up the accordion, then piano. It started out because I didn't want to do the piano since my mother already did. I played the accordion for a while, but then I turned to the piano because I wanted to play pop music. My uncle Bill, who worked for my father when he returned from the West Coast, had been a barroom piano player and knew Joplin; he taught me how to play ragtime. Then I found sheet music for it, which I took to my piano teacher, and I learned how to play "Maple Leaf" pretty well, really.

CD: You had music too. Your father was in what business?

SS: He manufactured women's clothing.

CD: He probably wanted to steer you in some sort of business direction.

SS: He wanted me to go to business school and inherit his company, as it were. No one foresaw that there would be a Korean War or anything like the draft, and the world began to change.

CD: You were too young to fight in World War II.

SS: I was thirteen.

CD: So you were draft age by the Korean War, and that was also just when you were entering college at Yale, where you were also in the ROTC program.

SS: This was 1951; everyone was hot and bothered by the Korean conflict. If you weren't careful you might get drafted and go to Korea; we didn't want that. So I did it partly to please Dad and because there was a classmate of mine, Dave Adams, who was doing it too. So we joined. It was eight weeks, and you got a rating out of it for the summer before college. There was a naval air station at the airport; my summer turned out to be a boot camp. I was too young for it, I eventually realized. It was a little brutal. I was just not ready. I succeeded in it, but I saw some things that at seventeen I should probably not have had imprinted on my mind. Some of those were described in certain poems.

CD: Can you think of one poem in particular?

SS: Just a minute while I look. . . . So I went down to New Haven and was a freshman there. I joined the NROTC, thinking, in my ignorance, I could transfer 424 90 59, my serial number in Minneapolis, to Yale and the NROTC there. Golly gee whiz! The naval lieutenant in charge came over to me and shouted, "You're already in the navy!" And I answered that I was in such-and-such a program. And he said, "No. You're already in the navy and you applied to our NROTC, and we took you. But you can't be in two branches of one service at the same time, so you are in trouble." And so on. This bureaucratic snafu went on all through freshman year and finally, through string-pulling and whatnot, the captain, my father's friend, did this and that, and I was discharged from the NROTC program at the end of freshman year. This status problem persisted until I got out of graduate school. Meanwhile, I made some friends among those driven fellows, chosen officers-to-be but not in Korea, like Jerry Dole, later of Reader's Digest; or Pete Wilson, who became governor of California. And then hero's pledges: I realized I wanted out of NROTC anyway, not to sign all those moral promissory notes to glory, so to speak. It took a while. And then I got drafted.

CD: You got drafted after all that?

SS: Well, I sure did. September 12, 1955.

CD: Is there one poem here that you can read a little bit from? That would be great.

SS: This is the third part of my poem "Tyros," which recounts a boot camp scene from that time.

> In boot camp once they were
> marched to sick bay; seated
> in a scoured lobby to wait

for vaccine and a wanton
Yellow fever shot
should they be sent to Asia.
It was one more hurry-up-
and-wait line, ennui of mud
on boots drying to powder.
And strapped to a gurney there
in the hall, on center stage,
untrousered, a man lay, prone.
The very agenda of pain,
of power, grew manifest.
The doctor was to do
his spinal tap soon now

and obedient, they sat
receiving this bit of training
by means of visual—and soon
audible—aids as the doctor
held up the needle, long
as a dipstick, checking it
by the strip of fluorescent light
in the hall painted neutral grey.

Dispensing with anesthetic
he went to work and eased
the needle home. The gasps
of pain grew more, tormenting
the ammoniated air,
though in modesty the man
had turned his face to the wall
away from the boys' eyes,
bug-eyed recruits who followed
orders, waiting turns
to step up, as the Captain said,
step up, step up like a man.

That's from *Thanksgiving over the Water*, which came out in 1992, if I remember, so almost...

CD: Thirty, forty years after, so you're remembering this with impressive detail.

SS: That's something that you don't forget. I was at an impressionable age.

CD: You must have feared being deployed to Korea.

SS: Yes, that was the big thing that folks were trying to handle.

CD: Did you have a college deferment, or how did it work then?

SS: I didn't have a college deferment—I was very innocent then. I just got on the train and went down to New Haven with my footlocker; I got settled, and one thing led to another. I got a deferment later. You were allowed to miss only four reserve meetings; if you didn't go to meetings, they threatened you with being called to active duty. But for some reason I wasn't very worried about that, because, you know, when you're eighteen, anything can happen and you can deal with it.

CD: So all of this was going on, this military musical chairs, while you were in your freshman year and after, trying to adjust to Yale.

SS: Yeah, but the great wave of experience of going to college was wonderful, I just was eating it up, and I was very busy and hard at work. So I didn't worry about that too much. I loved the courses I was taking, except for naval courses, which were either silly or incomprehensible.

CD: Was your interest in China still there?

SS: I wanted to major in East Asian studies. I really wanted to until somebody, probably my professor Chitoshi Yanaga (I was taking a course in the history of the West Pacific rim) said that "in order to major in Asian studies, you have to pick a country, and if you want China, you must take two years of intensive Chinese, and that will largely eliminate taking anything else." I had gotten interested in English, I was writing poetry, and I had "gone out" for the *Yale Literary Magazine*, and so on. I decided that China would have to be postponed because time lacked. A normal load was four courses, and devoting two of them to one language would not be feasible.

CD: So you ended majoring in English, but you were studying Chinese on the side?

SS: No, I didn't have the time.

CD: Anyway, you clearly continued to enjoy Chinese poetry and Chinese culture.

SS: Yes.

CD: I'm just trying to figure out that abiding interest and association.

SS: Nobody ever has, so it must be that my grandmother, although she didn't have money, seems to have done well enough to give a little bit of help; she said I could get something in New York if it was in the hundred-dollar range. I found a Chinese painting, which in those days cost a hundred dollars even for a signed piece. When it arrived at Pierson College, mounted of course on its scroll, it was too long to hang in my room, which was too small for it anyway, since it was about the size of your dining table. So I returned it and traded it for a Veracruz head. Sad, since I loved that sixteenth-century scroll, a wise man in the snow, and it was worth something even then.

CD: So you started writing poetry more in earnest at Yale where you were a member of Manuscript, a literary secret society.

SS: I was a member of Manuscript senior year. A "secret" club. It ended up not being secret; they tried by example to break open and end secrecy in the secret societies. They invited faculty, women, made them honorary members, and they challenged the boring Masonic Victorian elitism of the nineteenth-century societies, so Manuscript isn't secret anymore.

CD: You really started writing seriously at Yale, more and more seriously, as you went through your years there.

SS: Yes I was trying to write serious poems, but I was doing what Keats called "making plans." No great poet ever wrote a more downbeat introduction to a poem than Keats to "Endymion," and it is very interesting. His mind shines through, but he says in effect, "this is horrible, why am I publishing it? But maybe I am still making plans." I guess that was happening to me—it's a wonderful phrase for it. To "die away, a sad thought for me, if I had not some hope that while it is dwindling, I may be plotting, and fitting myself for verses fit to live. This may be speaking too presumptuously, and may deserve a punishment: but no feeling man will be forward to inflict it."

CD: I've never made the connection here before. "Fitting myself for verses, fit to live" is almost the exact same phrase that Dickinson uses when writing to Higginson, "tell me if my verses live," remember? I wonder if she'd read that.

SS: I am not an Emily scholar, but yes, I guess someone of her sort would've read "Endymion" as a matter of course. Then there's this . . . he had another paragraph added here I think is so interesting: "The imagination of a boy is healthy, and the mature imagination of a man is healthy. But there is a space of life between, in which the soul is in a ferment—the character undecided, the way of life uncertain, the ambition thick-sighted. Thence proceeds mawkishness and all the thousand bitters, which those men I speak of must necessarily taste when going over the following pages."

CD: He thought there was too much juvenilia in "Endymion"?

SS: Perhaps; the point is, he feels just miserable. This happens at a time when his brother Tom's inherited tuberculosis has come to the fore. If it were not for Tom, we could think of Keats as expressing Romantic irony—that perilous pull between self-abasement and self-confidence.

CD: So he's about twenty-three or so when he wrote it.

SS: Yes, and Keats knowing that he's . . . got much to do and to face, he begins thus: "Knowing within myself the manner in which this poem has been produced, it is not without a feeling of regret that I make it public."

CD: Well, he's not feeling good about "Endymion."

SS: To put it mildly. Very "down," as we say. On the other hand, this response might be a good example of Romantic irony. You know, the first title of "Sleep and Poetry" was "Endymion." It's been so long since I've read a biography that I can't tell you; the first book in 1817 was badly received, but nothing like how badly "Endymion" was received. "Endymion" was 1818, then "Isabella" and "Saint Agnes" were published later.

CD: But back to that passage about "mawkishness" and that sort of nebulous period between childhood and adulthood. He quickly emerged from that around the age of nineteen or twenty. Do you relate to that period yourself?

SS: I think we all should.

CD: When you were at Yale or beforehand?

SS: I think there's a period of enterprise that every writer imagines or feels, which can never be fully finished. It's like giving love—you can't stop being there. I feel that, in terms of Keats's categories, I was pleased with the poems I wrote, and I hoped I could write that purely after college. The Academy of American Poets felt that way too because I got their Yale college prize in senior year. Same year as Sylvia Plath at Smith! Then I needed to build bigger and better foundations. About the time when I got to *Black Box*, which came after *The Thread: New and Selected Poems*, I felt a freedom or maturity or something like it just to write that collection.

CD: Which contains a tremendous amount of recollection and thinking about poetry and how you came to be writing poetry. But it was published in 1999, long after your time at Yale and Harvard.

SS: I've doubtless spent too much time in my life being a graduate student and then teaching and advising, or doing the kind of counseling you once did. But I can't apologize for that or deny it—I mean, that's what I did. I chose.

CD: You had to support yourself as well.

SS: Yes, there's always that. As Frost said, "That too, that too." Plans have to be made.

CD: You were also beginning to write seriously at a time when the literary culture in this country, especially in poetry circles, was pretty formal and academic, in the fifties. There was a lot of pressure then coming from critics to write within the tradition of received forms.

SS: No doubt. "Overseas Highway" (a poem I wrote on my own when an undergraduate) comes to mind; it owes a debt to Hart Crane but not to academics, a debt to a Midwest summer digging ditches—not to Yale. I read Crane on lunch breaks. "Overseas Highway" was a lyrical presentation in rhyme, beginning as pastoral. It relates an experience that occurred. It might have been a rhymed version of some experience in Lowell's *Life Studies* or the like, though it was composed a decade before that.

CD: You could read a little bit of it if you want.

SS: One section:

> Beside the nearly shadeless shadow
> Of a twig-laced Poinciana tree,
> On the cordial shore, their El Dorado,
> They wondered by a sun-white sea
>
> Of the ocean's multiplicity,
> What Pleistocene, unhurried day
> Cast the sea so carelessly
> Back from their shallow place of play.

Anointed, unmindfully they lay
Burning on the altar-golden shore,
Oblivious in their careful way
To the always silence and the sometime roar.

CD: Lowell had a big influence on you, but not until you were at Harvard, right?

SS: That's much, much later.

CD: Was "Overseas Highway" the poem that won the academy prize?

SS: I think it was. There was another poem as well. Then in Cambridge, I felt that I was moving on, and "New England Graveyard" was the first poem I published in—as they say—a "big" magazine, in this case *The Atlantic*.

CD: So *Stresses in the Peaceable Kingdom*, your first book, came out when you were still a graduate student at Harvard?

SS: Just after. That collection came out in the summer of 1967, when I was going to Japan, and everyone said, "Oh jeez, stay here so you can push the book!" And I said, "But I'm committed to going to Japan. I'm a Fulbright teacher there and I can't renege. It'll wait 'til I get back." I was invited to go that summer to Bread Loaf as a fellow too; I had to turn them down. Craig Wiley wrote me a very nice letter and said, "Sorry you have to give up this pleasant occasion for something important like that."

CD: That was a momentous year for you. You went to Japan, and you were nominated for the Pulitzer and National Book Award as well.

SS: Yes, and soon I met Virginia and had left Harvard. I hadn't thought about it, but moving away from North Bennington just last year reminded me of the departure from Harvard for Japan.

CD: And Harvard had become such a cultural home for you.

SS: Yes. Good old Jack Bate, he was chair of the department. When he offered me the job at Harvard, he said, "Now you know a lot about poetry, and you're a pretty good poet in our view, but don't ruin your career by staying at Harvard. You sure as hell won't be able to write poetry here." I took that to heart, perhaps too much, but in any case he said, "now I want to make clear you have this job, but it's not good for more than three years." He also said after my orals—we ended up walking into Harvard Yard—"Sandy, I understand they opened a good vein and you bled well!"

CD: When you were writing *Stresses in the Peaceable Kingdom* in the mid-sixties while you were still at Harvard, a momentous sea change was occurring aesthetically in American poetry as a kind of reaction formation to the rage of formal verse that followed the modernists. Allen Ginsberg published "Howl" in 1955; James Wright, *The Branch Will Not Break* in 1962; Galway Kinnell, his groundbreaking book *What a Kingdom It Was* in 1962; and Robert Bly, *Silence in the Snowy Fields* in 1962. Bly's magazines also, *The Fifties* and *The Sixties*, wielded strong iconoclastic influence on your generation, "letting the dogs in" as Bly liked to say at the time, by which he meant such poets as Pablo Neruda, García Lorca, César Vallejo, Antonio Machado, and Juan Ramón Jiménez, along with other European and South American modernists. Young female poets were also breaking onto to the scene. Anne Sexton published *Starry Night* in 1961—the year after she had taken the same workshop as you with Robert Lowell at Boston University—and then *To Bedlam and Part Way Back* in 1962. Sylvia Plath's *Ariel* came out posthumously in 1965. The tightly wrought, often exquisitely formal poetry of the fifties had been abandoned by a new fiercely subversive group of younger poets who had started out as formal poets but turned to free verse in a very American rebellious manner. Robert Lowell wrote in 1960, just before the publication of many of the books I mention above: "Poets of my generation and particularly younger ones have gotten terribly proficient at these forms. They write a very musical difficult poem with tremendous skill. . . . It's become a craft, purely a craft, and there must be some breakthrough back into live." So it was a heady, innovative time to say the least, but also one that must have been terribly confusing for those poets who had placed such high stock in formal poetry. What were you thinking specifically in the midst of all this aesthetic upheaval? You knew Sylvia Plath and Anne Sexton; you studied with Lowell at Harvard. You were trying to find your own voice and style as a young poet yourself with the strong tradition of formal verse pulling you one way and the exciting new wave of free verse poets pulling you another.

SS: I was trying to keep my nose to the grindstone, as it were. I'd just say, keep the blinders on your horse, because if you don't have blinders on your horse, he'll see all the stuff coming at him, you know? The optical term for the horse is a "prey animal"—that is, it's the prey of others, and its eyes are on the side, always checking things out, as opposed to an attack animal, which has its eyes in front so it can focus like the big cats. I couldn't think about what was going on everywhere. I held off for a while, probably until Lowell, looking at a suite of poems I was writing, set in Boston and Cambridge and each in one form or another, said, "where are you from, anyway?" in that peculiar voice of his. "I don't think you're from Boston." I said, "I grew up in Minnesota." He said, "Well, I think you should write me some poems about Minnesota then. Something you know about."

CD: You wrote "Hiawatha."

SS: In fact I'd been writing that before. But probably Cal's words and "Hiawatha" were contemporaneous, and I don't suppose I took Lowell's word for everything.

CD: Those are beautifully wrought poems in *Stresses in the Peaceable Kingdom*.

SS: Thank you! People these days want to shake and rattle.

CD: What did you think about a lot of the free verse that was being written in the sixties? You were not really doing that, but there were enormously accomplished poets who were, such as Lowell by that time and Wright and Plath?

SS: Oh, yes. I liked it very much. But it seemed defeating in a way. I thought of Lowell as relying to an extent upon his ornate family. I liked his poetry very much—beautifully written. I think about

"Skunk Hour" all the time because we have skunks. I was in MacLeish's seminar; he was a good influence on me—a pretty big one. I tried several times to truly talk with him, and I finally did. It was only when he said to me privately how other people in that class were not doing quite so well. One got a certain amount of momentum from the luster of being in Robert Lowell's class, but MacLeish's seminar was more altitudinous yet.

CD: Who else was in there with you?

SS: A novelist named Carter Wilson was in that seminar and had been in my freshman gen-ed A class, and that seemed rather weird, but then Jonathan Kozol was as well, and he was a respected critic, having just published *The Fume of Poppies*—a quotation from Keats by the way. I was going to leave Harvard because there was no avenue for my creative work. I had met Bill Alfred and saw him maybe once a week on Athens Street. He would go out to the kitchen to make us martinis and then come back and say, "I was gone so long you probably thought I was boiling a rhinoceros. Here you go!"

CD: I didn't know he had a brogue like that.

SS: Oh, he could put it on, and he did; after all he was Irish.

CD: He was in the theater department, wasn't he?

SS: He was a professor of English. They didn't have a theater department when I got there. He taught Old English. He was very much an Anglo-Saxon specialist. Later he moved over into the theater. I think he was supposed to be the heir to the elderly F. P. Magoun, but then he was drawn into the theater and they hired someone else. He said, "I think you should have a workshop to go to and some contacts. I'll arrange this with Cal, and you can go in and sit in on his course at BU." So that's where I went. It wasn't until I had come back from Japan that I would come up to go to Cal's class, when he was quite out of his box. . . . I can tell you stories about that . . . but those who were in that BU seminar with me included George Starbuck, Anne Sexton, Kathleen Spivack, and a couple of other people. I went fairly regularly, and if you have access to Peter Davison's book, *The Fading Smile: Poets in Boston, 1955–1960*, from Robert Frost to Robert Lowell to Sylvia Plath...

CD: That's a beautiful book. There's a passage in that book about Lowell sharing the first drafts of "For the Union Dead" with his workshop at BU. He quotes one of your eloquent journal entries on this class at length, which is worth requoting here:

It was long trip by subway and trolley; the distance seemed to evaporate the exhausted formalities of Harvard so that the ambience of Lowell's classroom—relaxed intensity—meant a refuge that was faintly exotic and very welcome. Casual discussions on class poems were buttressed by comparison with earlier poems, obscure or great, recalled by Lowell, smoking cigarettes at all times, gesturing above the poems he addressed. He singled out individual lines to dissect; to excoriate and often then, surprisingly, to praise—almost in the same breath. The tone of those hours was set, dominated by Lowell's soft, tentative voice with its educated Boston vowels skewed by the Southern drawl and punctuated by periods of thoughtful stillness. The only writers whose work I knew were Anne Sexton, a regular, and George Starbuck, a rare visitor because he worked at Houghton Mifflin.

It is midday, bright and warm, early May 1960. Today the class meets in a room facing the Charles; Cal sits in front of the high window, his hulking silhouette a dark outline against the blue sky beyond. He has been asked to read a poem at the Boston Arts Festival in June, and though he dislikes commission work and is diffident about what he has done, he has written a poem he would like to share with us, get our views on. It's about to go into *The Atlantic* and final changes must be made. He passes duplicated copies of a four page text around the seminar table; for an hour we make a few comments (mostly from Sexton on my left) but largely listen, rapt to hear Cal read and then talk about what he is trying to do in "Col. Shaw and the Massachusetts 54th." Several think the title too topical and specific, going along with Cal's worry as to its "footnoteishness." By fall the poem will be called "For the Union Dead."

SS: More of those final pages were quoted from me than the quotation marks show. But that was a big experience there, and we felt very honored. Lowell went off the deep end in 1959, but before he did it was not difficult to mine what there was worthwhile in what he had to say. The two remarks I remember that he made to me—the first, you recall, was, "You're not from Boston! Why are you writing these poems about Boston?" The other he made lying on a bed in Quincy House. Kathleen Spivack and I went over to see him. Cal knew that Kathy had recently had a miscarriage, so he started to talk about Alan Tate and how he had been involved with a quondam nun. They had twins, and one strangled—caught in the bedclothes trying to climb out of the crib. That was an unkind, not to say gross, thing to bring up. Then Cal said he was to going to Israel, and he would write poems about Israel for Kathleen. I had recently returned from Japan; he asked me, "where's your collection of poems about Japan?" I said, "Not done yet, Cal," and he said, "if you won't do it, I will—since I'm going to Japan after Israel." Which of course he never did. But he was urging me onward, and I didn't forget it: "If you won't write that book, I will." So he also was behind people he knew, trying to expand relationships.

CD: What kind of impression did Archibald MacLeish make on you?

SS: Archibald MacLeish didn't make such an impression on me because he, well, I think that he was rather depressed because in and of himself, he said, "I can't make the fire light." It's like going down to the farm and trying to start a fire with twigs and blowing on it and just not making it; it wouldn't go. He had already done *J.B.*, and it was pretty much the end of his poetical career, but otherwise those people were people who just happened to be in my way so to speak. I thought taking those people in order might make it, saying so-and-so impressed me very much and helped me go along, and then when it came to Bly we argued in letters for a long time and he shat all over me and I said, "well, if that's the way you want to be, okay."

CD: Because he . . .

SS: Well, he thought I needed to, I suppose, become much more of an obedient cohort to his feelings. I had sent some poems first to

The Fifties and then to *The Sixties* and he said, "this is not good." I had met him when he came to Harvard to give a reading. Bill Alfred introduced him and said he was a very unlikely Harvard person, but he was really great. There was this aura in Harvard Hall 1, which was filled with people, that he had prevailed upon—that would be the word, he had *prevailed* upon—Bill Alfred to get him a reading and introduce him and so on. I was ready to leave Harvard because I wasn't terribly impressed and I wanted to go to Iowa, where you went. I must have gone and seen Jack Bate, who was the chairman then. He was so nice and a great scholar and a very wonderful teacher, and he was from Minnesota of course. He said, "this isn't my business but I don't think that we want to lose you, so I think you should go and talk to Bill Alfred." That was how I met Bill Alfred, and he invited me down for a drink near Harvard Square, 31 Athens Street. I took some poems for him and he read them and he said, "These are pretty good. I'm too busy teaching Old English and all these other things, but why don't you go down to BU and join Cal Lowell's class? That's the best one in town." I said I would like to go but I'd never met him, couldn't even pick him out of a crowd if I didn't see his photograph in a book, and he said "don't worry about a thing, I'll arrange it," and so he did. And I went down there and that was his famous seminar and there were all these interesting people there and it was very interesting. And so then at some point, I'd given him poems I'd written that involved the subway, some pretty good poems, and he said, "you're not from Boston, you're not from around here, why are you writing these poems? I want you to write about what you came out of." He was in a harsh mood; he got very dictatorial. I finally realized that that was extremely good advice, at least for the time being, and that's where "Hiawatha" came from. I could point out the book that the poem's in. My first book that was written as a result of that meeting with him; it was coffee and cigarettes for an hour and that was basically it. I came up and visited that class—anyone was always welcome once they'd been there—when I was teaching at Brown and I had just gotten back from Japan. He had become very much more dictatorial and it was more of a performance and it was strange. In each case it strikes me that circumstances brought to me those people who were an influence, those poets I could work around to Allen Ginsberg and the Beat poets and so on. Mostly scissor and paste, I may be forgetting somebody but, you know, "well, if you want to do this you just have to go and see so-and-so." Bate and Alfred said, "you don't want to go to Iowa," and I sort of did because my family was all from Iowa and my parents weren't terribly well. I was just trying to go down that road and find out what I could do.

CD: When you say cut and paste and work yourself toward Ginsberg, you mean after meeting with Lowell and writing about your own roots in Minnesota, you felt you could incorporate Ginsberg's raw Whitman-like style and voice into your own work?

SS: Well, sure, but the thing was he came famously to Harvard and he was not allowed to give a Harvard-wide reading but he took over the Lowell Common Room and gave a reading there and then he stayed for two weeks along with Peter Orlovsky. They were staying just down the block from where my quarters were, cramped as they were, when I first went to Dunster House, and I could look out my window down that street. They were staying at Sidney Goldfarb's, if I remember correctly. I wrote some sonnets about that, one in particular where I met Allen up in Harvard Square, because that's where he went to talk to people all night long, and I talked everyone into going home. Ginsberg still seems to have been out in front of everyone. Ginsberg will always be an exception of sorts because he was driven, to begin with, by religious obsessions and his desire to explore the concomitantly human spirit and psyche. I speak of a vast tide of poetry being published.

CD: So Ginsberg came to Harvard after writing "Howl" and if I remember correctly, Lowell in the very early sixties once commented that he wished he could write like Ginsberg.

SS: I never heard that, but I bet he said it. Ginsberg was pouring out all these poems and he was one of those people who didn't see any barrier between his psyche and yours or anybody else's. If he had ever met Lowell—I'm sure he had but not for an extended period—I don't know, Lowell might have been too huffy. Allen was just like somebody you have known for a long time, and he always made things sound so simple. But I was referring to his having seemed out of his window at Columbia and his religious quest. Because he was still wearing his neckties and suits and he was trying to bring those two sides of himself together. But that was a formative moment for me because I had sort of poo-pooed Ginsberg for a long time, but then he seemed like a shining light after you spent three hours with him talking about this and that. And another time when I had been to MOMA and was just walking down Fifty-Third Street, I heard this voice from a great distance shouting "Stephen! Stephen!" and I thought, I wonder who that is, you know, who that Stephen is, because nobody knows me down here. Finally it got closer and closer and I turned around and it was Allen Ginsberg, breathless, and he said, "I saw you back there, cup of coffee, come on."

CD: Can you describe the ambivalence you felt toward Ginsberg's work?

SS: I wanted to be able to write so much with such apparent ease, and join the crowd, but then I could not.

CD: Have your feelings changed over the years?

SS: Well, coming up to the present, Bill Morgan just gave a talk at Chapel Hill on "Kaddish" and when we were talking about that before he left, I said I thought that "Kaddish" was his best poem, his strongest poem. It is an elegy, and it does the things an elegy is supposed to do, and Bill said, "I guess I agree with you; thank you for saying that because that's something I can get at. They asked me to talk about this, his mother, who had mental problems and died alone in a mental hospital."

CD: Yes, Naomi.

SS: Naomi. Thus he had an occasion built in for writing "Kaddish." That's one thing that I could not do because my mother was jumping up and down, saying, "Where I come from people don't say 'either' they say 'either.'" So what I think has happened for me, at long last, is that I've become willing to write out of the person that I am.

CD: I think you must have first realized that when you were at Harvard and in Lowell's workshop at BU after meeting Ginsberg, namely, that you couldn't write like Ginsberg as much as you enjoyed the ease and frankness with which he wrote about political and social subjects. But you've experimented with many different forms.

SS: And writers. But I don't think it was at Harvard; I didn't really know what I was doing at Harvard other than the technical business of graduate school. I think that that's when it sort of came to me, who I was, when I got married, you find out who you are and some of it is just giving up things. Another circumstance that I thought about, running through these things, was when I was in Japan at a poetry conference. I had read *Riprap*, which was basically all Gary Snyder had published. I read through that many times and I admired it, and "Mid-August at Sourdough Mountain Lookout" for years was a poem that I had always taught in this way or that way because it does so many things so simply and it was such an accomplishment. I was a little late getting there off the train, and there were maybe a hundred people there, and I found a seat and I sat down and I realized I was sitting right behind Gary. He had already done his talk and he had this big notebook and I could see, without really being nosy, because he was small and those chairs so crammed together, and he kept writing the word *humility*. "Remember humility." And that was not unimpressive. And then everybody stopped for dinner. I didn't know you had to have a ticket for supper and so there was nothing for me to eat, and Snyder gave me his dinner and he said, "I can't eat this." It was chicken or something like that, I don't know; it was a pretty good meal from a Western point of view. He was being Zen. We had talked and he was going to talk again and he didn't want to eat.

CD: When was it that Jack Bate advised you to leave Harvard?

SS: That had happened when he was still chair in 1963, and he had offered me the job and said, "Don't get any big ideas! You're a pretty good poet, I hear. But you can't stay at Harvard, and I wouldn't recommend it."

CD: Who were you reading mostly then?

SS: I was reading the Romantics. I took the courses you had to take, one in each period.

CD: You've maintained an elegant formal voice over the years that's also become increasingly plainspoken, like Wordsworth in *Lyrical Ballads*, only in contemporary American English. Have you gone back to him again and again throughout your career as a lifelong influence?

SS: A great poet is a foundation for building any house of writing; for me, it's writing poetry. I'll be anecdotal again and say that just as I was leaving Yale, I met a junior named Mark Reed; he was working for Frederick Pottle, the Boswell scholar, and had been given the task of doing a chronology on three-by-five cards of everything that was known of Wordsworth's life. Then he ended up at Harvard in graduate school; actually, he got there first since I was in the army. Reed once opined that Wordsworth was the greatest poet of the nineteenth century in any language. And I said to myself, "now there's taking a stand!" Thus I began to study him and other Romantic writers.

It was a journey, and I know teachers at Harvard were perhaps stuffy compared to those performers at Yale. I took Romantic poets first, with Douglas Bush; he was tired and about to retire. But then there was Jack Bate and all these other men who at length one discovered. It was an influence on me to identify with Wordsworth. I was more than deeply impressed by "The Prelude." I had not warmed to the *Lyrical Ballads*, but the more autobiographical Wordsworthian texts I studied the more I understood that he was questing quietly for some kind of salvation, some way of living in the world, while exploring larger and finding—confirming—ultimate larger truths. I found this Romantic framework very moving and almost, I might say, familiar. Of course, later on in one's career, there you are—teaching and ending up at a college where you can (eventually) choose anything you want to teach. You're not limited to Milton, for example. For some people, all they ever do is to teach a specialty. So among other subjects I tackled, such as Asian culture and Homer, were the Romantic poets. I probably learned much more eventually about Keats, Wordsworth, Shelley, and Coleridge by teaching them than I knew from a student's glimpse. As they say, "if you want to learn about something, teach it."

CD: But there's a big difference between being impressed by a poet and reading him for literary reasons, which is particularly pertinent in relation to Wordsworth and his peripatetic poetry. You reprise many of Wordsworth's themes and strategies in your work, particularly the strategy of encountering anonymous wise men in your local environs, like Wordsworth's leech gatherer in "Resolution and Independence" and Coleridge's ancient mariner, and recording not only their stories, but their wisdom as well.

SS: When am I doing that?

CD: There are many examples in your work of such encounters—for example, the beggar in your poem "The Tack," Stephen Fels in your poem "Around Our Table," Robert Frost—not so anonymous—in "Place and Fame," the beachcomber in "Beachcomber," the man in "Man in the Open Air," Myron in "The White Oak of Eagle Bridge," and Malcolm Cowley in "Survivor Walking," to mention only a few.

SS: Good grief!

CD: I find it wonderful and telling that you didn't take a more confessional route as many of your peers did, choosing to adhere so strongly to the more Romantic notion, which doesn't obviate the self but, in a very English way, concentrates on public subject matter, the other rather than the self, for enlightenment.

SS: When I first met Anne Sexton—what a beauty!—she was pretty wild in her manner, as well as extremely gifted. My response to this combination of traits was not to be articulated back then. Her work was not well directed nor her figures always adequate. And why not go around and talk to people in the fields, though I can't think of a poem in which that takes place. There must be some permission, some "why not?," a device to speak through someone else. You could say that probably the most Wordsworthian of the poems is "The Tack," written long after all of this back in Cambridge, but that poem has Coleridge and certain points of reference in the outer world that give the voice of the poet a presentation of inner thoughts, awarenesses, and what has been discovered.

CD: And contemporary influences at the time?

SS: I suppose the fact that John Berryman had taught my brother and was living about six blocks from us in Minneapolis meant that I was enthralled by his wonderful "Henry" poems, but I realized that I couldn't do that. I was just trying to keep eyes peeled, but I didn't have anyone that I particularly wanted to be or copy. There was Starbuck's *Bone Thoughts* and Anne Sexton's *To Bedlam and Part Way Back*.

CD: In addition to Sexton you also meet Peter Davison in Lowell's workshop.

SS: Yes, a fine poet who I think also influenced me. I'd send him poems and he'd say, "Not this! But that!"

CD: Was he the poetry editor of *The Atlantic* then?

SS: Yes, and he was a very good editor, but I quarreled with his judgment. I think a lot of it was who was in in the academic situation; by now we have three hundred MFA programs. I thought a lot about becoming a poet who was a legitimate poet—I don't know fully what I mean by that—not a bastard poet. Poetical legitimacy meant you needed to find a path for yourself and continue on it. There are always going to be these kinds of influences, to which you must say, "no, that's not for me; I'm doing this." Russell Banks said that you have to understand the difference between your work and your career. Your work is what you are working on, and it's right before you; your career—you can't determine your career. You completely control your own work, but you can't control your career—for example, who ends up hiring you or who reviews your book. What you're not in control of includes, also, the fact that when you are in school, it just so happens that Archibald MacLeish is teaching there or Cal Lowell is sitting around in Boston trying to figure out where he's going.

CD: In addition to writing your own poetry and attending Lowell's famous workshop, you were also writing your dissertation on the eighteenth-century novel at the same time.

SS: Yes. Sterne, Fielding; then Scott, Austen, Radcliffe, *The Castle of Otranto,* and so on. I got my PhD in 1963, which is when I started to teach. Then I left in 1967; originally I was going on a Fulbright to Egypt; they had an apartment for me near the University of Alexandria, and a maid had been engaged. Then a telegram came from a Mrs. Hatch at the State Department, saying "Suggest you resume your position." The Six-Day War was raging in 1967. So I called and said, "I've rented my house, stopped teaching; I'm all packed—what do you suggest?" She said, "We'll look around for you." I ended up in Japan.

CD: There were several poets just ahead of you who were breaking new ground—poets like Galway Kinnell, Allen Ginsberg, Robert Bly, James Wright, John Ashbery, Ruth Stone, James Merrill, Donald Hall, Howard Nemerov, whom you replaced at Bennington in 1969— all of whom were about ten years older than you.

SS: I think of them as being a generation ahead of me.

CD: Even though they were only ten years older?

SS: Ten years might be a long time!

CD: Did you converse with them? Did you read their work?

SS: I loved Galway's work but didn't meet him for years—not until I got to Vermont—because he was somewhere else. I met him at a gathering at Goddard College. Now Howard Nemerov—he was at Washington University in Saint Louis. We met at Harvard in a state of mutual inebriation; inadvertently I said I was a better poet than he, which dumbfounded us both. I was sorry about that. He smiled; I apologized.

CD: You must have been impressed with his exquisite formal work, not to mention his wit.

SS: Indeed. He wrote a book I liked greatly called *The Salt Garden,* which was dedicated to one S.M.S. I didn't know who that was, but those are my initials, so I could fantasize that S.M.S stood for me.

CD: You have really followed a unique path in the latter part of the twentieth century, as far as your contemporaries and other poets are concerned. You taught at Harvard, went to Japan, spent your career teaching at Bennington, and maintained an accomplished and stunning formality in your work while also writing innovative free verse.

SS: Thank you!

CD: I'm curious to know what influence Japan had on you specifically in 1967. How did that Asian lens on the Northeast and the United States in general provide a unique distance from your own isolation? I'm borrowing Philip Larkin's line here from his poem "Talking in Bed."

SS: Well, I just kept on going. I began to write as soon as I got to Japan, and most of it was in journal form because it was all so strange. It was clearly a deeply different culture, and I was making all sorts of judgments. A friend from Minneapolis who was there, a linguistic genius, Bob Cote, picked up the various Japanese modes of address, class dialects and all. I would tell Cote what this or that meant and how impressed I was. He looked at me studiously and replied, "You should write down all these things because you know more now about Japan than you ever will again."

CD: Why?

SS: Cote was modestly putting me in my place with that. But still everything was contradicted. If you think this, just wait, and it will be that.

CD: Returning to your attitude toward formal verse in the early sixties, I'm curious about why you'd not want to continue writing in form exclusively if you were so accomplished at it, as well as successful, receiving academy prizes and publishing in reputable journals. I could quote from many poems, but here is just one example of your fluid, plainspeaking style in blank verse from the opening of "New England Graveyard":

> Back of the church the busy forsythias bow
> And scrape to May and all these blessed stones
> Stiff in their careful finery of words;
> The mess of markers makes me go and browse.

SS: Well, I never assumed that I was that good at it, and one of the only avenues that I had to go down to get to the judgment bureau was quarterlies and magazines. I think that the tide had really shifted to a more popular and less demanding sense of what a line was, what a whole poem was, and so on. What it then comes to is what is the theme and what is the occasion of the poem? I think poetry is a very serious thing; it is a serious art form, maybe the most serious, because it uses words. As Eliot said, "I have to use words when I talk to you," and that's what we have forgotten. We can't talk to each other without using words that mean important things, and I thought that poetry had to be considered as a vessel for the continuing understanding of the important terms of our existence and of our hopes and our loves. I think that with the free verse that began to take over, along with Allen Ginsberg and others in the mid-sixties . . .

CD: And also mid- to late fifties. "Howl" was published in 1956.

SS: Well, Ginsberg would always be a kind of exception because he was driven in the first instance by religion, or religious questions anyway, and his desire to explore the spirit and the psyche and so on. I had, not to speak of Allen but of the vast wash of poetry being published, a sort of a love-hate relationship because you wanted to be able to do that and join the crowd, but then you couldn't. So what I think has happened at long last, and with much water under the bridge, is that you have to be willing to do what you are able to feel comfortable with, that is to say, what is true to yourself.

CD: Every poet goes a little bananas, don't you think?

SS: Oh, yes. I've been bananas frequently.

CD: When did you go bananas?

SS: The first time I ever saw Bly was at Harvard when I was a graduate student and in Harvard Hall 1, and he was giving a reading and the room was just packed, and Bill Alfred introduced him and said that he had been one of his favorite students long ago and that it was so hard to think of him having gone to Harvard. He was wearing one of his get-ups, you know, very colorful South American things, and it was very interesting, but I wondered, "What was going on here?" I remember that clearly.

CD: This was after he'd published *Silence of the Snowy Fields*?

SS: Yeah. I was always convinced that he had prevailed upon Bill Alfred to get him a gig at Harvard. He did go to Harvard, that's right, and it's sort of in the same way that Robert Creeley went to Harvard, and he only had sight in one eye, and he gets up and . . . I don't know . . . He was a kid from Arlington, Massachusetts, and it was very hard to get adjusted to the grandeur and pretensions of Harvard. I felt that way myself.

CD: Yeah, you must've.

SS: And Bly, goodness, yes.

CD: Both you and Bly are from Minnesota, and James Wright was also from the Midwest and Martins Ferry, Ohio, but lived and worked in Minneapolis as well in the early and mid-sixties, and of course, John Berryman, who was at the University of Minnesota from the mid-fifties until his death in 1972. But perhaps Alan Grossman, who lived just down the street from you in Minneapolis, was your most influential local influence.

SS: Yeah. We went to the same school. There was a little touch point there because he loved old books. He refused that school ethic of *ra, ra, ra, ra!* Just refused it and went off to Harvard then.

CD: If I could step back a minute at this point from your biography and view the body of your work. There's a fascinating progression in your work that moves from themes of topoi or commonplaces in your first two books to a sharper focus on others—your children, neighbors, your father, proprietors, et cetera—in an objective way that resists the popular confessional impulse of your generation.

SS: Oh, really? I'd like to hear it.

CD: In the first couple of books, *Stresses in the Peaceable Kingdom* and *Roofs*, you write a lot about places, such as "Hiawatha" and "New England Graveyard." Also "Duck," "Dissolve," and "Declension," where you are often, it seems, dealing with subjects outside yourself. Again, you're not being confessional in the least in these books and poems—and you often struggle with the idea of yourself, or the self, in poems such as "Some Flowers," where you declare "we plunge ahead, as the light / Changes, against ourselves."

SS: There's a spiritual traffic sign.

CD: In your poem "Intersections," you write, "We do not belong to ourselves." And "Et Quid Amabo," the full title being "Et Quid Amabo Nisi Quod Aenigma Est," which is from Giorgio de Chirico, meaning "But what will I love if not the enigma?"

SS: Meaning the face.

CD: So on the whole I think there's this wonderful notion of the enigma and the face being one. There's a fascinating struggle with the self in a lot of those early poems. The places, as I mentioned earlier, the lyric—but not lyricized experience only, just almost the pure lyric in poems such as "Dissolve" or "Wild Ducks." Then with *Thanksgiving over the Water*, you really start placing others before you. You do a little bit in some of the early poems, like "Her River," which is a fascinating poem, but again that's . . .

SS: Lowell loved that.

CD: It is mesmerizing—like a dazed lover talking to himself in shock about what's happened, with that wonderful double refrain—"people are so careless with each other / It takes so long I don't know what it means"—that repeats with slight variation in every stanza. But beginning with *Thanksgiving over the Water*, suddenly there are elegies, there are poems about children, there are poems about little animals—the poem about the mole funeral or "Her Yard" with your daughter playing by herself in the backyard. There are beautiful elegies also in your fourth book *Riding to Greylock*. I'm thinking in particular of "Command Performance" and "Station 41" about your father, "Bridge of Abandonment" about Anne Sexton, and "The Second Law" about an AIDS victim.

SS: I'm very happy and rewarded that you can say those things.

CD: These are midcareer poems.

SS: Yeah, and Harry Ford, my editor at Knopf then, called up and said, "Okay, what's your title, Stephen? I'm going to do this book Monday." He designed all those books and then sent them down the funnel at Knopf, and I didn't have a title for that collection, and I finally took that piece of the liturgy—it's from baptism—and you make me think that it is appropriate after all.

CD: *Thanksgiving over the Water.*

SS: Yes. I do like that, but I don't think anyone else did.

CD: You once mentioned humorously that someone thought the book was about a man with "prostrate difficulties." But no, there are so many other poems: "Earth Day Story," "The Tack" is the best example. Let's see, "Charlie" and . . . there are just too many to mention here, but suddenly you're incorporating voices of others in the poems, and of course your poem "Nativity" about Clare's birth. William Blake once said that "there is no more sublime act than to place another before you." You follow this strategy repeatedly in your last four books, *Overlook, Weathers Permitting, Surface Impressions*, and *Black Box*, which you once mentioned to me was your favorite.

SS: Yeah, it's a favorite, although probably the thing that was most important for me to write was *Surface Impressions*, which also had a title problem.

CD: Your ambition has increased with each new book. In the book-length poem, *Surface Impressions*, as well as in many of the poems in *Black Box*, and others also, such as "Allegheny," "Station 41," and "Nativity," which you wrote in the eighties, you take on larger and larger themes in long poems that grapple with such subjects as apocalypse, birth, environmental disaster, and death.

SS: Someone said, "There are many poems that it is important to write, and fewer poems that it is important to have written." There's a third part to that: "and there are fewer still that it is important for others to read," meaning that if you've written a poem, it is there for other people to read.

CD: Could you just talk a little about your book *Surface Impressions*, which marks a bold departure from your previous books?

SS: It is a poem in eight parts, in which I just let myself go and wrote what came into my mind, because I had a deep feeling that I had to say something and I didn't know what it was.

CD: You found out?

SS: And I found out.

CD: What was it?

SS: I wanted to be able to write a poem in which everything was somehow embraced, and came out with . . . Well, I think that the beginning and the end sort of say it. Buzby was the name of my next door neighbor's dog. They're taking down the cross from the church and it's in pieces in the garden. That's sort of what happened to Christianity. The beginning goes back to childhood, when they put you out in order to remove your tonsils, and you blew up this great big balloon that had laughing gas or some kind of thing that left you completely out of touch with the world or in a new world in which you're trying to understand what is going on. Then our daughter wanted to go, and she joined the Peace Corps and was eventually sent to Madagascar, so I wanted to include that as a limit. Imagine being in Madagascar because we were trying very hard to keep up with this person, our daughter, who was at the opposite end of the globe, literally, and in this fascinating place with all these species that didn't exist anywhere else in the world. Something like a third of the species alive in the world are native to Madagascar. I just put myself in the place of her being there. So that's the kind of thing that makes me think of Defoe, or someone like that, just taking a journey and experiencing as much as you can of what it is. There are a lot of little hints, or little images, dropped through it, sort of religious items like triptych, and so on. Then there's this scene in the Native American bar in downtown Minneapolis, which is not a nice place to go, but the Chippewas are notoriously subject to alcoholism and everyone was drunk all the time there, and I went down there, and who should I find but Alan Grossman! I was trying to decide whether it was this way or that way, and [inaudible] a sort of life as I had known it so far, without getting into the military. It also tries to gather together a lot of the concrete images of a life like cufflinks.

CD: So it's really kind of a memoir of sorts?

SS: Well that's a very misused term these days, isn't it? Everything is a memoir! "I want to write a memoir because I can't get my novel to work!"

CD: Well, so you'd been waiting to write that book for a long time. You didn't know this, it seems, but had been working toward writing a book-length poem, especially after your children left home. I think you had also just retired or were about to retire when you started to work on it.

SS: I didn't retire until 2004, and this was published in 2002.

CD: After your children left home and you stopped writing poems about them and pastoral subjects—I'm thinking about such poems from the late seventies, eighties, and nineties as "Some Flowers,"

"Egyptian Onions," "Ray's Garden Shop," and "Condensation"—you begin using the third person pronoun much more in your books *Black Box* and *Weathers Permitting, Surface Impressions,* and *Overlook.* I'm curious if you made a conscious decision to avoid using the first person singular in those poems and for personal or strategic reasons started using second and third person pronouns.

SS: I don't know about that, but I do know that I was conscious of having too much natural history in my poems, and finding a flower or weed or animal...

CD: A lot of pastoral imagery. Also a lot of macadam in such poems as "After a City Shower," "Letter from Stony Creek," "Condensation," "Northway Tanka," "Around Our Table," "Thanksgiving over the Water"...

SS: Oh, God.

CD: These all have images of shining roads in them.

SS: Well, a shining road is different than a shining path. But yes, trying to get on with it and all at that point. I had a feeling that I had written too much about nature, and "Little flower, I pluck thee out of the cranny," as Tennyson would say.

CD: But again you have to write about what you have to write about.

SS: But there was an effort to get more human drama into the other poems, and I guess *Surface Impressions* is partly what that's using as a way of getting at that.

CD: But you also had many poems like "Ray's Garden Shop" where you just confront another and listen to him. I have to say that this isn't so present in a lot of your earlier work; it's as if you discovered gold in a strategy of encountering others in the poems in *Thanksgiving over the Water* where you begin, really for the first time in any consistent way, to place others before you, prompting you to incorporate colloquial speech into your poems, whether it's Ray in his garden shop or the beggar in "The Tack" or Myron in "The White Oak at Eagle Bridge"—your neighbors, in many cases. These recounted encounters influenced your style in a way that increased your verbal velocity—made your lines more spoken but still poetic without sacrificing the elegance in your voice. I was wondering if you were aware of this turn that occurred in your work in the eighties and early nineties.

SS: Not in any memorable way, but that's very good of you to point this out. The encounters perhaps give too much gilding to my humble blooms. Of course, I was aware that you can't really adopt others' speech habits unless you want to pretend to be Robert Frost, a whole other kettle of pretense. Centrally, I wanted to get away from iambic pentameter.

CD: But you never really do.

SS: Well, look at "Ray's Garden Shop," which consists of twenty-eight syllabically correct haiku.

CD: I stand corrected, but there is still an iambic stress there.

SS: But isn't the English language iambic? There's only two meters: strict iambic and loose. Didn't Frost say that?

CD: Your early poem "Hiawatha" is the only example I can think of where you follow the Finnish poet Elias Lönnrot's use of trochaic tetrameter in the Kalevala, as Longfellow also did in his "The Song of Hiawatha." But you're right, your lines are mostly iambic.

SS: It comes from long and, I suppose, careful readings and stuffing oneself with the five-beat line, the basic line in English. Of course, if you look over what is happening—out in the world—at this moment, you'll have no sense of that rigor, because they haven't read the work of great writers, it's not in the mind's ear for them. They don't have a sense of tradition, and I have found it hard to make a connection with poets not shadowing forth any tradition, or the tradition, whichever.

CD: Could you elaborate a bit on this connection?

SS: There are two major traditions in the language, whether it's

Chaucer, Shakespeare, Milton, Pope, Wordsworth, Tennyson, Frost, and so on. Many poets when I was, shall I say, maturing, were writing without a tradition or just pouring out feelings and reactions or they're consciously fighting against any familiar manner of exposition or response. A lot of poetry being written today in America is in some ways sitting back with Marianne Moore and Louis Zukofsky and such, who are making a specific attempt not to write in a given meter. I have started to read again the *Aeneid* as translated by William Morris. He was doing it in six-beat lines and fourteeners and rhyming it, fecklessly changing back and forth whenever he felt like it, well, not carelessly, but carefreely moving back and forth. In the long run, that doesn't seem to work in contemporary English. You can't make up a work of any length in six-foot or seven-foot or longer lines. And Morris is a good poet. I guess in some sense, if you have an ear, which some contemporary poets lack, at least in this country, the ear is trained or has grown into a certain ability—or shape or conception—of how the language is heard. Then it just stays dormant. It is annoying when you read poets who are trying to do something with English that they don't really know how to do. I was just thinking, though, of Whitman and later Jeffers, and what those wonderful, great poets have is a style of voice, which we're all told to find when we go to one of our populace of poetry degree programs. Whitman or Jeffers, who just come to mind, have a floor or base in the standard meter. They wrote in it just to show that they could, and then they moved onward . . . like Emily Dickinson.

CD: But meter and form . . . the echo of it is still very strong?

SS: The echo of it is there, although the rest may not be.

CD: It seems to me that you make a very strong argument for that connection to the legacy of poetry and present work, including you own in your poem "Thatch," where you conclude:

> When men stopped watching them—began to live
> In the high wattage of what they were doing.
> Once everyone knew thatch, like dark, like fire,

Presences under foot, or overhead
And fossil, to be killed, like dust. Now he knows it:
Strong as wire, tender almost, a life
Surprised, because it was there all the time
Shy, smiling, asking with its dead lights.

So, if "Thatch" is a metaphor, in a way, for form, it seems that form suffers the contumely of contemporary critics over and over again but somehow holds up throughout the ages.

SS: Well, very good, sir! "Thatch" is a metaphor there, yes.

CD: But an extended metaphor.

SS: "Thatch" gets to be very thick and smelly and not waterproof either.

CD: Right.

SS: I can't remember if it was in England or Japan where they use thatch too, and they change it rigorously every eighteen years.

CD: I just thought that maybe you were writing almost unconsciously about form . . . which may be the best way to write about something you're feeling so strongly about all along.

SS: Only if you knew the years I spent trying to get out of that. It suddenly makes me think of a person who spent his life in the military, and it's very hard finally to quit it.

CD: It's interesting that you say that because you've really seem to have had a lovers' quarrel with form. I think every healthy poet should have a lovers' quarrel with how or what he or she is writing. But you always seem to come back to writing what you have to, and what you're hearing is your breath, it's who you are, and it's your initial influences and how they encouraged you to write, from Wordsworth on.

SS: We had better write, in the long run, from what we must write.

That's a point very well taken. Nothing shows up more quickly than writing without purpose, without inspiration.

CD: I think you've tried that, and everyone tries that, and you have to. I mean, it can be very healthy at times. But in rereading all of your books...

SS: What a task!

CD: No, it's been a great pleasure. I hear you coming back not so much to a line that you can't escape, but a way of hearing, which is a better way of putting it.

SS: Yes. When I am writing, one does hear it, and then one writes it down. It's reasonably ineffable—I don't see how to explain it without taking hundreds of words, and even then that wouldn't do it. But you have a sense of being, as it were, "in the groove," or that you must take this down because a voice is speaking, though you don't want to say that that actually happens, and you feel inspired to write something down. It doesn't matter if you don't know what it means—it just does.

CD: I was wondering, at the beginning of your career, if you didn't have some strong reaction to those, say, like James Wright or Robert Bly, who were making such fun in their magazine, *The Fifties* and *The Sixties*—of people who were writing academic poetry, some strong reaction that was at odds with what they themselves were doing. They were obviously trying to introduce a lot of European and South American modernists into American poetry. Wright broke away from form in 1961–1962 with his book *The Branch Will Not Break*, and you have a wonderful, it seems to me, parody of what he's doing in your poem "Tom and Henry, Camping Out," when you write: "We knew if we could step out / Of our bodies they would fill up with those garnets," which mimics these lines from Wright's poem "A Blessing": "Suddenly I realize / That if I stepped out of my body I would break / Into blossom."

SS: Really, I never considered that. When I was in college after sophomore year, I got a job in Minneapolis with the gas company digging down to the gas mains and sealing where they leaked at their joints. I spent every lunch hour reading Hart Crane. The other workers were friendly but not, at the end of the day, "compatible," as one might say.

CD: Would you say you took to him with the same ferocity as you took to Wordsworth?

SS: Was I ferocious with Wordsworth? But Crane is different. There's a sort of fustian quality and lots of excitement about big words and *music*, music, music in his poetry that is just absolutely splendid.

CD: But you must have felt that you could write enough like him to try.

SS: You can always try to equal but really can only try. If you use Beethoven for inspiration it doesn't mean that you're going to write like him.

CD: Phil Levine has a wonderful story about trying to write like Dylan Thomas at the beginning of his career and failing, but in his failure also realizing that his natural style was much plainer and more narrative. He claims that Hart Crane and Dylan Thomas are the two most gifted musical poets of the twentieth century.

SS: Not Stevens?

CD: He didn't mention Stevens, but I think he could have.

SS: I loved Dylan Thomas and liked Stevens a lot, but of course he—we shared a name—died on my birthday in 1955. I fantasized, well, his spirit entered me. Bullshit!

CD: Yes, Stevens, Crane, and Thomas were really the three, and I'm not being terribly deliberate about this, but I think the influence is obvious here. Here's a stanza of Crane's from "O Carib Isle!":

> The tarantula rattling at the lily's foot
> cross the feet of the dead, laid in white sand
> Near the coral beach—nor zigzag fiddle crabs

Side-stilting from the path (that shift, subvert
And anagrammatize your name)—No, nothing here
Below the palsy that one eucalyptus lifts
In wrinkled shadows—mourns.

And here's a stanza of yours from "Oyster Cove":

The macadam is flaking and the lilac
Too big to bloom
Fingers a cobweb of smoky light from the terrace,
Grazes the sun-chalked cedar shakes. And no surprise.

Gone the lady, to Athens or Anjou. Her sunroom
Oozes silence. The paisley over the back
Of a wicker rocker. The pedals of her grand hover
Above the calm sea of the tiled floor

There's a very similar elegance and exoticism there.

SS: Well, okay, but I wasn't thinking of that, it was perhaps from the ear's subconscious. The "crashed glass" and then there's "wicker rocker"—onomatopoeia. I feel that this poem is well written and does what it tries to do, but at last, it's showing off a bit. I remember feeling that way and that it was written to offer an explanation to those who kept wanting to know what a pergola was and a gazing globe.

CD: Was it the pergola in this one?

SS: Yes, and I actually thought that that poem was trying to explain the feeling of pergolas, and then more folks at that time were asking what a "gazing globe" was.

CD: I think the danger of trying to emulate Crane or Thomas is showing off. You get seduced by language in a way where "sometimes the violin knows it's a violin," as Lorca said.

SS: I would agree, yes. But with Crane it isn't showing off so much— he's doing what he can do . . .

CD: Just so easily.

SS: Doubtless through his horrible hangover, he's trying to make everything fit together in some way.

CD: Yes, with such extraordinary music in his language. Unequaled really.

SS: Unequaled . . . yes, it's beautiful. I taught a class with Alvin Feinman and he got quite fierce in defending the utter greatness of "The Broken Tower." Alvin after all was the one who suggested Crane's phrase "the visionary company of love" to Harold Bloom as the title for his key critical study of Romantic poetry.

CD: If we could go back to some of the early poems and the decision you made in the late fifties and early sixties essentially to remain a formal poet. You have obviously felt the pressure throughout your career to write in free verse, as many of your peers have, while at the same time understanding the importance of remaining connected to the legacy of poetry and traditional English poetry.

SS: Well said.

CD: I know that throughout your career you have been very enamored of John Ashbery, who hasn't written very formally, though he did write several beautiful poems in received forms early on in his career before he started writing exclusively in the fluid, insouciant style of free verse for which he has become so famous.

SS: My Ashbery indoctrination began about 1971. He was brought up to Bennington by Georges Guy to interview for a job and I had to introduce him, hence to read him, and to get a discussion going with the students. That was where it started but not before that. Of course that was back pretty much at the beginning of his career. Now, in some degree the "new imagination" of Robert Bly was Spanish in origin, and that makes me think that the reason Spanish became so popular, not only in the Southwest where it had a right to be, but it was a language that you could excel in, if you had to take a language; Spanish was relatively easy. So Spanish spread rapidly, and now of course there are Hispanics living everywhere. Thus it was not so difficult to write poems out of one's experience of the South American poets, the Latin American poets.

CD: Neruda was probably the most popular.

SS: Yes, Neruda and Paz in particular but others as well, and it was an opening of a door where your work could be open to all. So there's a difference there between what's going on in the tradition of the English language and what's going on in the tradition of the Spanish language—and the Spanish language of Latin America had been, if I'm not mistaken, somewhat simplified and lyricized by not being part of the peninsular Spanish tradition of tightly written formal poetry. I can't elaborate on it further because Spanish is not my tongue. That may have something to do with it. Robert Bly has Spanish, and I assume Wright did.

CD: Wright had more German.

SS: Of course, German—that's how Franz Wright got his name. But then Wright was living at Robert Bly's.

CD: They lived together on Bly's farm near Bly's friend William Duffy in Pine Island, Minnesota. But it's interesting because if you think about Wright and Bly, Wright could write in form magnificently, as we see in *The Green Wall* and *Saint Judas*, those first two books of his that came out in the fifties, and he writes circles around almost everybody. Bly was never a great formalist—he just never had a great ear. He found his voice after going to Norway in the early sixties, then in 1962 publishing *Silence in the Snowy Fields* that contained spare free verse poems. So they were two very different poets. Bly revered Wright for his manifold gifts as both a formal and free verse poet, but they were really very different poets. I'm so fascinated by what you were doing at the same time in the early sixties, maybe later sixties, when Bly and Wright and Kinnell were trying to let the dogs in. A lot of confessional poetry was being published in free verse at the time as well. It was in fact the heyday of confessional poetry. Sylvia Plath had published *Colossus* already, and *Ariel* was published posthumously in 1965. Anne Sexton was writing up a storm, and Robert Lowell had also begun to write confessionally after being influenced by his student W. D. Snodgrass's Pulitzer Prize–winning volume *Heart's Needle* in 1959. I think it's fascinating what you said earlier, that you felt writing in form was like the military to you in a way, which was so hard to get out of. It was difficult for you to write outside of form, but at this point you must feel like you had made some peace with it. I'm not sure; I'm presuming this.

SS: With the military or with form?

CD: With both, actually.

SS: Yes, I made peace with it, but it is an interesting figure. I spent years trying to get out of the military—literally—and I've spent years trying to get out of the formal verse.

CD: Do you know why?

SS: Well, because I wanted to live my life!

CD: As Robert Lowell claimed, free verse helped one to "create a breakthrough back into life." I feel, as your reader, that I'm entering your later poems—those since the publication of *The Thread* in 1998—in media res. I have to figure out exactly where that point is. You avoid the first person assiduously, which in turn forces you to live in the other, as if you're wary of being too solipsistic or narcissistic in creating a self-absorbed rather than a transpersonal speaker.

SS: I think that I would say it's more painterly to have a *he* or a *she* there in that. I try to make it all the more impersonal in some way.

CD: But again you've always been that way. It's interesting that you haven't used that style as much, though if you go back to the early poems, you are reluctant to use the first person or talk about yourself in an "American" way—it's American to say "I did this" or "I went here" or "I, I, I."

SS: Well, you know, I think that has to do with poetry workshops where the kids were saying "I went to the bathroom" and so on. I remember I kept telling a lot of students—also in gen-ed A or the basic composition courses, you know—I had these little ideas for how to write poems, and I said, "Don't use the first person. Just steer clear of it, and after a while ... and so on." But then you see that for people like Lowell or Shakespeare the *I* is never the true *I*.

CD: But in addition to saying what I just did about the arc of your work, I also find this tendency occurring throughout your work of concluding with profound observation—what Richard Howard aptly calls in his blurb for *Black Box* "sweet reason and/or beautiful imagery." Of course you have that influence of going back to your undergraduate days at Yale of reading a lot of Chinese and Japanese poetry and learning to appreciate the power of imagery. You wrote a book, *Netsuke Days*, in 2003 in which you rely on evocative imagery entirely in one brief poem after another. This book didn't, in my opinion, receive enough attention. Here are two of my favorites from this collection:

> Icarus: his two white legs
> sticking out of the
> sea, making a victory sign.

> Get what you ask for
> by and large
> according to the sticker—
> someone's horse
> smarter than your son.

SS: The Japanese are so conscious of not belonging that they have no Emersonian self-reliance. My friend Takano has always said something like that. "We can't stand alone—we have to do what we are told to do." He ended up by being the chairman of the English department at this huge university, yet he was arrested falsely for demonstrating, even peaceably, and he was in jail for a little while. He got out and he didn't have anything to do with anybody. But they feel so strongly like that—like they are part of a group, of a complex, of a family.

CD: Well, you say this in "A Short Account of the Japanese"—"Still in step, arm in arm, the Japanese do nothing, not even skiing, alone."

SS: Yes.

CD: The full line, or the full sentence, about "ourselves" in your poem "Intersections" compares our intractable if ironic foreignness from ourselves in this metaphorical way: "We do not belong to ourselves; / even the night soon belongs to a morning." That's the kind of profound observation or "sweet reason" that Richard Howard was talking about and that you are able to pull off repeatedly in the endings of your poems with the belief that images, unlike explanations or telling, contain what Ezra Pound called "intellectual and emotional complexes in an instant of time." Another poem in which you do this so successfully is "Stony Creek."

SS: You gave me that poem, sir.

CD: Well, no, I didn't—you wrote it.

SS: Yes, but you took me there.

CD: Yes, I took you there, but you found the words for it and this conclusion: "Lichens peel, and you see in; / the light on the water trembles, rises." So there are many poems like this where you are admirably patient with the image, realizing its power. That there is no more telling you can do or should do at that point in the poem. The showing is absolutely enough. I think you learned this from your immersion in Japanese and Chinese poetry during your Fulbright and beyond.

SS: I'm sure that yes, I did, but if somebody gives you the right substance, and you don't know about it, you can see down into stone from rock, and that's been a very important image for me.

CD: Right. To quote one more poem, "Station 41," which is an elegy about your father and concludes also with a powerful image:

The mottling and the cyanosis had begun.
I would not comprehend the urgency,
He was so strong, headstrong; strongest of men,
He'd stay among his three at least till one
At bedside, daughter or son,
Hugged him to speech, to bless
From his high wilderness
His child, but toiled then, now with joke, now rage.
At last it was mine to be next: to disengage
And sing, as the tenor, called to his loveliest
Work, brightens the stage
Alone and sings, by the dark hall possessed.

Such beautiful music. The occasion isn't overwhelmed by verbal showing off or sentimentality. There's an exquisite mastery of form here also that's in the service of the occasion, enhancing the pathos of your father's passing and your concomitant awareness of being next.

SS: So at the last section of that poem I felt that I had finally gotten there.

CD: I mentioned to you earlier that I'm fascinated by your religious sensibility that is never overt in your poems. Maybe there are a few examples that I'm overlooking—can you think of one where you address the subject of religion directly?

SS: "Ray's Garden Shop."

CD: In which Ray says near the end of the poem:

> He dropped to his knees
>
> and said, I don't know
> what your beliefs are, I don't
>   want to offend you

but I believe that
heaven and hell are right here
    on this earth. Mind you

I'm no atheist
but, see, after flesh-and-blood
    it's bye-bye baby.

Incidentally,
friend, just look, this marvelous
    stuff growing away

right on the shoulder
right in the oil and sand and all
    this dust. He bent his

old dry body down
and held a head of dust-white
    hen-and-chickens for me to see.

I think that speaks a huge amount about the dialectic that runs
throughout your work. You've been an Episcopalian throughout
your life, and yet here in this poem you have this gardener speaking
in a kind of double way about not being an atheist, on the one hand,
but believing that "heaven and hell are right here," as he points to a
flower—the hen and chicks—nobody really notices by the side of the
road.

SS: You have to pay attention, as you know, to what one writes about
and what one does not. That is different from saying what I write
about and what I don't write about. You can't get away with it because
it somehow lacks seriousness, it lacks wit, it lacks attractively dis-
played perception.

CD: You mean religious writing?

SS: Yeah. I mean, it's just straight out of a prayer book, or something, or an event from the Bible, which is already handled better in the Bible. I think that sometimes . . . well, Archibald MacLeish did well with Job in *J.B.*

CD: What about Eliot's "Four Quartets"?

SS: Well that's very different: a.) because he gets away with it, and b) because it's deeply personal, and Eliot, as he is quoted in one of his letters to, I guess, John Middleton Murry, is as far as he's concerned damned and going to hell because he couldn't do right by Vivienne. He was in a place, as we say, where he felt very stiff and depressed and so on, and he worked very hard at publishing in order to do a good job there, but he was not having a real life there. So he was able to deal with that, and then "Little Gidding" was very much his state of mind, and he quoted Julian of Norwich's famous aphorism, "All shall be well and all shall be well and all manner of things shall be well," and the big charming part of that was when he writes to Virginia Woolf, "Come to tea on Wednesday, tea on Tuesday, or dinner Wednesday night." She writes back, "You must come on Wednesday for dinner." He writes back and says, "That is wonderful, and I can teach you the basics of the Grizzly Bear, and a couple of other dances that I can't remember the name of after dinner." They danced later, which was unimaginable for Virginia Woolf or Eliot, but he was known as a great fan of the burlesque theaters and the minstrel shows. In Boston we used to go all the time! When I was teaching twentieth-century poets at Brown, I've no memory of doing it, but I danced up on the stage or podium and did a little Charleston or something, and I did things for this rather large crowd I had there. It was just an act in passing, and, I think, talking about "Four Quartets" and so on, there were those two sides of Eliot. As I'm always saying to myself, "Well, X could get away with that because of his experience and because of his craft."

CD: Well, you have both.

SS: Well, maybe I don't have the confidence, who knows.

CD: It's interesting because your views seem to be different from your religious tradition or the deity of your religious tradition. You know, the traditional view of God within the Episcopal tradition is at odds, say, with the muse or what your speaker says in "Ray's Flower Shop." There's a freedom that you must feel when you're writing poetry outside of the religious tradition—you put words in your speakers' mouths that are consistent with your Episcopal faith, but that doesn't mean you necessarily feel contradictory or schizy about what you think or believe. Do you ever feel that your writing *is* your religion?

SS: No. It's not a religion; it's literature.

CD: The difference is?

SS: It's a question of degree, I guess. I don't know. The difference is that poetry is what you can do, and religion is what somebody else can do with more power and with more perspective than I could possess.

CD: You say "somebody else" meaning the church?

SS: The church, the whole history of the varied histories of the religions. I think it's possible to find in Christianity a sort of way to understand how some religions seem to be or how practices seem to be truly pagan or something of that sort. At the same time, in Japan it's a religious world in some way. The Japanese believe that no religion is a final club—you know what I'm saying? All of the Christians in my society are all finalists who can't . . . you can't be a Baptist and also be a . . . there's a community of Lutherans in the Episcopalians, but I don't care about any of that stuff. But they have the Shinto practices and the Buddhists, of which there are six different sects—sometimes very different—in Japan. They also allow people to be Episcopalians and so on. They don't care about that—it's all the same. I don't quite feel that I live in that world because of the intolerance of . . . I mean, the United States has a society that I know is one of the more intolerant ones.

CD: I'm thinking of certain poets besides, let's say, Eliot, who tried through their poetry to reach or to achieve some sort of salvation in the act of writing itself, outside of the traditions of various religions. I'm thinking of "A Dolphin" by Lowell or maybe "Asphodel, That Greeny Flower" by Williams or "Trial by Existence" by Frost and Coleridge's "The Ancient Mariner," where poets, not so much through religious avenues or with religious language, attempt to work toward some sort of salvific goal in their poems.

SS: Coleridge had a terrible time facing anything, and one feels his religious concerns, starkly so when he was young, finally leveling off into a kind of, well, not complacency, but a treaty with the world in which he lived, when he found that he could be happy in a situation where there was a doctor to care for him and to give him the occasional shot of morphine or whatever. He talked a great deal about metaphysical ideas and organizations of the world, but he became what I think is a very agnostic, very civilized agnostic person, who just lived his life up in northern London and enjoyed the birds and the bees.

CD: Before we end I'd like to ask you about the state of American poetry. Where would you begin?

SS: I can't imagine the rattled poetry competition, with thousands of submissions, coming up with a winning poem called "Ode to the Mother of a Dispossessed, Crazy, Lesbian Daughter" and have the runner-up be a poem called "Jane's Garage Sale." It just makes you think, "oh, goodness, how we have become involved with the sociopolitical questions of our time, or the minor economic front of having a tag sale," or something like that. But where is the serious and accomplished writing, rhetoric, meaning, and ground of the poetry that exists as an important part of our lives? Where is it in those things? It's like people have focused their snapshots better and call that art, or something. So I think that there are just as many, if not more, very good poets writing today as ever, but it's very hard to put your finger on them because we have this explosion of topical forgettable poems.

CD: The "big tent" of American poetry? The explosion of MFA programs and schools here and there and journals and publications and small presses publishing everything under the sun.

SS: Yes, publishing has become terribly easy—anybody can do it, but it can't be distributed. I got a subscription to *Poets and Writers* just to behold what's going on, and it's just unbelievable! You can apply for a scholarship if you're someone who writes about uninhabited country—places in Minnesota, for example. There are all these kinds of things in there.

CD: So you feel that there is a real dearth of knowledgeable arbiters these days.

SS: Publishing is a business. The technological breakthrough that has occurred over the past thirty years, which enables anybody with a few hundred dollars to publish a pamphlet, has created a surfeit of poems in the open market. But then how does it get distributed? Well, it doesn't, except online. I for one have absolutely no idea how this is all going to pan out—I think the idea of what I would define as poetry, classical poetry, or great poetry would be very different from that of a lot of students. I'm auditing this course in the Baroque, and there are very bright kids in there. This kid I was sitting next to had his little machine out. I said, "Please don't do that, especially when you're right next to me, because it gets confusing with what I'm trying to say." "Oh, I was trying to find . . ." But the last Friday he came up to me in class—he's really such a very nice and bright person—and he said, "I wanted to thank you" and mentioned, "I saw your poem in *The New Yorker*, and isn't that just great?" I said, "Well, it's very small, but thank you very much!" He said, "And it was so funny!" I guess it was funny, but I don't know in what regard.

CD: Well, I guess I'm a little curious about how you feel, as someone who has aspired to write memorable poetry; has worked his whole life on mastering form and inventing your own forms, creating your own memorable language with a clear connection to the legacy of poetry; has been mindful of the music and the meaning and imagery in your poetry in a way that connects, again, to the legacy of poetry but in a way that you've tried to "make new" yourself; and has spent your whole life, fifty years or more, publishing widely and receiving a lot of acclaim and are now witnessing a poetry scene that has become more and more demotic while at the same time creating a very blurred line between synchronic and diachronic writing. I guess my question is, what's a poet to do? What's a poet with your interests and your kind of talent and your record to say to the director of an MFA program today? What do you do or say?

SS: We can't possibly know what effect the death of privacy and birth of an electronic everything will have on us. I think that what one can only do or must do is simply carry on with his or her project. Since the age of eight I've been writing poems, and I probably will continue, although I have to get settled a little bit. One always goes through dry places—another one of my desert places is everywhere. I think it's part of our lives. I don't really approve so much of how these writing programs—all of them, apparently, as far as I can determine—are telling their students, "you must write every day." Well, that doesn't mean you should write poetry every day; you need to keep your books, write your checks. But I'm not sure that you should; there should be many days when you don't. If you feel life is not worth living, if you do not have a stream of poems coming out all the time, you get some pretty bad work, and I can give you a list of names. You can come to some of them yourself.

CD: If you were going to talk to a young writing student today and had to tell him or her the importance of reading, of connecting himself or herself to the tradition of poetry, what exactly would you say to them about why that's important?

SS: Well, I've told innumerable college students whom I've taught just to do that, and I've written many, many reading lists out and so on. I used to always recommend that you should not go to an MFA program. If you just want a degree and can afford it, then fine, but if you have other needs then you should go to graduate school in biology or something so you'll learn a different set of terms and rules and everything. I think that's the wise thing to recommend, but it does seem to me at times that all the people I've most thoroughly told not to go to MFA school did.

CD: Because they felt they had to?

SS: Well, it's something to do, and of course MFAs authorize those who take them to become semi-authorized authors. "I'm a legitimate poet or essayist or fiction writer"—whatever that means. It puts a seal of approval on one's effort to become a writer. If you're already a winner in that regard then no problem, but, you know, I don't suppose it does any harm until the numbers approach millions.

CD: But why read Coleridge, Wordsworth, Donne, Shakespeare when I'm enjoying writing the story of my life right now?

SS: Yes, well, they tell you that the great human experiences have always been duplicated on a smaller, lesser plane and a smaller scale than they were originally done. You have to imbibe the tradition.

ACKNOWLEDGMENTS

I'm deeply grateful to the following people who were instrumental in helping me complete this book: Janet Masso, Chelsea Puffer, and Maggie Burke for transcribing these interviews; Alex Wolfe and Sarah C. Smith for their invaluable editorial skill and thoroughness; and finally, but not least, my wife, Liz, for her tireless support and sharp ear.

Interview with Natasha Trethewey: *World Literature Today*
Interview with Galway Kinnell: *American Poetry Review*; also
 appeared in *Sad Friends, Drowned Lovers, Stapled Songs, Conver-*
 sations and Reflections with 20th Century American Poets
Interview with Carolyn Forché: *World Literature Today*
Interview with Jane Hirshfield: *World Literature Today*
Interview with Anne Wright: *American Poetry Review*
Interview with Ed Ochester: *Poetry International Online, Florida*
 Review
Interview with Martín Espada: *American Poetry Review*
Interview with Stephen Kuusisto: *Story Preservation Initiative*
Interview with Peter Everwine: *The Iowa Review Online*
Interview with Stephen Sandy: *Poetry International Online*
The biographical sketches, with the exception of Anne Wright's, were
 taken from the Poetry Foundation website

Chard deNiord. Photo by Liz Hawkes deNiord